You are about to begin reading. . . Relax. Concentrate. Dispel every other thought. Let the world around you fade. Best to close the door; the TV is always on in the next room. Tell the others right away, "No, I don't want to watch TV!" Raise your voice—they won't hear you otherwise—"I'm reading! I don't want to be disturbed!" Maybe they haven't heard you, with all that racket; speak louder, yell: "I'm beginning to read!"

—ITALO CALVINO

Publisher
DRUE HEINZ
Founding Editor
PAUL BOWLES
Managing & Associate Editor
LEE ANN CHEARNEYI
Design & Promotion Manager
JENNIFER MCDONALD
Assistant Editor
KATHLEEN REDDY
Editorial Assistants

| LEA BAECHLER | JENNIFER GRIFFIN |
| K.T. KORNGOLD | ALICE ROTTERSMAN |

Contributing Editors

ANDREAS BROWN	STANLEY KUNITZ
JOHN FOWLES	W.S. MERWIN
DONALD HALL	EDOUARD RODITI
JOHN HAWKES	MARK STRAND

Antæus *is published semiannually by The Ecco Press, 26 West 17th Street, New York, N.Y. 10011. Distributed to bookstores in the United States by W. W. Norton & Company, Inc., 500 Fifth Avenue, New York, N.Y. 10110; to newsstands in the United States by B. DeBoer, Inc., 113 East Centre St., Nutley, New Jersey 07110; in England and Europe by W. W. Norton & Company, Inc.*

Antæus *Contributions and Communications: 26 West 17th Street, New York, N.Y. 10011. European address: 42A Hay's Mews, London, W. 1, England. Four-issue Subscriptions: $20.00. Back issues available.*

ISSN 0003-5319
Printed by Wickersham Printing Co., Inc.
ISBN 0-88001-144-0
Library of Congress Number: 70-612646
Copyright © 1987 by Antæus, *New York, N.Y.*

Cover painting: **Man Reading** *by Wayne Thiebaud, 1963*
Collection: Allan Stone
Dena Santoro should have appeared in *Antæus 58* as a Fiction Reader.

Publication of this magazine has been made possible in part by a grant from the National Endowment for the Arts.
Logo: Ahmed Yacoubi
Page 212 constitutes an extension of the copyright page.

Antæus

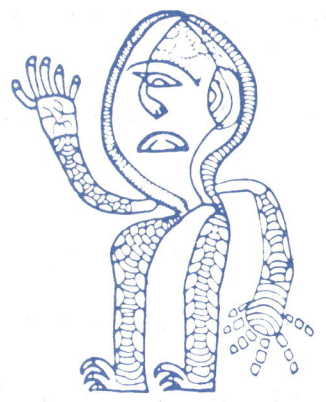

EDITED BY

DANIEL HALPERN

TANGIER/LONDON/NEW YORK

NO. 59, AUTUMN, 1987

CONTENTS

LITERATURE AS PLEASURE

NOTES ON PLEASURE

I

JOYCE CAROL OATES / *Literature as Pleasure, Pleasure as Literature* 21

LEE ZACHARIAS / *In the Garden of the Word* 31

RICHARD FORD / *Reading* 39

GUY DAVENPORT / *On Reading* 52

DAVID LONG / *On Rereading* 62

JAMES PURDY / *Rereading: Not for Pleasure Alone* 69

II

JOSEPH CONRAD / *Books* 73

JOSEF ŠKVORECKÝ / *The Pleasures of the Freedom to Read* 79

STANISLAW BARANCZAK / *The Revenge of a Mortal Hand* 85

III

ROY BLOUNT, JR. / *Reading Appreciation* 95

DONALD HALL / *The Way to Say* Pleasure 101

GAIL GODWIN / *What's Really Going On* 110

JONATHAN HOLDEN / *Poetry, Baseball: The Pleasures of the Text* 115

MADISON SMARTT BELL / *Literature and Pleasure: Bridging the Gap* 127

CHARLES SIMIC / *Reading Philosophy at Night* 135

IV

JAMES LAUGHLIN / *The Pleasures of Reading the Classics in Translation* 145

A. L. ROWSE / *Literature as Pleasure* 168

MARY KINZIE / *Nocturnal Habit: On Literary Addiction* 176

CALVIN BEDIENT / *Sensible Ecstasies* 185

WILLIAM S. WILSON / *loving/reading* 200

Contributors / 211

Books from The Ecco Press are available to *Antæus* subscribers at a 20% discount. Please write for a catalogue: The Ecco Press, 26 West 17th Street, New York, New York 10011.

Notes on Pleasure

If it ain't a pleasure it ain't a poem.

— WILLIAM CARLOS WILLIAMS

There is only one way to read, which is to browse in libraries and bookshops, picking up books that attract you, reading only those, dropping them when they bore you.

— DORIS LESSING
The Golden Notebook

What is written without effort is in general read without pleasure.

— SAMUEL JOHNSON

I wish thee as much pleasure in the reading, as I had in the writing.

— FRANCIS QUARLES
Emblems

No man is a hypocrite in his pleasures.

— SAMUEL JOHNSON

The Poet writes under one restriction only, namely, that of the necessity of giving pleasure to a human Being possessed of that information which may be expected from him, not as a lawyer, a physician, a mariner, an astronomer or a natural philosopher, but as a Man.

— WILLIAM WORDSWORTH
Lyrical Ballads

The proper and immediate object of science is the acquirement, or communication, of truth; the proper and immediate object of poetry is the communication of immediate pleasure.

—SAMUEL TAYLOR COLERIDGE
"Definitions of Poetry"

The pursuit of happiness by means lawful and unlawful, through resignation or revolt, by the clever manipulation of conventions or by solemn hanging on to the skirts of the latest scientific theory, is the only theme that can be legitimately developed by the novelist who is the chronicler of the adventures of mankind amongst the dangers of the kingdom of the earth.

—JOSEPH CONRAD
"Books"

There is no happiness where there is no wisdom. . . .

— SOPHOCLES
Antigone

. . . style, "the only thing that is immortal in literature," as Sainte-Beuve has said, a still unexpected energy, after all that the argument or the story needs, a still unbroken pleasure after the immediate end has been accomplished.

—W. B. YEATS
"Poetry and Tradition"

Play, we found, was so innate in poetry, and every form of poetic utterance so intimately bound up with the structure of play that the bond between them was seen to be insoluble.

—JOHAN HUIZINGA
Homo Ludens

To *name* an object is to take away three-fourths of the pleasure given by a poem. This pleasure consists in guessing little by little: to *suggest* it, that is the ideal.

—STÉPHANE MALLARMÉ
"Réponse à une enquête sur l'évolution littéraire"

It should be of the pleasure of a poem itself to tell how it can. The figure a poem makes. It begins in delight and ends in wisdom. The figure is the same as for love. No one can really hold that the ecstasy should be static and stand still in one place. It begins in delight, it inclines to the impulse, it assumes direction with the first line laid down, it runs a course of lucky events, and ends in a clarification of life—not necessarily a great clarification, such as sects and cults are founded on, but in a momentary stay against confusion.

—ROBERT FROST
"The Figure a Poem Makes"

Hearken unto a Verser, who may chance
Ryme thee to good, and make a bait of pleasure.
  A verse may finde him, who a sermon flies,
And turn delight into a sacrifice.

—GEORGE HERBERT
"The Church-porch"

Text of pleasure: the text that contents, fills, grants euphoria; the text that comes from culture and does not break with it, is linked to a *comfortable* practice of reading. Text of bliss: the text that imposes a state of loss, the text that discomforts (perhaps to the point of a certain boredom), unsettles the reader's historical, cultural, psychological assumptions, the consistency of his tastes, values, memories, brings to a crisis his relation with language.

Now the subject who keeps the two texts in his field and in his hands the reins of pleasure and bliss is an anachronic subject, for he simultaneously and contradictorily participates in the profound hedonism of all culture (which permeates him quietly under cover of an *art de vivre* shared by the old books) and in the destruction of that culture: he enjoys the consistency of his selfhood (that is his pleasure) and seeks its loss (that is his bliss). He is a subject split twice over, doubly perverse.

—ROLAND BARTHES
The Pleasure of the Text

But when a creative writer presents his plays to us or tells us what we are inclined to take to be his personal day-dreams, we experience a great pleasure, and one which probably arises from the confluence of many sources. The writer softens the character of his egoistic day-dreams by altering and disguising it, and he bribes us by the purely formal—that is, aesthetic— yield of pleasure which he offers us in the presentation of his fantasies. We give the name of an *incentive bonus,* or a *forepleasure,* to a yield of pleasure such as this, which is offered to us so as to make possible the opinion, all the aesthetic pleasure which a creative writer affords us has the character of a forepleasure of this kind, and our actual enjoyment of an imaginative work proceeds from a liberation of tensions in our minds. It may even be that not a little of this effect is due to the writer's enabling us thenceforward to enjoy our own day-dreams without self-reproach or shame.

—SIGMUND FREUD
"Creative Writers and Day-Dreaming"

In some traditions "pleasure" has been understood as the absence of pain rather than as itself an actively experienceable condition, while in others it has been understood as a discrete sensory phenomenon the experience of which does not depend on the prior presence (or even anticipated presence) of pain. Even in the second case, however, it has tended to be understood as a *bodily* state in which something other than the *body* is experienced. . . . Thus the two conceptions of pleasure are not as deeply at odds with one another as they may at first appear, for in each (overtly in the first case, less overtly but recoverably in the second) it is a condition associated with living beyond the physical body, or experiencing bodily sensations in terms of objectified content.

— ELAINE SCARRY
The Body in Pain

. . . no verse can give pleasure for long, nor last, that is written by drinkers of water.

— HORACE
The Epistles

Appetite grows by eating.

— RABELAIS
Gargantua

Music is to make people happy.

— BUNK JOHNSON

Most men pursue pleasure with such breathless haste that they hurry past it. They fare as did that dwarf who kept guard over a captured princess in his castle. One day he took a midday nap. When he woke up an hour later, the princess was gone. Quickly he pulled on his seven-league boots; with one stride he was far beyond her.

— SØREN KIERKEGAARD
Either/Or

Pleasure is labour too, and tires as much.

— WILLIAM COWPER
"Hope"

Waiting for one's pleasures is tiresome work.

— PETRONIUS
Satyricon

Each is dragged along by his pleasure.

—VIRGIL
Eclogues

Pleasure's a sin, and sometimes sin's a pleasure.

—LORD BYRON
"Don Juan"

A cigarette is the perfect type of a perfect pleasure. It is exquisite, and it leaves one unsatisfied. What more can one want?

—OSCAR WILDE
The Picture of Dorian Gray

. . . can it be that pleasure makes us objective?

—ROLAND BARTHES
The Pleasure of the Text

It is an uneasy lot at best, to be what we call highly taught and yet not to enjoy: to be present at this great spectacle of life and never to be liberated from a small hungry shivering self—never to be fully possessed by the glory we behold, never to have our consciousness rapturously transformed into the vividness of a thought, the ardour of a passion, the energy of an action, but always to be scholarly and uninspired, ambitious and timid, scrupulous and dimsighted.

—GEORGE ELIOT
Middlemarch

Not the poem which we have *read,* but that to which we *return,* with the greatest pleasure, possesses the genuine power, and claims the name of *essential poetry.*

—SAMUEL TAYLOR COLERIDGE
Biographia Literaria

According to [Hemsterhuis (1720–90)], beauty is that which gives most pleasure, and that gives most pleasure which gives us the greatest number of ideas in the shortest time. Enjoyment of the beautiful, because it gives the greatest quantity of perceptions in the shortest time, is the highest notion to which man can attain.

—LEO TOLSTOY
"What Is Art?"

A thing final in itself and, therefore, good:
One of the vast repetitions final in
Themselves and, therefore, good, the going round

And round and round, the merely going round,
Until merely going round is a final good,
The way wine comes at a table in a wood.

And we enjoy like men, the way a leaf
Above the table spins its constant spin,
So that we look at it with pleasure, look

At it spinning its eccentric measure. Perhaps,
The man-hero is not the exceptional monster,
But he that of repetition is most master.

—WALLACE STEVENS
"Notes Toward a Supreme Fiction"

People can have many different kinds of pleasure. The real one is that for which they will forsake the others.

—MARCEL PROUST
Remembrance of Things Past

Of course, she said to herself, coming into the room, she had to come here to get something she wanted. First she wanted to sit down in a particular chair under a particular lamp. But she wanted something more, though she did not know, could not think what it was that she wanted. She looked at her husband (taking up her stocking and beginning to knit), and saw that he did not want to be interrupted—that was clear. He was reading something that moved him very much. He was half smiling and then she knew he was controlling his emotion. He was tossing the pages over. He was acting it—perhaps he was thinking himself the person in the book. She wondered what book it was. Oh, it was one of old Sir Walter's she saw, adjusting the shade of her lamp so that the light fell on her knitting. For Charles Tansley had been saying (she looked up as if she expected to hear the crash of books on the floor above), had been saying that people don't read Scott any more. Then her husband thought, "That's what they'll say of me;" so he went and got one of those books. And if he came to the conclusion "That's true" what Charles Tansley said, he would accept it about Scott (She could see that he was weighing, considering, putting this with that as he read.). But not about himself. He was always uneasy about himself. That troubled her. He would always be worrying about his own books—will they be read, are they good, why aren't they better, what do people think of me? Not liking to think of him so, and wondering if they had guessed at dinner why he suddenly became irritable when they talked about fame and books lasting, wondering if the children were laughing at that, she twitched the stocking out, and all the fine gravings came drawn with steel instruments about her lips and forehead, and she grew still like a tree which has been tossing and quivering and now, when the breeze falls, settles, leaf by leaf, into quiet.

It didn't matter, any of it, she thought. A great man, a great book, fame—who could tell? She knew nothing about it. But it was his way with him, his truthfulness—for instance at dinner she had been thinking quite instinctively, If only he would speak! She had complete trust in him. And dismissing all this, as one passes in diving now a weed, now a straw, now a bubble, she felt again, sinking deeper, as she had felt in the hall when the others were talking, There is something I want—something I have come to get, and she fell deeper and deeper without knowing quite what it was, with her eyes closed. And she waited a little, knitting, wondering, and slowly those words they had said at dinner, "the China rose is all abloom and buzzing with the honey bee," began washing from side to side of her mind rhythmically, and as they washed, words, like little shaded lights, one red, one blue, one yellow, lit up in the dark of her mind, and seemed leaving their perches up there to fly across and across, or to cry out and to be echoed; so she turned and felt on the table beside her for a book.

> And all the lives we ever lived
> And all the lives to be,
> Are full of trees and changing leaves,

she murmured, sticking her needles into the stocking. And she opened the book and began reading here and there at random, and as she did so she felt that she was climbing backwards, upwards shoving her way up under petals that curved over her, so that she only knew this is white, or this is red. She did not know at first what the words meant at all.

> Steer, hither steer your winged pines, all beaten Mariners

she read and turned the page, swinging herself, zigzagging this way and that, from one line to another as from one branch to another, from one red and white flower to another, until a little sound roused her—her husband slapping his thighs. Their eyes met for a second; but they did not want to speak to each other. They had nothing to say, but something seemed, nevertheless, to go from him to her. It was the life, it was the power of it, it was the tremendous humour, she knew, that made him slap his thighs. Don't interrupt me, he seemed to be saying, don't say anything; just sit there. And he went on reading. His lips twitched. It filled him. It fortified him. He clean forgot all the little rubs and digs of the evening, and how it bored him unutterably to sit still while people ate and drank interminably, and his being so irritable with his wife and so touchy and minding when they passed his books over as if they didn't exist at all. But now, he felt, it didn't matter a damn who reached Z (if thought ran like an alphabet from A to Z). Somebody would reach it—if not he, then another. This man's strength and sanity, his feeling for straightforward simple things, these fishermen, the poor old crazed creature in Mucklebackit's cottage made him feel so vigorous, so relieved of something that he felt roused and triumphant and could not choke back his tears. Raising the book a little to hide his face, he let them fall and shook his head from side to side and forgot himself completely (but not one or two reflections about morality and French novels and English novels and Scott's hands being tied but his view perhaps being as true as the other view), forgot his own bothers and failures completely in poor Steenie's drowning and Mucklebackit's sorrow (that was Scott at his best) and the astonishing delight and feeling of vigour that it gave him.

Well, let them improve upon that, he thought as he finished the chapter. He felt that he had been arguing with somebody, and had got the better of him. They could not improve upon that, whatever they might say; and his own position became more secure. The lovers were fiddlesticks, he thought, collecting it all in his mind again. That's fiddlesticks, that's first-rate, he thought, putting one thing beside another. But he must read it again. He could not remember the whole shape of the thing. He had to keep his judgement in suspense. So he returned to the other thought — if young men did not care for this, naturally they did not care for him either. One ought not to complain, thought Mr. Ramsay, trying to stifle his desire to complain to his wife that young men did not admire him. But he was determined; he would not bother her again. Here he looked at her reading. She looked very peaceful, reading. He liked to think that every one had taken themselves off and that he and she were alone. The whole of life did not consist in going to bed with a woman, he thought, returning to Scott and Balzac, to the English novel and the French novel.

Mrs. Ramsay raised her head and like a person in a light sleep seemed to say that if he wanted her to wake she would, she really would, but otherwise, might she go on sleeping, just a little longer, just a little longer? She was climbing up those branches, this way and that, laying hands on one flower and then another.

"Nor praise the deep vermilion in the rose," she read, and so reading she was ascending, she felt, on to the top, on to the summit. How satisfying! How restful! All the odds and ends of the day stuck to this magnet; her mind felt swept, felt clean. And then there it was, suddenly entire; she held it in her hands, beautiful and reasonable, clear and complete, the essence sucked out of life and held rounded here — the sonnet.

But she was becoming conscious of her husband looking at her. He was smiling at her, quizzically, as if he were ridiculing her gently for being asleep in broad daylight, but at the same time he was thinking, Go on reading. You don't look sad now, he thought. And he wondered what she was reading, and exaggerated her ignorance, her simplicity, for he liked to think that she was not clever, not book-learned at all. He wondered if she understood what she was reading. Probably not, he thought. She was astonishingly beautiful. Her beauty seemed to him, if that were possible, to increase.

> Yet seem'd it winter still, and, you away,
> As with your shadow I with these did play,

she finished.

"Well?" she said, echoing his smile dreamily, looking up from her book.

> As with your shadow I with these did play,

she murmured, putting the book on the table.

—VIRGINIA WOOLF
To the Lighthouse

I

Joyce Carol Oates

Literature as Pleasure, Pleasure as Literature

I have always come to life after coming to books.

—JORGE LUIS BORGES

It might be argued that reading constitutes the keenest, because most secret, sort of pleasure. And that it's a pleasure best savored by night: by way of an ideal insomnia. At such times, lamplight illuminating the page but not much else, the world is writ small, deliciously small, and words, another's voice, come forward. *What I love about wakefulness* the insomniac says *is being alone, and reading.*

Insomnia is a predilection, a skill, a way of being, best cultivated young: in early adolescence if possible. To begin in adulthood would be a pity since, at the very least, so much precious solitude (i.e., occasions for reading) has already been lost.

You know it's poetry, Emily Dickinson says, when it takes the top of your head off. Or when, to use Randall Jarrell's metaphor, you're struck by lightning—as a reader. All great poetry is enhanced by the occasion of its discovery, and by the occasion of its savoring: a poem by night is far more powerful than a poem by day. And there are certain mysterious poems, like this by Walt Whitman—atypical Whitman, it should be noted—that can only be read by night.

A Clear Midnight

This is thy hour O soul,
   thy free flight into the wordless,
Away from books, away from art,
   the day erased, the lesson done,
Thee fully forth emerging, silent, gazing,

>   pondering the themes thou lovest best:
> Night, sleep, death and the stars.

Love at first sight/hearing—however delusory in human romantic terms it is nearly always reliable, in fact irresistible, in literary terms. A certitude that darts into the soul by way of the eye; provokes an involuntary visceral effect. Not always "pleasant" in the most benign sense of that ambiguous word but always, always exciting.

When you haven't realized you have memorized another's words, poetry or prose, and then, as if unbidden, the words assert themselves. Coleridge's "knowledge returning as power . . ." As, one evening in Princeton, a poet-friend and I discovered that we could recite in unison an early poem of Yeats' most admirers of Yeats would consider marginal, if, in its angry percussive rhythms, it could have been written by no one else—

> *To a Friend Whose Work Has Come to Nothing*
>
>   Now all the truth is out,
>   Be secret and take defeat
>   From any brazen throat,
>   For how can you compete,
>   Being honor bred, with one
>   Who, were it proved he lies,
>   Were neither shamed in his own
>   Nor in his neighbors' eyes?
>   Bred to a harder thing
>   Than Triumph, turn away
>   And like a laughing string
>   Whereon mad fingers play
>   Amid a place of stone,
>   Be secret and exult,
>   Because of all things known
>   That is most difficult.

This too is a poem best savored, perhaps uniquely savored, by night. Like other great poems of Yeats'—"The Magi," "The Circus Animals' Desertion," "The Cold Heaven," "The Wild Swans at Coole," the Crazy Jane poems—to name only a few—which I first discovered in protracted, headachey, but utterly ravishing insomniac spells of reading in my late teens. How hard to maintain the keenest degree of consciousness after having been awake most of the night; how hard, how *willful* the task, to take daylight as seriously as night—! Yeats' magisterial imperatives have the authority, shading into contempt, of words engraved in stone: tombstone, maybe. Like those famous lines at the end of "Under Ben Bulben"—

> Cast a cold eye
> On life, on death.
> Horseman, pass by!

"A book is an ax," Franz Kafka once said, "for the frozen sea within." Curious metaphors—particularly the ax. But we know what he means.

* * *

There are pleasures in reading so startling, so intense, they shade into pain. The realization that one's life has been irrevocably altered by . . . can it be mere words? Print on a page? The most life-rending discoveries involve what has in fact never been thought, never given form, until another's words embody them. Recall the ingenuous Dorian Gray of whom it is said he was "seduced by a book." (The book being Huysmans' masterwork of decadence, *A Rebours*.) And have there been innumerable others who were seduced by that book, and Wilde's own masterwork *The Picture of Dorian Gray*? And what, at a morbid extreme, of the young killers Leopold and Loeb, who, having read Nietzsche as undergraduates, decided in the manner of Dostoyevsky's Raskolnikov to experiment with taking a human life—having ascended, as they thought, to the level of absolute moral freedom Nietzsche's Zarathustra preached? Is this pathology, or the greatest possible empathy? The least resistance to the "pleasure" of being overcome by another's voice?

Consider the phenomenon of reading, that most mysterious of acts. It is the sole means by which we slip, involuntarily, often helplessly, into another's skin; another's voice; another's soul. One might argue that serious reading is as sacramental an act as serious writing, and should therefore not be profaned. That, by way of a book, we have the ability to transcend what is immediate, what is merely personal, and to enter a consciousness not known to us, in some cases distinctly alien, *other* . . . This morning I open a new hardcover book, of moderate size, modestly packaged, not guessing how, within minutes, in fact within seconds, my heart will be beating more quickly; my senses alert to the point of pain; an excitement coursing through me that makes it virtually impossible to stay seated. The book is *The Collected Poems of William Carlos Williams*, volume I, 1909–1939, edited by A. Walton Litz and Christopher MacGowen (New Directions, 1986), the poem I begin to read is "Paterson: Episode 17" with its haunting, percussive refrain "Beautiful Thing"—first read how many years ago? and reread how many times?—yet still possessed of its uncanny original power. And there are the great "raw" poems we all know, and have memorized, "By the road to the contagious hospital," "The pure products of America/go crazy," "The Widow's Lament at Springtime," that poem in honor/awe/terror of America—

> The crowd at the ball game
> is moved uniformly
>
> by a spirit of uselessness
> which delights them—
>
> all the exciting detail
> of the chase
>
> and the escape, the error
> the flash of genius—
>
> all to no end save beauty
> the eternal—
>
> So in detail they, the crowd,
> are beautiful
>
> for this
> to be warned again
>
> saluted and defied—
> It is alive, venomous
>
> it smiles grimly
> its words cut—
>
> The flashy female with her

24 / Joyce Carol Oates

mother, gets it—

The Jew gets it straight—it
is deadly, terrifying—

It is the Inquisition, the
Revolution

It is beauty itself
that lives

day by day in them
idly—

This is
the power of their faces

It is summer, it is the solstice
the crowd is

cheering, the crowd is laughing
in detail
permanently, seriously
without thought
      (from *Spring and all*, 1923)

Elsewhere—

What are these elations I have
at my own underwear?

I touch it and it is strange
upon a strange thigh.
     (from *The Descent of Winter*, 1928)

And: I enter an empty classroom in the old Hall of Languages Building, Syracuse University, sometime in the fall of 1956, discover a lost or discarded book on ethics, an anthology of sorts, open it at random, and begin reading . . . and reading . . . so that the class that begins in a few minutes, whatever remarks, long-forgotten, by whatever professor

Joyce Carol Oates / 25

of philosophy, also, alas, long-forgotten, is a distraction and an interruption. How profoundly excited I am by this unknown new voice, this absolutely new and unique and enchanting voice!—though I am familiar, I suppose, with some of the writers *he* read, and from whom *he* learned (Shakespeare, Dostoyevsky, Emerson), I am not at all familiar with Nietzsche himself—only the name, the word, the sound, mysterious and forbidding. This philosopher who is an anti-philosopher; a poet; a mystic (and anti-mystic); whose genius expresses itself in aphorism and riddle—"philosophy with a hammer." To have read Nietzsche, aged eighteen, when one's senses are most keenly and nervously alert, the very envelope of the skin dangerously porous, to have heard, and been struck to the heart, by that astonishing voice—what ecstasy! what visceral unease!—as if the very floor were shifting beneath one's feet. Late adolescence is the time for love, or, rather, for passion—the conviction that *within the next hour* something can happen, will happen, to irrevocably alter one's life. ("*The danger in happiness:* Now everything I touch turns out to be wonderful. Now I love any fate that comes along. Who feels like being my fate?") Whatever books of Nietzsche's I then bought in paperback or took out of the university library—*The Birth of Tragedy, Human, All-Too-Human, The Gay Science, Thus Spake Zarathustra, Beyond Good and Evil, Twilight of the Idols*—I must have read, or devoured, quickly and carelessly and with no sense of their historical context; under the spell of an enchantment I had every reason to think was unique. And for me Nietzsche *was* unique—one of those voices out of a densely populated world that define themselves so brilliantly, in a way so poignantly, against that world, they become—almost—assimilated into one's very soul.

(Nietzsche died mad. But, mad, lived for a long time—eleven years. In January 1899 on a Turin street he saw a coachman flogging a horse, ran to protect the horse, flung his arms around it and collapsed; and never recovered. And in his madness, even, what radiance, what bizarre and heartrending poetry—signing himself "The Crucified" and "Dionysus"—writing letters like this one, to Jacob Burckhardt: ". . . In the end I would much rather be a Basel professor than God; but I have not dared push my private egoism so far as to desist for its sake from the creation of the world. You see, one must make sacrifices however and wherever one lives. . . . What is disagreeable and offends my modesty is that at bottom I am every name in history. With the children I have put into the world too, I consider with some mistrust whether it is not the case that all who come *into* the kingdom of God also come *out* of God. This fall I was blinded as little as possible when I twice witnessed my funeral. . . . We artists are incorrigible." And, in a postscript: "I go everywhere in my student's coat, and here and there slap somebody on the shoulder and say, 'Are we content? I am the god who has made this caricature.'")

And: I leaf through a bulky anthology of poetry, too many years ago to calibrate though I was probably still in junior high school, and the names are mostly new, mysterious, lacking all associations, therefore talismanic, pure. No mere opinionizing went into the assemblage of this book — no literary politics — surely not! — so far as a thirteen-year-old might guess. If I noted the absence of women I have no memory of it and rather doubt that I did, since poetry even more than prose seemed to me then, and seemed to me for many years, a wholly neutral, or do I mean neuter, genderless activity. (I might have thought — perhaps I still think — *That's the beauty of the enterprise!*) And it would have struck me as rude, vulgar, insipid, trivializing, a profanation of the very page, to read the poetry that excited me most as if it were the product, even, of a human being like myself; as if it were the product of what would one day be called a "female consciousness." For didn't it mean that, being a poet, having been granted the imprimatur of poet, Emily Dickinson had in fact transcended not only the "female" but the "human" as categories?

> I hide myself within my flower,
> That fading from your Vase,
> You, unsuspecting, feel for me —
> Almost a loneliness.

I don't remember the first Dickinson poems I read except to know that this exquisite verse was not among them: it wasn't then, and isn't now, one of the anthology items. Very likely they were the same poems we all read, and reread, and were puzzled and haunted by, as by a child's riddle of such evident simplicity you feel you must understand it — yet can't, quite. Of the frequently anthologized poems it was the darker and more mysterious ones that struck me as embodying poetry's very essence. (Cheerfulness, even the cheerfulness of genius, has always bored me, since who needs it? — we have enough of our own.) The Dickinson who fascinates most is the Dickinson of the great elegiac poems, the poems of "madness," the terse elliptical statement poems that carry with them an air very nearly of belligerence, they are so short, and complete—

> The competitions of the sky
> Corrodeless ply.

And:

> Fame's Boys and Girls, who never die
> And are too seldom born—

And:

> We outgrow love, like other things
> And put it in the Drawer—
> Till an Antique fashion shows—
> Like Costumes Grandsires wore.

All good poets resist paraphrase; Emily Dickinson frequently resists simple comprehension. And should we "sense" her meaning we are inevitably excluded from her technique, marveling at the rightness of certain images, sounds, strategies of punctuation—the ellipses of a mind accustomed to thinking slantwise—yet unable to grasp the poem's ineluctable essence. (And the identity of the poem's narrative "I," shifting as it does from poem to poem.) When we read Dickinson the nerves tighten in sympathy, and wonder. Fragments leap out at us as powerfully as fully realized poems—

> It is the Past's supreme italic
> Makes this Present mean—

*

> Silence is all we dread.
> There's Ransom in a Voice—
> But Silence is Infinity.
> Himself have not a face.

*

> Oh Life, begun in fluent Blood
> And consummated dull!

*

> The Brain, within its Groove
> Runs evenly—and true—
> But let a Splinter swerve—
> 'Twere easier for You—
>
> To put a Current back—
> When Floods have slit the Hills—
> And scooped a Turnpike for Themselves—
> And trodden out the Mills—

* * *

Franz Kafka in his stories, parables, fragments, and journal entries rather more than in his incompletely realized novels . . . Virginia Woolf in her diary and letters, in which her voice sounds forth quicksilver and inimitable, rather more than in her frequently stilted, always self-conscious prose fiction . . . Henry James when he is most Jamesian (as in *The Wings of the Dove*) and then again least Jamesian (as in the unabridged *Notebooks* in which he addresses himself without artifice, sometimes in melancholy, sometimes in triumph, speaking to his muse whom he calls "mon bon" as if he, or it, were a lover) . . . William James in that great work *The Varieties of Religious Experience* in which you will find yourself in one or another chapter ("The Religion of Healthy-Mindedness," "The Sick Soul," "The Divided Self, and the Process of Its Integration") . . . Hardy's great novels, prose-poetry as narrative, *Tess of the D'Urbervilles* and *Jude the Obscure* in particular . . . Robert Frost despite the distracting regularity of certain of his rhymes (which mitigate against, in the ears of many admirers, the deeper music of his art) . . . D. H. Lawrence in his poetry no less than in his prose, and in such "minor" work as *The Lost Girl* as well as in the "major" novels . . . James Joyce in the very excess of his genius, word-maddened, besotted, not so much crossing the line between sanity and craziness as erasing it—at least in art. And there are the others, the many others, the flood of others, the voices of strangers closer to us than the voices of friends, more intimate, in some instances, than our own. Literature grants us few of the consolations and none of the vatic promises of religion but *is* our religion nonetheless.

* * *

The expression on the young man's face—I am haunted by it, not envious (of it, or of its cause) but wondering, bemused: was it simple surprise, at the masterpiece of short prose fiction we had taken up in our workshop; was it awe?—sheer *interest?* And his eagerness to read more by Hemingway, more of these short tight perfect narratives, written when Hemingway was (as I tell my students gently) not much older than they. The story is "A Very Short Story," one and a half pages of laconic prose, bitten-back rage, "One hot evening in Padua they carried him up onto the roof and he could look over the top of the town. . . ." and it's perfection of a kind, of a kind Hemingway himself only infrequently achieved. It is a young man's record of being wounded, the death of romance, of hope, as powerful in its way as the novel it would later become, and far less sentimental. And the young, very young writers in my workshop to whom "Ernest Hemingway" has always been a name or a reputation are allowed to see that there was a Hemingway who did not know himself Hemingway, could not, so young, have guessed it would turn out as in his most aggressive childlike fantasies he'd dreamt it would: he *was* the real thing, wasn't he. And one of them remains after class wanting to say something further, not wanting the talk of Hemingway to end, or the talk, in any case, of *this* Hemingway to end, this page and a half of perfectly honed and seemingly immortal prose; wanting to ask me something but not knowing what to ask, as at all crucial moments in our lives we want to speak without knowing what to say. What can I tell him of the unfathomable mystery of personality? Of personality transcribed and made permanent in art?—in mere finite *words?* Perhaps the young man wants to ask, Can I do it too? Can I try, too? but he would not ask such a thing, would not expose himself so rawly, that isn't Princeton's style. He says, the book still open in his hands, his voice rather vague, searching, "It's so short. It does so much." And I'm thinking, yes, this is the real thing, this is love, that look on your face, again, always, what pleasure.

Nietzsche never married, had no child. It is believed his madness was caused by syphilitic infection contracted when he was a student or while nursing wounded soldiers in 1870. (The translation used here is by Walter Kaufmann.)

Lee Zacharias

In the Garden of the Word

Fiction is about what it is like to be human.

—DORIS BETTS

1

The weather is sweet. In this town that has, like so many others, a Market Street, the median is planted with trees called weeping cherries; they are weeping the palest pink blossoms. In my yard the daffodils and forsythia are already fading into azaleas and dogwoods, whose uncurling green fists promise the spectacular white lace of spring. Even the sidewalk is fragrant with the earth warming beneath it. I have opened a window in my study, for on this fine afternoon I am inside, writing a novel.

I am imagining another spring day, twenty-two years ago, a day on which 25,000 people gathered on the grassy slope behind the Washington Monument under a bright blue dome of sky with the warmth of the sun soaking into their shoulders. They are protesting the Vietnam War, but it is 1965, the war is young, and on such a day neither I nor the character I have singled out from that crowd can summon anger. She cannot know of the bitterness to come, the mood of protest turning from hope to blind fury. The scene is already written, but I surprise myself by adding these lines: "It is not possible to believe in evil on a perfect spring afternoon, and in its absence, one places faith not in the tangle of conditions between, but in good. It is in this error that we come to be moral."

2

But what do I mean by that, exactly? As a writer, I operate by the rules of two thumbs: two lines of omniscience; get out. Pronouncements are as final to a scene as the tonic note to the musical phrase. But the composer is under no obligation to explain his structure, for its meaning is contained in its sound. My obligation is to imply the clear and impalpable thought in the palpable word.

I'm not sure that those two sentences do the job, which will fall to all the words that have lesser pretensions, the *he said* and *she said* and all the little flashes of gesture, detail, and mood that leave most of what they should say unspoken. But I, who have the obligation to know every word that isn't said, am thinking about what it is like to be human.

What do I mean by "this error"?

Something like this: if to be human is to be fallible, it is precisely because no other creature makes the mistake of assuming itself to be moral. Nature admits of design, but not of motive. In search of one we claim an identity apart, which is both our grandeur and sorrow, for we die in the company of dust, but live in the crux of good and evil.

3

I am writing this novel by day, for I am on leave from my job, and at night I discover a luxury I haven't known for years. I close *Curious George,* call Daddy, who sings "Hail to the Redskins" far better than I do, kiss my small son good night, and climb into my bed, free to read anything I want, for hours. It is an ornate iron affair, my bed, picked up for ten dollars from some *junque* shop beside an Arkansas highway fifteen years ago, and it requires four fat pillows to keep its medallions from printing their whorls on my spine. But imagine — four fat pillows, a quilt worn soft drawn up under my arms, the hood of yellow light, the rose-colored walls, Steiglitz' *Flatiron* in its dusky mist of gum bichromate evoking the comforting sound of wheels on wet pavement, my husband's closet open and spilling ties. And on my bedside table whatever book I choose. I am a child again, propped up on the sofa, sick and home from school. My husband is kind — he brings me coffee soothed with milk; he is a reader too, and he understands that reading is, in the act itself, a sensory delight.

It is easy to forget that when you read, as we do, for a living: stories in search of publication, student manuscripts, the hundred pages you must teach tomorrow and have no time to savor. One finds pleasure in the best of these words too, but the act is not the same: I find some other place to do it, the desk where I write checks (never the one where I write fiction), the wing chair, a couch, the breakfast table. To reject a story, write a comment, or annotate an anthology in my bed is as unthinkable as sleeping on the stove or slicing onions in the bathtub. It is the place of sex and dreams; one may read happily in such a setting, but conduct business never.

					4

My appetite in reading is for narrative, my attraction to stories, any story, so instinctive that I cannot remember when it began. My mother claims to have toilet-trained me by threatening never to read to me again, and yet, once I was able to read to myself and the Little Golden Books of preschool were all packed away, I recall growing up in a house without books, save a few condensed novels from *Reader's Digest* and a paperback edition of *Peyton Place* my mother kept hidden beneath a clean white towel in the linen closet. My father worked double shifts at an oil refinery; my mother kept house, shopped for bargains, and sewed my dresses, strewing the living room with patterns, straight pins, and gaudy tufts of thread. We had a new television, and that was our frill.

It was by most counts, I think, a fairly standard childhood, given the time and place, and class, far too ordinary and intellectually impoverished for the standards of any child I know today. My own son is spoiled with the books and excursions and consideration of his questions that I wish I had had. Television is to him a VCR with a Disney classic or British actors playing Ratty, Moley, and Mr. Toad. What could my parents know of how I would look back? If they were children of the Depression, I was a child of their affluence. They were pioneers of the postwar cliché, astonished by the luck that work could bring them: a builder house, hands that fed their mouths, and at day's end an hour of Arthur Godfrey or Milton Berle. Settling the suburbs, we lived on the monochromatic frontier of the electronic age.

I went to the sort of schools where English meant another dreary day of linking verbs that the kids in the back row never seemed to master, in the sort of town where library cards were stamped *adult* or *child* and the librarian called your mother if you tried to check out *Jane Eyre* instead of the little orange biographies of Mary Mapes Dodge, Jolly Girl, and Boy Inventor Eli Whitney. I adored Maude Hart Lovelace, whose Betsy, Tacy, and Tib grew up with me. (Betsy wanted to be a writer!) I laughed at *Mrs. Piggle-Wiggle*, I wept and rewept over *King of the Wind*, all the Lassies and Black Beauties of true hearts and fickle masters, and, having failed to make a confidante of the steel-faced librarian, when I exhausted the emotions wrought by the children's section, I became addicted to Nancy Drew.

How can I describe the pleasure of an Easter Monday or any Saturday made special by a holiday dollar, when I squatted before a book rack in Goldblatt's to choose a new title? There are the smells—not ink and new paper, but jelly beans, Kandy Korn, and floor wax, the starched gray twill of men's workclothes stacked on counters, the leather of pocketbooks stuffed with tissue where the wallets and tobacco-shagged lipsticks belong. The sounds—the under-counter doors rattling across their aluminum tracks ("Let me see if I have an extra-large down here"), the dead chord of cash register keys marked dollars and cents and struck three together, the high bell of the elevator. But mostly there am I, sitting in the burnished gold-gray light on the floor of an alcove already sealed off as an entrance to a department store that has since been vacant for years, reading of Nancy's roadster and silk frocks, already doomed to nostalgia in a world committed to nylon and—though it doesn't know it yet—Toyotas.

I rode the bus home reading. By bedtime I would be finished, and on the next schoolday I would bring my new treasure to trade with my new friend Gulsum, another addict, a Turkish girl born in China who escaped the Reds with her father and grew up in Australia, where she had kept a pet kangaroo. Her mother had died in China, whether in childbirth or the civil upheaval I either do not recall or never knew. Her stepmother had just sued Lana Turner, whose daughter Cheryl had stabbed Lana's lover to death; the lover was Gulsum's stepmother's ex-husband and the father of Gulsum's stepbrother John. This last she never mentioned; I knew because *The Hammond Times* reported it, and in a school more accustomed to petty thieves than foreign students or Hollywood connections, I remember a whisper of scandal. What I don't remember is thinking her exotic, though I suppose some hideous little drawer in the rigid cabinet of a mind trained to think in linking verbs, in that unconditional grammar of nominatives where nothing ever happens, filed these facts. She lived in a tract house much like mine, ate her dinner at a similar formica and chrome dinette, endured the same dopey boys spitting mashed potatoes in the Woodrow Wilson Junior High cafeteria ("Look, I'm a pimple"), and marked the endless sentence of our humdrum girlhoods by a living room clock that is preserved in a picture in my album, where it summons all the hopeless innocence of an era when people realized dreams by saving S & H Green Stamps. No, she was not exotic to me, despite my impeccably eventless life; I think she was no more exotic to herself. How else to explain the avidity with which she took my latest Nancy?

Ah, Nancy Drew, now there was a world apart. We had "I Love Lucy" and English (*is, was, has been, will be*, with the boys in the back row throwing spitballs); Nancy had adventures. She was forever being knocked over the head to come to in a room stocked with black widow spiders or a house about to fall into the sea; she was less a real girl than a series of crises and rescues. But there was something else, beyond her freedom, beyond all the secrets and clues, the hidden staircases, leaning chimneys, and moss-covered mansions, that distinguished Nancy's world from ours. Hers was a world of absolutes, good and evil, with no moral murk between. Was Miss Dredge, the pink-haired old lady with one gray suit who ignored the spitballs and droned on (*is, feels, appears, seems to be*), good? Surely she was not evil, though we all hated her and called her Miss Drudge. Was my mother good? Was I? Was Cheryl, daughter of Lana, evil? What about my father, who suffered insomnia when he worked the night shift and came out of his bedroom raging whenever I made too much noise? "Your father is a good man," my mother would explain. "He's a good provider. Now look what you've done," she would say, and I would tell the neighbor at the door that she wasn't home while she crouched behind the armchair fingering her bruise. We lived a far cry from pretty Nancy, the good, golden-haired sleuth tracking an underworld of dark jewel thieves, counterfeiters, and forgers, a world in which the only passion was greed and good always won over evil. Even then we — Gulsum and I — knew that these mysteries we adored were useless as guides. What drew us to them was the fact that they were lies.

5

What a revelation college was to me, the discovery of a literature that dealt in truth — in the mysteries and measures of character, in the paradox of good and evil, not in a moral world but in moral vision — at the same time that I fancied I had discovered a life that was not a lie. I went home as rarely as respectable, wore jeans before they were fashionable, affected a lenseless pair of granny glasses, espoused unpopular causes with no real understanding of the issues, took odd courses, hung out at foreign films, read Ferlinghetti, and somehow figured all this made me an honest — i.e., moral — person. But I also read Chaucer, Shakespeare, and Milton, Keats, Wordsworth, Byron, Blake, Joyce, Woolf, Hawthorne, Hemingway, Faulkner, Fitzgerald, et al., for I majored in English, doubling up hours and taking correspondence courses to make up the fifteen credits beyond the forty-five maximum in any one subject that would count toward a diploma. My minor was more literature, comparative, and to this day I embarrass myself in French pronunciation, having been so busy reading that I taught myself the requisite languages from textbooks rather than take the time to slow down and learn them from the *croissant, Wurst,* and oral drill up in 101 classes. In those days I was into *ideas.*

I might have majored in philosophy if my freshman teacher hadn't had such a terrible case of dandruff or made such a clumsy near-pass. "You seem like such an interesting person," he said, explaining why he had summoned me to his office on the pretext of discussing my test, about which he had nothing to say. "Me?" I squeaked. When one is seventeen, out of such silliness decisions are made: he was no more interested in my mind than I was in his body, and I was shocked, because I admired his mind, but in my awareness of the white scurf on his sweater (he sat much too close), I understood that the body was precisely what I missed in his class, where we made sense of life without the pleasure of experiencing it first through the senses. I chose English, and in that choice nearly all the turns my life has taken since, because what I read in those classes was at once intellectual and visceral.

That is what I say about the choice now. At the time I had no such word in my vocabulary. I made it on instinct, the same that led me to decide in second grade my ambition to be a writer. I liked stories; I liked poems; I liked the illusion they gave me of learning things firsthand. *Learning* would have been a key word then, for I was serious and did not know I could seriously admit that I chose literature for the pleasure of it.

One discovers—and deepens—that pleasure by stages. If the readers who make best-sellers never leave the first and second stages, in which one reads for entertainment or the satisfaction of an emotional need, serious students know the third: the thrill of honing in on the meaning, the triumph of discovering that all great literature has a theme and that the theme nearly always has to do with morality or, in its narrower sense, ethics. Perhaps even then I knew there was a fourth, the appreciation for style, that grace of the accurate word and true rhythm. The appreciation for what writers call texture, that *sine qua non* of sensory detail, often comes later, for, although the tools are available to any six-year-old, it seems to take some knowledge of the craft to raise the appreciation to the level of conscious and legitimate delight. This fifth is not the last stage—there is another, in which all the pleasures unite and the work becomes whole for the reader—but the love for texture and the love for the language are the ones that seduce the writer.

6

Art, I sometimes tell my writing students, is a perfect and constantly changing balance of cruelty and nostalgia.

I am anxious to explain to them that by *nostalgia* I do not mean *sentimentality*, though likely I do. I am attached to the things of this world, which I suspect I measure more by my attachment than by their own worth, the eternal week of the weeping cherries, the starburst of time in an S & H clock. It is sentiment that makes phenomena of them, just as it is sentiment that lingers over the details of character, the cactuses on Emma Bovary's windowsill, Delores Haze's hand stretched out to take Humbert Humbert's figurative penny, long after the intellect has summed up the person. It is, to my mind, something akin to what Gertrude Stein means by the noun in that odd essay on poetry and grammar. Prose, she says, loves the verb; poetry loves naming. For me, the greatest pleasure of literature comes half from that poetry of naming, from the word that evokes not only the substance but also the emotions the writer would have us attach to it, a poetry that is as much a part of the best prose as of any excellent lyric. Literature serves the desire to possess the world by giving it a name.

It balances on our sense of loss.

For as much as nostalgia comes from loss—our impending sense of death, informed by all the little things we lose along the way—so does the cruelty that is our cold knowledge of it. One might call it irony, but it is also discipline.

Having named the thing, we subject it to the truth of action. The way in which it yields is all the pleasure.

7

The writer is the voice of humankind, speaking to the race of the individual and to the individual of the race, witness to the imagination, the intellect, history, and the life of his or her time. Literature is the record. By it I enlarge the bounds of my sympathy, for as it calls me to imagine that I am part of some other, I join company in a way that I cannot in any other social endeavor. I am permitted to know characters in mind, dream, and body, in a way that I will never know even those people who are so close to me as my husband and son.

Tonight I will read.

Tomorrow I will return to writing my novel.

These are not lonely acts.

By them, in their heightened moral climate, I cast myself outside the dumb glory of nature and come to know Eve. I have tasted the fruit. In truth I have found it most delicious. I reach for the word and invent my own garden.

Richard Ford

Reading

For H.S.B.

I learned to read—I mean learned to read carefully—in 1969, when I was twenty-five years old. I was in graduate school then and trying to figure out if I should begin to write short stories. I was married and living in a small apartment. I'd quit law school the year before. I had gone a long way from home—to California—and I did not know very much. I didn't even think I did.

Nineteen sixty-nine was an awful year in the Vietnam War and a bad year in the country. The Tet offensive had been the year before, and everyone saw the whole war as a loss. Among us graduate students there was a related and distinct unease, almost a squeamishness, about what *we* were doing—writing; an unease that manifested itself as a hot and unforgiving demand for relevancy in everything we said and intended and studied and, most important, asked of others. And, especially, we measured our courses that way. They needed, we felt, to be very, *very* relevant; to our lives, but to our dreads also, to our predicaments, our genders, our marriages, our futures, to the war and to the sixties themselves—an era we knew we were living through even as we did it.

And, naturally, nothing quite measured up. I had a course in the *Bildungsroman*, read Lessing, Rousseau, Mann, Henry Adams. And it all seemed just too bookish by half; too much to do with history and Freud, both of whose lessons we distrusted and made fun of as reductive. I read all of Hardy's poems after that, all seven hundred or so pages in the big green Macmillan edition, and couldn't bear them either. They seemed oldish, pale and insulated from my interests. What we did like, of course, we didn't need or mean to study: *Man's Fate*, a clear book of truth; both the wonderful Kesey books; *The Crying of Lot 49, At Play in the Fields of the Lord, The Ginger Man*—books premised in ironies, a mood more and more attractive when the sincere and practical connections between us and the world could not be convincingly drawn.

Contemporary writing itself had not been in much of a signifying mood. Donald Barthelme's stories were in our minds. Ron Sukenick's. Barry Hannah. William Kotzwinkle. They were all writing wonderfully. And the disjointures and absurdities, the hilarity, the word-virtuosity of those writers—all of whom I still admire—seemed right for our time and us. The world was a whacking wreck, California its damned epicenter. And we were stranded there, absurdly. And absurdity is never completely irrelevant to the facts of any life.

Exactly what we wanted is not clear to me. Though likely it was not one thing, alone. We were young. We were not particularly educated. And, like many beginning writers, for a time we were addicted to the new in everything. We were makers and less so takers-in, and we thought *ourselves* in the relevance business. Barthelme and those other guys were our colleagues, whether they knew it or not. And to be vulnerable to teaching suggested about us and these classics we resisted—tameness. Encapsulability. There wasn't time for Mann. *Irrelevant,* I have come to believe, is a word one often uses to put oneself forward. And what I truly think is we wouldn't have recognized relevance if it had come up and kissed us on the lips.

Part of my school training as a writer, however, provided that I could learn how to teach. It was felt by my teachers—writers themselves—that if we students ever became the real things, we would probably never be able to support ourselves that way and so could teach as a fallback while we busied ourselves toward agents, book contracts, editors, movie and paperback deals, big bucks—whatever else is at the end of that line of hopes. And strange to say, if my classes did not seem spot-on relevant to me, this prospect of teaching somehow did. Teaching *was* a kind of practical preparation for life, after all, and it did not seem hard to do. It had pleasures. It involved the admiration of others—something I wanted. And teaching literature seemed allied to writing it in some way abject studenthood did not. And so I said I would do it, and in fact was very glad to do it.

What exactly this teacher training entailed was going before a class of undergraduates, asking them to read several short stories and novels chosen and discussed among us assistants by an overseeing professor, and then, for three days a week, teaching. Teaching fiction. And what I found my problem to be was that I couldn't imagine the first thing to do, because I didn't, in any way I could convey to another human, know how to read.

Oh, I'd read plenty. I felt I was *a reader,* and I expected to be a writer. I'd been an English major at a big midwestern university and escaped with good grades. I had actually "taught" high school English a year and worked as an assistant editor for a Hearst Corporation magazine, and had, it seemed, experience to make me worth the risk of being put in a classroom full of eighteen-year-olds. Only as I began to prepare I was drawing a blank.

I can still say the things I knew about fiction then—most of it brought along from college. I knew several terms: Characters were the people in fiction. Symbols were the objects in stories to which extra meaning adhered (the raft in Huck Finn, for example, was a symbol). Point of view, I understood, referred not to a character's opinion about something, or the author's, but to what means the story was told by. First, third, omniscient. I knew that beginnings were important parts of stories and, as in "The Lady with the Pet Dog," sometimes they contained the seeds of the entire story (I did not know why that mattered, though). I knew primitive myths sometimes underlay fairly simple-seeming stories. I knew irony was important. I knew, nervously, that the language of a story or novel often meant more or less or even something entirely different from what it seemed to, and that understanding it—the story—meant understanding all the meanings at once. Meaning itself was a term, though I'd never been altogether sure what it meant.

And I knew other things. I knew how to "read like a writer." We talked about such things in our workshops. Certain books had practical lessons to teach. Nuts and bolts: how to get characters efficiently in and out of fictional rooms (Chekhov was good here); how to describe efficiently that it was dark (Chekhov again); how to weed out useless dialogue ("Hi, how are you?" "I'm fine, how are you?" "I'm okay. Thanks." "Good to hear it." "Good-bye." "Good-bye." That sort of stuff). I learned that a good opening ploy in a novel was to have Indians —if there were any—ride over a hill screaming bloody murder. I learned that when in doubt about what to do next, have a man walk through the door holding a gun. I learned that you couldn't get away with killing off your main character in a short story—though I was never told why, and neither, I guess, was Hemingway.

All these hands-on lessons were things I was mulling. Yet they didn't really seem worth teaching to young readers, people for whom making literature was not yet a career selection, nor was reading it even a given in their lives—in fact was possibly as disagreeable as a dentist's visit. Going about teaching literature in this way seemed like teaching someone to build a sleek and fast car without first treating them to how it felt to split the breeze in one. They'd never know exactly what it was all good for.

What seemed worthwhile to teach was what I *felt* about literature when I read it—those matters of relevance set slightly aside. That was why I wanted to write stories, after all. Literature was pretty and good. It had mystery, denseness, authority, connectedness, closure, resolution, perception, variety, magnitude—*value*, in other words, in the way Sartre meant when he wrote, "The work of art is a value because it is an appeal." Literature appealed to me.

But I had no idea how to teach its appealing qualities, how to find and impart the origins of what I felt. I didn't even know when to bring in my terms, or if they were right. I quickly came to feel that being an intermediary between an expectant mind and an excellent book is a conspicuous and chancy role to play. And I imagined myself sitting behind a metal desk staring at them, *Madame Bovary* open before me, passages underlined, silence commanding every molecule of the still air, and having nothing whatsoever to say, while being certain something should be said. Or worse—having only this to say: "What's the point of this book?" And *then* having nothing to say when the right answer came and as a voice inside me screamed, *mystery, connectedness, authority, closure, magnitude, value.*

These first preparations for teaching occurred over the Christmas holidays, in 1968. I went to my tiny graduate-student office and pored over my stories, over and over and over, without advance. "A Guest of the Nation"; "Death in the Woods"; "The Battler"; "Disorder and Early Sorrow"; "The Wind Blows." I could practically recite them. But I had no idea what to say *about* them. I still can feel the panic of pure inessentialness cold on my neck as literature rose against me like a high wall behind which was a deep jungle. I was to take people through there not just safely but gainfully, only I had no business even setting out.

In an office down the hall from where I was panicking that winter was a man named Howard Babb. I knew him because he was to be the chairman of our English department the next fall, and he was director of the course I was readying to teach. Mr. Babb liked us writers—even more, we felt, than he liked the Ph.D. types whose literary training he saw over. We seemed like true amateurs to him, not even serious enough to be gloomy, and it was in his good character to think of himself, or at least to portray himself, in precisely that way. Later, when I knew him better in the few years before he died, and I was his young colleague, I would overhear him say again and again to some student, about some piece of literature he was instructing, "Now, of course, I don't pretend to know a goddamned thing about any of this business, mind you. I would only in a simpleminded way venture to say this . . . " And then he would go on to say what was truest and best and smartest about a story or a novel. He merely did not claim to be an expert, and possibly he wasn't, though he knew a great deal. Simplest just to say that his mind stayed remarkably open to literature, whereas an expert's sometimes does not.

I will say a word or two about Howard Babb here because he was a singular man—human and inspiring—and because his influence over my life as a writer and as a reader was direct and unqualifiedly good. A day, indeed, doesn't go by now that I do not think of him.

At that time, I knew about him only a very few things, as was once the case between students and their professors—no first names, no dinner invitations or ball games attended together. He was a big yankee man—in his late forties—with a Maine accent, a bluff, good temper and a deep, murmurous voice with which he would occasionally talk loudly for effect. He had left college to be a sailor, and cursed like a sailor, though he was not undignified. He had tattoos on his arms that you could see when he rolled up his white sleeves. He smoked Tareytons in secret when he was at school, and sometimes drank at faculty parties and talked even louder. He'd been a student of Walter Jackson Bate at Harvard, and later a colleague of John Crowe Ransom and Peter Taylor at Kenyon. He was married and had a son. He walked with a heavy, hod-carrier's purposive gait—bow-legged, arms a little out from his shoulders, as if he was always stalking something. He seemed like a tough guy to me, and I liked him the first moment I saw him.

Toughness aside, though, he loved Jane Austen and George Eliot. He loved Conrad and Richardson and the eighteenth century. He knew a world about narrative and wrote and talked about it smartly, though he never became famous for it. He was, I thought even then, as out of place in southern California as a man with his history and affection for lasting virtues could ever be. And possibly to accommodate those divisive forces—though maybe the line of cause runs exactly opposite—he immersed himself with a fury in literature: reading it, teaching it, and talking about it. And for our purposes—his students—his fierceness, his zeal for teaching, his fervor for literature and its importance to us, comprised his entire attitude toward life, his whole self. No discrepancies. No ironies. No two-mindedness about how he felt, say, when the Irish soldiers kill their poor prisoner in "A Guest of the Nation," and how he might feel were such an awful dilemma ever to be his own. Or our own. Literature had direct access to his everyday life. The day, in fact, that he read aloud to me those fearsome final words of O'Connor's, sitting alone in his shadowy office on a winter afternoon almost twenty years ago, I listened without moving. And when he was finished he just stared at the floor, leaning on his knees, the book opened in his big hands, and maybe for five minutes we did not speak a word—not one word—so large were both our feelings for what we'd heard. And what I knew was that anything that happened to *me* afterward, after that seized moment, I would never feel the same about again. Here, I think, was relevance, first encountered, and here was pleasure of a quite rare kind.

But before then, back on that cheerless snowless Christmas, I had yet to encounter it. And what I did, at my wits' very end, was pick up my book of stories and walk down the empty corridor to Mr. Babb's office at the end of the hall. He was there through those holidays, reading alone without overhead light, making his minute margin notes, preparing for his courses while his colleagues were elsewhere—on their sailboats or skiing or attending conventions. I stood in his open doorway until he looked up and saw me. He stared a moment. "Well," he said softly, "what in the hell do you want? Shouldn't you be off farting around back in Mississippi, or wherever it is you're from?" This was friendly.

"No," I said, "I have a problem here."

"Well okay, then." He sighed and closed his book. "Come on in and sit down." And that is what I did.

Not surprisingly, if I could not teach those stories, neither could I say to Mr. Babb how or why I couldn't. This seems axiomatic now—proof of ignorance. But even more awful was that I didn't want to admit I didn't know. Silence has always been the accomplice to my ignorance; and ignorance, unsuitedness, unpreparedness always my coldest, most familiar fears. I have never approached anything difficult and truly new without expecting to fail at it, and quickly; or without generalizing how little I knew and dreading being told.

What I said was this: "I am having trouble knowing *exactly* how to go about teaching this Anderson story."

The Anderson story, as I've said, was "Death in the Woods," one of his great, signature stories, written in the thirties and separate in style and sympathy from the famous "Winesburg" tales from fifteen years earlier and the aftermath of the war. In "Death in the Woods," as in those few other Anderson masterpieces, "I Want to Know Why," "The

Egg," "The Man Who Became a Woman," an adult narrator tells a series of events recalled from his childhood, a seemingly simpler time, when the speaker was but a receptor—though a keen one—for whom life's memorable moments became the stuff of later inquiry and recognition. It is a classic story structure, one I have come to know well.

In Anderson, a man remembers a woman he saw once years earlier, in the small town where he was a boy. The woman was poor and poorly treated by her brute husband and her brute son. Yet she fed and provided for them on their poverty farm while the two men went off drunk and carousing. On a certain trip back from town, where she had traded eggs for meat and flour, the woman—named, sadly, Mrs. Grimes— pauses to rest at the foot of a tree, and surprisingly though painlessly freezes to death as snow and then clear night set on. In a spectral and unforgettable scene (one the narrator imagines, since he could not have witnessed it) Mrs. Grimes' dogs begin to run wild circles around her body and eventually drag her out into the night radiance and feed themselves on the provisions she was bringing home—though not, it should be said, on Mrs. Grimes, whose palely beautiful body goes untouched— " . . . so white and lovely," the speaker imagines it, ". . . so like marble."

Much is plain in this wonderful story, even to the least lettered reader. When I first read it, in 1969, it seemed longer and complexer than when I read it today. But its large concerns seem the same ones I must've known then, if intuitively: the cruelty inherent in us all; our edgy similarity to the spirit of wild beasts; the uncertain good of advancing civilization; the mystery and allure of sex; adulthood as a poor, compromised state of being; the ways by which we each nurture others; the good to be got from telling. Mystery, closure, connectedness, magnitude— value. Anderson wrote inspired by all these grand disturbances and their literary conceits. I think of him still as one of our great, great writers.

And I meant to teach him. He was on the syllabus, though I could not then have found the words I've just said.

"Tell me, Mr. Ford," Mr. Babb said, still softly, when he'd sat in silence for a while, flipping pages through the story in my anthology, glancing at my underlinings, raising his eyebrows at my notes, sniffing now and then, humming at a line of Anderson's he admired. He knew the story by heart and loved Anderson. I knew that in the way a graduate student must know the tastes of his professors and assume them shamelessly. "Tell me just this," he said again, and looked up at me quizzically, then at the ceiling, as if he'd begun rehearsing some life of his own from years ago, which the story had pleasantly revived. "What, um, what do you think is the most interesting formal feature of this story? I'm, of course, not talking about anything particularly complicated. Just what *you* think about it." He blinked at me as though in the mists of this marvelous story and of his own memory, he couldn't quite make me out now.

And at the instant I write this, I know what was in his mind—though I have never known it before, and would've guessed it was something else; that I would give him the wrong answer, or an incomplete one, and that our talk would commence there. But I understand now that he was certain I had no idea in the world what he could be talking about, and that our tasks would begin from that point—the perfect point of origin. Zero. The place where all learning begins.

"I don't know what you mean by 'formal feature,'" I answered in a good, clear voice. And with that I gave up some large part of my ignorance. I must've sensed I'd learn something valuable if I could only do that. And I was right.

"Well," he said, bemused. "All right." He nodded and sighed, then turned in his swivel chair to a green chalkboard on the wall, stood, and with a chalk wrote this list.

Character
Point of View
Narrative Structure
Imagistic Pattern
Symbol
Diction
Theme

These, of course, were words I'd seen. Most of them had been swirling around my thinking for days without order or directive. Now, here they were again, and I felt relieved.

These expressions, Mr. Babb said, sitting back in his chair but still looking at the list, described the formal features of a piece of fiction. If we could define them, locate them in a particular piece of fiction, and then talk about any one of them in a careful and orderly way, reliant on the words of the story and commonsense, asking perfectly simple questions, proceeding to deductions one by one, perhaps talking about other features as they came to mind—eventually we would involve ourselves in a discussion of the most important issues in a story, or in a novel.

In every story he himself read, he said, some one formal feature seemed to stand out as a conspicuous source of interest, and he could investigate the story that way. *The Great Gatsby,* for instance, was *narrated* in a way he thought especially interesting. Point of view was then the issue: Who was Nick Carraway? Why was he telling this story? What peculiar advantage or disadvantage did he have as its teller? Was our understanding of the story affected by the fact that he told it? If so, how? Did he — Nick — judge other characters? How? Was he always telling the truth? What if he wasn't? Why did I think so?

In "Silent Snow, Secret Snow," the lustrous, enigmatic master-story by Conrad Aiken (also on the syllabus), how could one make sense of this unusual snow that seems increasingly to buffer the child whose life is at the story's center? Is it actual snow? Why do we think it is or isn't? Could we reasonably imagine it to represent anything besides itself? Only one thing? What did this have to do with other features of the story? The child's character? The setting? His parents? Here we were investigating an image.

Story to story, each had a path-in signaled by a prominent formal feature, with one feature's effects and our observations about it implicating another — point of view leading naturally to an interest in character, leading onward to some wider sense of how, as the story progressed through its own structural parts (scenes, settings, flashbacks), character and image and narrative strategy intertwined and formed the whole, until by our directed questioning we could say what seemed most complexly at issue in the story. Theme, this was — though no one should hope to identify that matter succinctly or to say it in a phrase. It was last but not foremost. Foremost was one's intimacy with the story.

In the Anderson, Mr. Babb said, one might start with a simple-minded set of questions and observations about who it was who told that story to us. Was it just a straightforward matter of an anonymous voice telling a story in the most unembellished way? *No.* Wasn't the teller a character? *Yes.* Did he tell it as it happened? *No.* Could one, on close examination of the very words chosen in the story, distinguish different concerns — even preoccupations — of the speaker besides just the facts of the old woman's death? *Yes, yes, yes.* And with each answer elicited couldn't we reasonably say, "And how does this materially contribute to my understanding of the story?" Or, in plainer words: "So what if this is true?" "So what if this is not?"

What opened for me in the course of this single conversation was a large number of small lights, partial recognitions I could only partially appreciate, but that over the years have developed and seemed among the most important I've ever made and, toward reading literature, the most important of all. Mr. Babb, naturally, never told me exactly what to do, and our talk never left the plain of the hypothetical/conditional ("one *might* ask this; isn't it possible to wonder that? surely this is not completely irrelevant . . . "). But he taught. He taught me not only an orderly means to gain entry to and intimacy with a complex piece of narrative, but also that literature could be approached as empirically as life, to which after all it was connected. As in life, our literary understandings, even our failures at understanding, were founded on a series of commonsense responses — not necessarily answers — that were true to the small facts, the big movements, and the awes and dreads and pleasures we all felt as we made our way along. Literature was not only accessible, but relevant to life, inasmuch as the same matters were of issue in both: How do I love whom I love? How can I go on each day with or without those persons? How will this day end? Will I live or will I die?

It will be understood that when I left Mr. Babb's office that late December afternoon, I did so with a much less clear view of reading literature than I have today, even though my view now is still clouded by the ignorance of all I've yet to read and will never read, and by the "complicating" experience of having spent the next eighteen or so years trying to make stories as good as those Anderson ones I loved and that affect me to this moment. Still, I went away feeling confident — pleasurably confident — that the method I'd just seen practiced bore an utterly natural relationship to any piece of fiction I would ever read, examine, or teach. I believed that the stories which had pleased me, awed me, frightened me with their interconnected largeness were actually *constructions of* those formal features Mr. Babb had described. Good stories — whether or not they were made so intentionally by authors — were basically arrangements of knowable images, word patterns, of dramatic structure and symbols. They were *made of* characters and points of view and possessed themes. Moreover, reading any story with this knowledge amounted to the truest experience of knowing it. I'm certain I taught my first students that, and taught others, too; made discovering forms and verifying them an end, not just a pedagogy, a device. It is almost inevitable I would, given my novice's need to order a universe and since fiction can be fitted in so nicely to this symmetry. My mind rested there, I suppose I can say. And many people, I suspect, students and their teachers, too, never get beyond that static, intermediate stage of reading—knowing which point of view is which, sensing what an old symbolizing animal man is, comparing and contrasting poor Jake Barnes and lucky Bill Gorton *as characters;* never get around to asking what all this has to do with life—asking the final question of relevancy: So what?

Thinking back to then, I'm sure Mr. Babb didn't believe in such a pat, synthetic view of literature, but instead that we synthesize these forms in an effort to organize our progress through difficult writing, tracing their shapes like constellations in a wild heaven. The proof was the awe he preserved, the affection, the eagerness with which he returned to the same passages and stories over and over, still curious, pleasantly baffled, willing to be amazed, reverent of all that the books continued to give him. It was I—not smart enough and just beginning—who championed a method before the method's full use and limits could be understood.

And it is—I suppose appropriately—only because of writing stories rather than being an excellent reader that I figured out that this formalism was a faulty account of how stories of any length got made and are best known.

Stories, and novels, too—I came to see from the experience of writing them—are makeshift things. They originate in strong, disorderly impulses; are supplied by random accumulations of life-in-words; and proceed in their creation by mischance, faulty memory, distorted understanding, weariness, deceit of almost every imaginable kind, by luck and by the stresses of increasingly inadequate vocabulary and waning imagination—with the result often being a straining, barely containable object held in fierce and sometimes insufficient control. And there is nothing wrong with that. It doesn't hurt me to know it. Indeed, my admiration for the books I love is greater for knowing the chaos they overcame. But there is very little I can say, then, about the experience of writing stories that will make the experience of parsing them formally seem a completely apt way to know them. Even the word—formal—seems wrong-spirited to such an amateurish and un-formal business. *Characters,* those "rounded" people in good books whom we say we recognize and know like our cousins, are at heart just assemblages of sentences, ongoing, shifting arrangements of descriptions and purported human impulse and action hooked to a name—all of it changeable by adding and subtracting or forgetting words—yet hardly ever sharply convincing to me as "selves." Point of view, that precise caliper for measuring meaning in Mr. Babb's scheme, is chiefly an invented mind's voice which I can hear and "write through," and whose access to language and idiom seems, at least to start, adequate for some not quite certain telling. Imagery — at best — is a recurrence of sentence patterns and emotional tics and habits I would often rather trade in for more diverse and imaginative resources in language. And symbol. Well, symbol is anything the reader says it is.

And for every writer it's different; different means and expectations, different protocols under which a story accumulates, different temperaments and lingo about how to do it — different work in every way — as should be.

A formal template for studying narrative can guide us orderly into such creations as these, permit a desired intimacy with sentences, aid our confidence and encourage our thinking by abstracting us from parts of the story we can't grasp yet, then in due time leading us to the other parts, so that eventually we see and can try connecting all that's written. But an organizing or explaining system which doesn't illuminate the haphazard in any story's existence can't be a real comprehension. Such schemes are always arbitrary and unstable — wrong (if still useful) in that at their worst they reduce a complex story to some matter of categories, and pose as cure-alls to our natural wonder and awe before great literature — reactions that originate less in ignorance than in the magnitude of the story itself; reactions we shouldn't relinquish but hold on to for dear life — as pleasure.

But pleasure can arise even from this very friction between the story read and the story written. And not a single, simple pleasure, but several, with shadings and history. Even as unsevere and practical-minded as the formal procedure taught me when I learned to read closely is in some sense an imitation of its subject — one with a consoling use, in this case. And imitation has always appealed to us: "The pleasure . . . received is undoubtedly the surprise or feeling of admiration occasioned by the unexpected coincidence between the imitation and its object." That was Hazlitt's idea. And Addison takes it straight to the point: " . . . Our imagination loves to be filled with an object or to grasp at anything that is too big for its capacity" — which is what happens when a method of knowing cannot altogether account for its natural subject in all its complexity.

This friction between my school method and my experience might just as well be renamed pleasure. Each is valuable to me, each quickens interest in the whole truth, and each can accommodate the other. Pleasure, in this scheme, arises when what was unknown, or unknown as pleasure, can be perceived that way; when, in a sense, pleasure is reinvented.

I still feel dread and wonder in the face of literature from time to time — usually in a novel, often so much that I can't parse it with satisfaction. Maybe my spirit for parsing has been worn down. Joyce makes me feel that way. Ford Madox Ford, sometimes. Céline. Gide. Pynchon: awestruck — although I think these writers' aim is to make me feel that. And I simply experience chaos — literary chaos, the story's apparent nearness to its own disorderly beginnings — more agreeably than I once did. I try to accommodate the story read to the one written, which is what Mr. Babb did and would've had me do from the beginning. He probably knew, however, that there's pleasure in first learning and then unlearning, that it is one of literature's other great relevant lessons for life. And I am satisfied that his pleasures have finally become mine, and that I was at least a willing student. For that I could not be more grateful.

Guy Davenport

On Reading

To my Aunt Mae — Mary Elizabeth Davenport Morrow (1881–1964), whose diary when I saw it after her death turned out to be a list of places, with dates, she and Uncle Buzzie (Julius Allen Morrow, 1885–1970) had visited over the years, never driving over thirty miles an hour, places like Toccoa Falls, Georgia, and Antreville, South Carolina, as well as random sentences athwart the page, two of which face down indifference, "My father was a horse doctor, but not a common horse doctor" and "Nobody has ever loved me as much as I have loved them" — and a Mrs. Cora Shiflett, a neighbor on East Franklin Street, Anderson, South Carolina, I owe my love of reading.

Mrs. Shiflett, one of that extensive clan of the name, all retaining to this day the crofter mentality of the Scots Lowlands from which they come, a mixture of rapacity and despair (Faulkner called them Snopes), had rented a house across the street from us formerly occupied, as long as I could remember, by another widow, Mrs. Spoone ("with an *e*"), she and her son, whom we never saw, as he was doing ten years "in the penitencher." But before Mrs. Shiflett's son, "as good a boy to his mother as ever was," fell into some snare of the law, he had been a great reader. And one fateful day Mrs. Shiflett, who wore a bonnet and apron to authenticate her respectability as a good countrywoman, brought with her, on one of her many visits to "set a spell" with my mother, a volume of the Tarzan series, one in which Tarzan saves himself from perishing of thirst in the Sahara by braining a vulture and drinking its blood. She lent it to me. "Hit were one of the books Clyde loved in particular."

I do not have an ordered memory, but I know that this work of Edgar Rice Burroughs was the first book I read. I was thought to be retarded as a child, and all the evidence indicates that I was. I have no memory of the first grade, to which I was not admitted until I was seven, except that of peeing my pants and having to be sent home whenever I was spoken to by our hapless teacher. I have even forgotten her appearance and her name, and I call her hapless because there was a classmate, now a psychiatrist, who fainted when he was called on, and another who stiffened into petit mal. I managed to control my bladder by the third grade, but the fainter and the sufferer from fits, both classmates of mine through the ninth grade, when I quit school, kept teachers edgy until graduation.

No teacher in grammar or high school ever so much as hinted that reading was a normal activity, and I had to accept it, as my family did, as part of my affliction as a retarded person. The winter afternoon on which I discovered that I could follow Tarzan and Simba and some evil Arab slave-traders was the first in a series of by now fifty years of sessions in chairs with books. I read very slowly, and do not read a great deal, as I had much rather spend my leisure painting and drawing, or writing, and I do not have all that much leisure. And as a teacher of literature I tend to read the same books over and over, year after year, to have them fresh in my mind for lectures.

From *Tarzan*, which I did not read efficiently (and Burroughs' vocabulary runs to the exotic), I moved on to available books. My father had a small library of a hundred or so, from which I tried a *Collected Writings of Victor Hugo*, mysteriously inscribed in my father's hand, "G. M. Davenport, Apr. 24, 1934, Havana, Cuba," where I am positive my father never set foot. Under this inscription, he (or somebody) drew a cube, in ink that bled through to appear on the other surface of the page, on Victor Hugo's forehead in a frontispiece engraving. But Hugo is not Edgar Rice Burroughs, and I could make nothing of him.

Aunt Mae had inherited, with pride, the small library of my uncle Eugene, a soldier in the First World War, buried in France a decade before my birth. This contained a complete Robert Louis Stevenson and James Fenimore Cooper, both of whom proved to be over my head. But there was a picture book of Pompeii and Herculaneum, which opened a door of a different sort, giving me my first wondering gaze into history and art. Aunt Mae was herself addicted to the novels of Zane Grey, whom I lumped in with Victor Hugo as a writer unable to get on with what he had to say, as bad at dawdling as Cooper.

And then I made the discovery that what I liked in reading was to learn things I didn't know. Aunt Mae's next-door neighbor, Mrs. McNinch, belonged to the Book-of-the-Month Club, which in 1938 — I was eleven — sent its subscribers Antonina Vallentin's *Leonardo da Vinci*. Mrs. McNinch, a woman of fervent piety and a Presbyterian, had chosen this book because of *The Last Supper*. She lent it to me. I had not known until the wholly magic hours I spent reading it, all of a wet spring, that such a man as Leonardo was possible, and I was hearing of the Renaissance for the first time. I read this difficult book in a way I can no longer imagine. I pretended, I think, that I was following the plot and the historical digressions. I have not reread this book, and yet I can, in lectures, cite details of Leonardo's career from it. Or think I can. I have read some forty studies of Leonardo since, and many books about his epoch, and may be fooling myself as to which source I'm remembering. But I can still see all the illustrations, the codex pages in sepia, the paintings in color.

When I returned the biography of Leonardo, the generous Mrs. McNinch lent me Carl Van Doren's *Benjamin Franklin*, also published in 1938, and a Book-of-the-Month Club selection. This was harder going, with phrases like "minister plenipotentiary," which I would mutter secretly to myself. It is a truism that reading educates. What it does most powerfully is introduce the world outside us, negating the obstructions of time and place. When, much later, I ran across the word *opsimathy* in Walter Pater, I could appreciate the tragic implications of late learning. All experience is synergetic: and Bucky Fuller should have written, and probably did, about the phenomenon of Synergetic Surprise. We cannot guess what potential lies in wait for the imagination through momentum alone. The earlier Leonardo and Franklin enter one's mind, the greater the possibility of their bonding and interacting with ongoing experience and information.

My childhood was far from bookish. I spent a lot of it hunting and fishing, searching Georgia and South Carolina fields for arrowheads, longing to work on the Blue Ridge Railroad, playing softball in the street, building tree houses. The hunting was done with my Uncle Broadus Dewey, on Saturdays, with a bird dog named Joe. Joe was gun-shy, and had conniption fits, with pitiful howls, when we took a shot at game. Many lives were spared, of squirrels and partridges and rabbits, to spare Joe's nerves. I myself never managed to shoot anything. What I liked was the outing, and the comradeship, and pretending to have Leonardo's eyes in looking at plants, rocks, the landscape. Back from hunting, I would try to imitate a page of the notebooks. On manila construction paper, from Woolworth's, I would draw in brown ink leaves in clusters, and rocks, and insects, hoping that the page resembled one by Leonardo.

When the first American paperbacks came along, they, too, opened other worlds: Sherlock Holmes and other detective fiction, leading me to read people in the Holmesian manner at the barbershop and on the street.

At sixty I have ample evidence for tracing synergies in reading. Summer before last I spent a beautiful day in Auvers-sur-Oise, standing by the graves of Vincent and Theo. The wheatfield is still unmistakably there, across the road from where they are buried against the cemetery wall, the Protestant place; and Gachet's house and garden. This day began with Irving Stone's trashy and irresponsible biography, and the hilariously vulgar film based on it, but one must begin somewhere. Opsimathy differs from early learning in that there are no taproots, no years of crossbreeding, no naturalization in a climate.

After I had taught myself to read, without reading friends or family, I kept at it, more or less unaware of what hunger I was feeding. I can remember when I read any book, as the act of reading adheres to the room, the chair, the season. Doughty's *Arabia Deserta* I read under the hundred-year-old figtree in our backyard in South Carolina, a summer vacation from teaching at Washington University, having lucked onto the two volumes (minus the map that ought to have been in a pocket in vol. II) at a St. Louis rummage sale. (The missing map was given me fifteen years later by Issam Safady, the Jordanian scholar.)

I read most of Willa Cather and Mann's Joseph tetralogy in the post library at Fort Bragg. The ordnance repair shop was on one side, the stockade on the other, and I was "keeping up my education" on orders from the adjutant general of the XVIIIth Airborne Corps, who kindly gave me Wednesday afternoons off specifically to read.

Proust I began among the spring blossoms of the Sarah P. Duke gardens in Durham, North Carolina, and finished forty years later by my fireplace in Lexington, Kentucky, convalescing from a very difficult operation to remove an embedded kidney stone. These settings are not merely sentimental; they are real interrelations. The moment of reading is integral to the process. My knowledge of Griaule's *Le renard pâle* is interwoven with my reading a large part of it in the Greenville, South Carolina, Trailways bus station. Yeats' *A Vision* belongs to the Hôtel Monsieur-le-Prince, once on the street of that name, as does *Nightwood* and *Black Spring*. *The Seven Pillars*, an Oxford room; *Fanny Hill*, the Haverford cricket field. And not all readings are nostalgic: the conditions under which I made my way through the *Iliad* in Greek were the violence and paralyzing misery of a disintegrating marriage, for which, nevertheless, the meaning of the poem is the more tragic for this abrasion. There are texts I can never willingly return to because of the misery adhering to them.

Students often tell me that an author was ruined for them by a high-school English class; we all know what they mean. Shakespeare was almost closed to me by the world's dullest teacher, and there are many writers whom I would probably enjoy reading except that they were recommended to me by suspect enthusiasts. I wish I knew how to rectify these aversions. I tell bright students, in conference, how I had to find certain authors on my own who were ruined for me by bad teachers or inept critics. Scott, Kipling, Wells, will do to illustrate that only an idiot will take a critic's word without seeing for oneself. I think I learned quite early that the judgments of my teachers were probably a report of their ignorance. In truth, my education was a systematic misleading. Ruskin was dismissed as a dull, preacherly old fart who wrote purple prose. In a decent society the teacher who led me to believe this would be tried, found guilty, and hanged by the thumbs while being pelted with old eggs and cabbage stalks. I heard in a class at Duke that Joyce's *Ulysses* was a tedious account of the death of Molly Bloom. An Oxford don assured me that Edmund Wilson is an astute critic. Around what barriers did I have to force my way to get to Pound, to Joyce, to William Carlos Williams?

All of this points to our having a society which reads badly and communicates execrably about what we read. The idea persists that writing is an activity of thoughtful, idealistic, moral people, called authors, and that they are committed to protecting certain values vital to a well-ordered society. Books mold character, enforce patriotism, and provide a healthy way to pass the leisurely hour. To this assumption there has been added in our day the image of the author as a celebrity, someone worth hearing at a reading or lecture even if you have no intention of parting with a dime for one of the author's books.

There is little room in this popular concept of writing for the apprehension and appreciation of style. I had, all along, I would like to think, been responding to style in my earliest attempts to read. I knew that the books I failed to enjoy — Scott's *The Black Dwarf* was the worst of these — were texts that remained foggy and indeterminate, like a moving picture experienced through bad eyesight and defective hearing. Style is radically cultural both linguistically and psychologically. I couldn't read Scott, Stevenson, and Cooper because I had not developed the imaginative agility needed to close the distance between me and the style of their texts. I could read, with excitement and a kind of enchantment, the biographies I encountered so early of Leonardo and Franklin not only because my curiosity about them was great, but because these biographies were in a contemporary, if academic, English.

My discovery of style came about through various humble books.

Hendrik Van Loon's whimsical history of the world (a Pocket Book, from Woolworth's) alerted me to the fact that tone makes all the difference. It was this book that began to make something of an aesthete of me, for I progressed to Van Loon's biography of Rembrandt (conflating the rich experience of the Leonardo biography with the pleasure of reading for style), a book I kept reading for the pleasure of the prose, despite my ignorance of his historical setting. In it, however, I saw the name Spinoza, which led me to dear old Will Durant, who led me to Spinoza's texts, and all fellow readers who have ever taken a book along to a humble restaurant will understand my saying that life has few enjoyments as stoical and pure as reading Spinoza's *Ethics*, evening after evening, in a strange city — St. Louis, before I made friends there. The restaurant was Greek, cozy, comfortable, and for the neighborhood. The food was cheap, tasty, and filling.

Over white beans with chopped onions, veal cutlet with a savory dressing, and eventually a fruit cobbler and coffee, I read the *De Ethica* in its Everyman edition, Draftech pen at the ready to underline passages I might want to refind easily, later. Soul and mind were being fed together. I have not eaten alone in a restaurant in many years, but I see others doing it, and envy them.

At some time, as a freshman in college, I would guess, my pleasure in style came together with the inevitable duty of having to read for content. I became increasingly annoyed with inept styles, like James Michener's, or styles which did violence to the language (and thus knew nothing of sociology until I could read it in French), with the turkey gobble of politicians and the rev. clergy. I began to search out writers whose style, as I was learning to see, was an indication that what they had to say was worth knowing. This was by no means an efficient or intellectually respectable procedure. I found Eric Gill's writing (all of which has evaporated from my mind), Spengler (all retained), Faulkner (then unknown to my English profs), Joyce (whose name I found in Thomas Wolfe), Dostoievsky.

A memory: I was desperately poor as an undergraduate at Duke, did not belong to a fraternity, and except for a few like-minded friends (Dan Patterson, who was to become the great student of Shaker music; Bob Loomis, the Random House editor; Clarence Brown, the translator and biographer of Mandelstam) was romantically and self-indulgently lonely. I was already learning the philosophical simpleness that would get me through life, and I remember a Saturday when I was the only person in the library. I took out Faulkner's *Absalom, Absalom!* (buff paper, good typography), and went back to my room. I felt, somehow, with everybody else out partying (Dan Patterson was practicing the piano in the basement of Duke chapel), Faulkner deserved my best. I showered, washed my hair, put on fresh clothes, and with one of Bob Loomis's wooden-tipped cigars, for the wickedness of it, made myself comfortable and opened the Faulkner to hear Miss Rosa Coldfield telling Quentin Compson about Thomas Sutpen.

So it went with my education. God knows what I learned from classes; very little. I read Santayana instead of my philosophy text (the style of which sucked), I read *Finnegans Wake* instead of doing botany (in which I made an F, and sweet Professor Anderson, that great name in photosynthesis, wrote on the postcard that conveyed the F, "You have a neat and attractive handwriting"). Instead of paying attention to psychology I made a wide study of Paul Klee and Goya.

On a grander scale I got the same kind of education at Oxford and Harvard, where I read on my own while satisfying course requirements. I can therefore report that the nine years of elementary schooling, four of undergraduate and eight of graduate study were technically games of futility. If, now, I had at my disposal as a teacher only what I learned from the formalities of education, I could not possibly be a university professor. I wouldn't know anything. I am, at least, still trying. I've kept most of my textbooks, and still read them (and am getting pretty good at botany).

Wendell Berry, that thoughtful man, once remarked that teachers are like a farmer dropping an acorn into the ground. Some years will pass before the oak comes to maturity. We give grades, and lecture, and do the best we can. But we cannot see what we have done for many years to come. In setting out to write about the pleasure of reading, I find that I have equated my private, venturesome reading with my education, such as it is. There's much to be learned from this. All useful knowledge is perhaps subversive, innocently and ignorantly so at first. I assumed, with the wisdom of children, that it was best not to mention to my fourth- and fifth-grade teachers, Miss Taylor (who made us all take a Pledge of Lifelong Abstinence from Alcohol) and Miss Divver, that I had read Antonina Vallentin's *Leonardo* and Van Doren's *Franklin*, and wanted very much, if I could find them, to read *Frankenstein* and *Dracula*.

I also read in those grammar-school years the nine volumes of Alexander Dumas's *Celebrated Crimes*, and a dozen or so volumes of E. Phillips Oppenheim, and the three-volume *Century Dictionary* (I have always accepted dictionaries and encyclopedias as good reading matter).

Last year I met a young man in his twenties who is illiterate; there are more illiterates in Kentucky than anywhere else, with the possible exception of the Philippines and Haiti. The horror of his predicament struck me first of all because it prevents his getting a job, and secondly because of the blindness it imposes on his imagination. I also realized more fully than ever before what a text is and how it can only be realized in the imagination, how mere words, used over and over for other purposes and in other contexts, can be so ordered by, say, Jules Verne, as to be deciphered as a narrative of intricate texture and splendid color, of precise meanings and values. At the time of the illiterate's importuning visits (I was trying to help him find a job) I was reading Verne's *Les enfants du capitaine Grant*, a geography book cunningly disguised as an adventure story, for French children, a hefty two-volume work. I had never before felt how lucky and privileged I am, not so much for being literate, a state of grace that might in different circumstances be squandered on tax forms or lawbooks, but for being able, regularly, to get out of myself completely, to be somewhere else, among other minds, and return (by laying my book aside) renewed and refreshed.

For the real use of imaginative reading is precisely to suspend one's mind in the workings of another sensibility, quite literally to give oneself over to Henry James or Conrad or Ausonius, to Yuri Olyesha, Bashō, and Plutarch.

The mind is a self-consuming organ, and preys on itself. It is an organ for taking the outside in. A wasp has a very simple ganglion of nerves for a brain, a receptor of color, smell, and distances. It probably doesn't think at all, and if it could write, all it would have to say would concern the delicious smell of female wasps and fermenting pears, hexagonalities in various material (wood fiber, paper) in the architecture of nests, with maybe some remarks on azimuths (for the young). Angels, to move to the other pole of being, write history and indictments only, and if Satan has written his memoirs, they would read like Frank Harris, and who would want to read them?

Music is as close as we will get to angelic discourse. Literature comes next, with a greater measure than music can claim of the fully human. I am on slippery ground here, as the two arts can share natures. *Don Giovanni* and the *Mass in B Minor* are both music and literature; all of what we now call poetry was for many centuries song. Even if we had all of Sappho's texts, we would still be without the tunes to which they were sung—like having only the libretto of *The Magic Flute*.

Guy Davenport / 59

Shakespeare's *Sonnets* and the Duino Elegies are a kind of music, in themselves.

By "fully human" I mean *The Miller's Tale* and the *Quijote*, Surtees and *Humphry Clinker*, Rabelais and Queneau. The fully human is suspect in our society; Kentucky high schools keep banning *As I Lay Dying*. We do not read enough to have seen that literature itself is not interested in the transcendental role society has assumed for it. The pleasure of reading has turned out not to be what our culture calls pleasure at all. The most imperceptive psychologist or even evangelist can understand that television idiotizes and blinds, while reading makes for intelligence and perception.

Why? How? I wish I knew. I also wish I knew why millions of bright American children turn overnight into teenage nerds. The substitution of the automobile for the natural body, which our culture has effected in the most evil perversion of humanity since chivalry, is one cause; narcosis by drugs and Dionysian music is another. I cannot say that an indifference to literature is another cause; it isn't. It's a symptom, and one of our trivializing culture's great losses. We can evince any number of undeniable beliefs—an informed society cannot be enslaved by ideologies and fanaticism, a cooperative pluralistic society must necessarily be conversant with the human record in books of all kinds, and so on—but we will always return to the private and inviolable act of reading as our culture's way of developing an individual.

Aunt Mae didn't read the books she inherited from Uncle Eugene, slain in France fighting for my and your right to read what we want to. She read *Cosmopolitan* and *Collier's* and "the *Grit*." And Zane Grey. She knew, however, that books are important, to be kept right-side up on a shelf in the living room, near her plaster-of-Paris life-size statue of Rin-Tin-Tin.

The world is a labyrinth in which we keep traversing familiar crossroads we had thought were miles away, but which we are doomed to backtrack to. Every book I have read is in a Borgesian series that began with the orange, black, and mimosa-green clothbound *Tarzan* brought to me, as a kindly gift, by Mrs. Shiflett in her apron and bonnet. And the name Shiflett, I know because of books, is the one Faulkner transmuted to Snopes.

And Aunt Mae, whose father was a horse doctor but not a common horse doctor, looked down her nose at the Shifletts of this world as common white trash (she was an accomplished snob, Aunt Mae). Year before last, exploring the Cimitière des Chiens et Chats in Paris, I came upon the grave of Rin-Tin-Tin, *Grande Vedette du Cinema*, and felt the ghost of Aunt Mae, who had always intended "to visit the old country," very much with me, for I'm old enough to know that all things are a matter of roots and branches, of spiritual seeds and spiritual growth, and that I would not have been in Paris at all, not, anyway, as a scholar buying books and tracking down historical sites, and going to museums with educated eyes rather than eyes blank with ignorance, if, in the accident of things, Aunt Mae and Mrs. Shiflett had not taken the responsibility of being custodians of the modest libraries of a brother and a son, so that I could teach myself to read.

David Long

On Rereading

That scene three-quarters of the way through *The Great Gatsby*: the principals all unhappily convened in a sweltering parlor suite at the Plaza, everything set to come undone. If, earlier on, we could read with a split vision, one eye on the story, the other watching Fitzgerald's craft, his sentences (Nick telling us, for instance, "I wanted no more riotous excursions with privileged glimpses into the human heart"), now we're undivided, too far inside the story to think. Overhead, in the real world, a little Cessna whines toward the city airport; we're oblivious. We're at the Plaza, sweating, hearing Tom Buchanan begin to needle Gatsby: "All this 'old sport' business. Where'd you pick that up?" A couple of squirmy pages later the scene hits critical mass, Tom finally coming out with the thing he's got to say: "What kind of row are you trying to cause in my house anyhow?"

OK, we think, burning ahead: Here's real trouble.

We don't know what comes next. Actually, we do know, or almost know, but narrative's such a potent stimulant we're too stirred up to imagine it precisely. Whole books can rely on this high-octane stuff— thrillers are, after all, thrilling. But all fiction moves forward, even as it moves sideways and backward, and even the most serene of tales gives off sparks where not-yet flashes into now. However much we appreciate the rest of a writer's act, first reading speeds us, paradoxically, toward the last page, where the excitement will end. And unless we manage to wipe all traces of what-happened from our memories, that excitement's more or less history—what a sinking feeling to discover, seventy pages into an old Lew Archer or Travis McGee, that you did read this one, after all.

So why *do* we reread?

My older boy has dawdled through the *Chronicles of Narnia* books maybe six times. "They're trustworthy," he tells me. Absolutely. They're loyal old friends who do not change. Seldom do we finish a book then flip straight to the front again. But let time pass. We find ourselves overtaken by a certain mood, a craving for a certain voice. We want some of John McPhee's handsome, self-effacing descriptions—of things we wouldn't have guessed we could care about, Switzerland's armed forces, for instance. Or we want the Faulkner of *Absalom, Absalom!*'s opening pages, Quentin sitting opposite Miss Coldfield in that closed-up room, motes of dead air blowing down, the language already starting its breathless accretion. Or, another time, a few minutes of James Wright's quiet sympathies, say "Small Frogs Killed on the Highway":

> Still,
> I would leap too
> Into the light,
> If I had the chance.
> It is everything, the wet green stalk of the field
> On the other side of the road . . .

Even the prickliest of voices can console, can offer its specific antitoxin. And it's not just the voices, of course, but the whole architecture of the work, especially its outcome. Each time, Shakespeare, the old buffalo in John Graves's story, "The Last Running," has to die, and each time, Tom Bird must turn to his great-nephew and say: "Damn you boy . . . Damn you for not ever getting to know anything worth knowing. Damn me, too. We had a world, once."

We count on it.

Still, if the writing doesn't change, we do. We reread, sometimes, to test ourselves, to see who we've become. There are writers we tried too young. Richard Ford remembers his first tangle with Fitzgerald's story "Absolution," still a freshman majoring in hotel management: *Puzzlement. Backed up by a vague, free-floating self-loathing . . .*[1] Reading's so invisible an art, we forget we've gotten better at it. Books still baffle us occasionally, but not nearly so often, and there are reasons for this bafflement—we're in a bum frame of mind, or the book's too technical for someone with our background, or maybe it's just written badly. In short, we've learned to know ourselves as readers. We've learned specific tricks, as well, how to adjust our reading style to the pages at hand. We slow-dance with some, others we ride like breaking waves. A few we don't go near without protective gear. It wasn't until I was loose in that no-man's-land after college that two of the more blindingly obvious illuminations struck me: That I couldn't read *every book* (and could leave

---

[1] Richard Ford, "The Three Kings: Hemingway, Faulkner, and Fitzgerald," reprinted in The Graywolf Annual Three *(St. Paul: Graywolf Press, 1986), p. 71.*

off torturing myself). And that, life being short, I could just plain quit a book if I wanted. Blasphemy!

But, anyway, what pleasure to find clarity and mystery where you remembered murk and mystification. I acquired a boxed paperback set of *The Alexandria Quartet* my own freshman year, 1966. I might've actually labored through *Justine* (I doubt it). But I was convinced I ought to read it, and I know I jumped ship more than once, mired in Durrell's showy vocabulary, his feverish working of ideas, and simply the foreignness of it all. The other three spines—*Balthazar, Mountolive, Clea*—stayed factory-smooth. But then, one gloomy November in the 1980s, I seemed to need it. Amazingly, I sailed straight through. Eleven hundred and nine pages: excessive, overlush, an intricately peopled construction for the mind and heart. As William Gass says: *We are so pathetically eager for this other life, for the sounds of distant cities and the sea; we long . . . to pit ourselves against some trying wind, to follow the fortunes of a ship hard beset, to face up to murder and fornication, and the somber results of anger and love; oh, yes, to face up*—in books . . .[2]

There are some books best read young. Guidebooks of one kind or another—sexual, spiritual, political. I have boxes full in the cellar, still taped from the last move, or the one before that. It's no discredit to the best of these to say we generally have the sense not to reread them in middle age. They jarred us when we needed a particular jarring, and that's enough. Still, it pulls us up short to come on writing we once thought splendid—*crucial*—and find it dull, badly dated, silly even. A measure of our growth maybe, but unsettling, too. Who were we when we raved about *this*?

Rereading, there's always the threat of disappointment, of having our judgment called into question. I page through *Essays of E. B. White*, looking for "Once More to the Lake," a piece I once bragged was all a person would need to teach a course in writing. It's White's account of returning, with his son, to a lake in Maine where his own father had brought him, summer upon summer. Really, a meditation on time. I find it just as keen with detail as I recalled—the Pond's Extract, the can of lime in the outhouse, the dragonflies lighting on the tips of the rods. I move carefully toward the last paragraph, remembering its punch:

When the others went swimming, my son said he was going in, too. He pulled his dripping trunks from the line where they had hung all

---

[2]William Gass, "The Concept of Character in Fiction" in Fiction and the Figures of Life *(Boston: David R. Godine, Nonpareil Books, 1980), p. 37.*

through the shower and wrung them out. Languidly, and with no thought of going in, I watched him, his hard little body, skinny and bare, saw him wince slightly as he pulled up around his vitals the small, soggy, icy garment. As he buckled the swollen belt, suddenly my groin felt the chill of death.

No need to worry, after all: very good writing persists in being very good. And we're reminded that, thankfully, there's something constant in us, too.

A certain amount of our rereading has simply to do with retrieving information, for some useful end, or for the sheer hell of looking a thing up. We recall that F. Lewis Allen opens *Only Yesterday*, his book on the social upheaval of the 1920s, with a nifty few pages cataloging a typical weekday in May of 1919; or that Jacob Bronowski, somewhere toward the end of *The Ascent of Man*, makes a chilling leap between the Heisenberg Principle in physics and the ash-filled pond at Auschwitz. But what did they actually *say*? We remember the general idea, and (if we're lucky) where to go after it. But our memories aren't just thin on the verbatim goods—they're tricky, inhabited by wisps and chimeras and a godless assortment of misrecollections. That passage isn't where we thought it was (toward the back, top of a right-hand page), and it's, well, pretty different. In fact, we remember not so much the words as the resonance they created in us—we remember an instant in our reading lives. Rereading, we try to reclaim that instant, the frisson it set off. I'm tempted to say it's a futile exercise, like most other tries at going back. But the funny thing is, some relationships *are* renewable, some pleasures defeat time. Hear White himself on rereading Thoreau:

> Hairshirt or no, he is a better companion than most, and I would not swap him for a soberer or more reasonable friend even if I could. I can reread his famous invitation with undiminished excitement . . . I find it agreeable to sit here this morning, in a house of correct proportions, and hear across a century of time his flute, his frogs, and his seductive summons to the wildest revels of them all.[3]

If we're writers ourselves, there exists a core of texts that please us intimately *as writers*. In a commentary to her short story, "Over the

---

[3] E. B. White, "A Slight Sound at Evening" in *Essays of E. B. White* (New York: Harper & Row, Harper Collophon Books, 1977), pp. 241–42.

Mountain," Gail Godwin talks about reading Mark Helprin's "A Vermont Tale":

> . . . when I came to the last scene between the boy and his grandmother and read the words, "For reasons I could not discern, I began to cry," something started hurting me but in an interesting way. I sat very still in the chair and kept repeating to myself "For reasons I could not discern . . . For reasons I could not discern . . ." Something from my own experience lay just beneath the surface of that phrase, but I couldn't get to it. I didn't know why, but the story made me want to write a matching story. An echoing story.[4]

An echoing story. That's it exactly. We're moved to write stories that are kindred — in subject, or in strategy, or perhaps just in the audacity of their execution. These works we so admire might well be daunting; instead they become our private store of encouragement and instruction.

There's no work of fiction I've reread as often — clear through, or a page or two on the fly — as William Maxwell's short novel, *So Long, See You Tomorrow.* Briefly: it's the story of two betrayals. In the first, a tenant farmer named Lloyd Wilson is shot and killed by his neighbor and one-time closest friend, Clarence Smith (some months before, Wilson had fallen in love with Fern Smith). Fifteen days later, Smith's body is fished from a gravel pit outside town. The other betrayal is of one boy, Cletus Smith, son of the murderer, by another, the book's narrator. An adolescent blunder, a moment's failure to act, remembered across a lifetime.

And it's about, as well, the vanished place which gave rise to these particular betrayals.

Right away I was inclined to like such a book. First, it's set in heartland America, between the world wars (Lincoln, Illinois, in this case, 1921). Second, it pivots on an old crime. It reads, at times, like memoir (and could well be), but surely it's a novel, a remarkable one. We know from the first page who's been killed, and not long afterward who accomplished it. Stripped of wondering how things wind up, we wonder, as we watch the singular, intimately detailed moments laid before us, why these good people couldn't stop the dismantlement of their lives. By the

---

[4]*Gail Godwin, in* New American Stories: The Writers Select Their Own Favorites, *ed. by Gloria Norris (New York: New American Library, 1986), p. 371.*

end, we believe we know as much as may be known, and this is enough to make us hurt at the tragedy, but not enough to explain away its mystery.

In *Screenplay* scriptwriter Syd Field talks about *context* and *content*. Context, he says, is where a scene falls in the story, what's at stake, and where things must stand by its end. Context is a cup waiting to be filled. Content's what we pour in. Trouble is, some days we don't have much to pour in, or we pour in stuff we have to dump right out again. We come smack against an essential writerly dilemma: You can understand and believe in the whole of your story without knowing its exact parts. We feel stymied, thickheaded, incapable of the ordinary problem-solving that gets other people through a day. Thus, the truest reason writers reread: To watch another writer's mind at work. To see how he or she overcame not-knowing and *got down the page*.

Reading Maxwell, I'm reminded how the best works of art feel saturated with what they're about, how each page—each square inch of canvas, each minute of screen time—contains the whole. These are Maxwell's specific instructions: solve the riddle of not-knowing by *inhabiting* athe scene; move the camera off-center until you find the one thing—strawberries left unpicked, a boy washing his hands beside a floor grate, a loop of fence wire in a man's hand—that starts you saying what you have to tell about next. And don't let it run an instant longer than it needs to.

Aren't these old lessons? Of course. But there's nothing like tutoring with a master.

Here's the moment when private misfortune turns public, as it must in a small town:

> Over the mirror in the barbershop there is a colored poster, framed, of a woman with a pompadour. Her ample bust emerges from a water lily. She is holding an eyedropper elegantly and advocating Murine for the eyes. On the opposite wall, a whole row of calendars for the year 1921. On the linoleum floor, swatches of straight light brown hair. A minute before they were part of Cletus Smith. Now they are waiting for the broom . . . Sitting in the barber chair, with his head pushed down so that his chin is resting on his collarbone, Cletus can only look sidewise. He sees a shadow fall on the plate-glass window and then withdraw abruptly.
>
> With a wave of his clippers the barber indicates the sidewalk, empty now. "Wasn't that your friend?"
>
> The question is not directed at Cletus but at his father, waiting

his turn under the row of calendars. When there is no answer the barber is not offended. People either answered prying questions, in which case you found out something you didn't know before, or they ignored them and if you bided your time you found out the answer anyway. Friend no longer, he remarked to himself. And then his eyebrows rose because of what he saw in the mirror: the boy was blushing.

Everywhere, a new resonance of the story's melody: things coming apart. But I think of the time before this passage existed, when it was only a morning's problem. I think of Maxwell sitting and imagining, testing a line: *Eventually, everyone knew* . . . and chucking it, trying others, working his way toward a particular public place, a barber's, and finally to two images—a man's shadow on glass, a boy's hair on the floor. I imagine the joy of composing a line such as: "A minute before they were part of Cletus Smith." It's the joy of surprising yourself, of writing an utterly simple sentence that speaks your entire story.

How I want to show off passages like this, how I want you to be as moved as I've been. Another pleasure of knowing a book inside out, and a fine one. But in the end it doesn't matter. If what we choose to read, in a time of rampant information, reflects the spectrum of our moods and curiosities, what we read again is an even more intimate expression, a distillate, of who we are: single lines, fragments marked off with a highlighter, a few whole works we own with as much authority as any of the stories we happen to have lived out. In those C. S. Lewis books my son loves, the four children who one day tumble through the back of a wardrobe into Narnia, and reign there for a generation, kings and queens, spill back just as abruptly into the England they left. They discover that, oddly, no time has passed. Imagine how they feel: stranded in childhood again, hoping Narnian magic might strike a second time. Still, they're not the schoolchildren they were—they know what they know. Lewis doesn't say so, but we can easily picture them turning to each other and trading memories, keeping their secret lives alive. And so it is with us.

James Purdy

Rereading: Not for Pleasure Alone

The books I have read again and again are not exactly those I associate with pleasure alone.

I must have read Cervantes' *Rinconete and Cortadillo* twenty times, sometimes in the Spanish, which is hard, and again in the pale English translations. Cervantes, like Melville, told only a fraction of what he actually knew. In *Rinconete and Cortadillo* he gives us a peek into the underworld of Seville with its brotherhood of cutthroats and thieves and its mysterious hideout mansions.

A short piece of fiction by Aleksei Remizov, *The Fifth Pestilence and the Tinkling Cymbal and Sounding Brass*, always puts me under a spell. (The 1928 Payson and Clarke Ltd. edition is beautiful.) I could read Remizov a hundred times. I know of course much of his humor is being lost in the English translation, but the outlandish picture of small-town Russia comes home with wonderful hilarity.

A tome which I am not certain I have read every word of is Doughty's *Travels in Arabia Deserta*. It is as toilsome to read as it must have been wandering in the Arabia of Doughty's time. The almost obsolete words and winding syntax are bewildering as a sandstorm. Yet whenever I open up the book I lose myself in its obscurity.

I wonder if another favorite of mine, Petronius' *Satyricon*, would be so teasing if we had the complete work. The fragments we do possess make one dream of what must have finally happened to the outrageous Ascyltos, Giton, and Encolpius.

Finally Paul Morand's *New York* reads as fresh and sassy as when it appeared in the 1920s. (Morand's short stories are perhaps even more brilliant.) I often wish *his* New York was the New York of today.

In this respect, I should mention that over a period of some years I consumed all fourteen volumes of the Loeb Classical edition of Livy's Roman history while riding the New York subways. Given the character of our underground, that should say a lot about Livy as a writer.

II

Joseph Conrad

BOOKS

1905

I

"I have not read this author's books, and if I have read them I have forgotten what they were about."

These words are reported as having been uttered in our midst not a hundred years ago, publicly, from the seat of justice, by a civic magistrate. The words of our municipal rulers have a solemnity and importance far above the words of other mortals, because our municipal rulers more than any other variety of our governors and masters represent the average wisdom, temperament, sense and virtue of the community. This generalisation, it ought to be promptly said in the interests of eternal justice (and recent friendship), does not apply to the United States of America. There, if one may believe the long and helpless indignations of their daily and weekly Press, the majority of municipal rulers appear to be thieves of a particularly irrepressible sort. But this by the way. My concern is with a statement issuing from the average temperament and the average wisdom of a great and wealthy community, and uttered by a civic magistrate obviously without fear and without reproach.

I confess I am pleased with his temper, which is that of prudence. "I have not read the books," he says, and immediately he adds, "and if I have read them I have forgotten." This is excellent caution. And I like his style: it is unartificial and bears the stamp of manly sincerity. As a reported piece of prose this declaration is easy to read and not difficult to believe. Many books have not been read; still more have been forgotten. As a piece of civic oratory this declaration is strikingly effective. Calculated to fall in with the bent of the popular mind, so familiar with all forms of forgetfulness, it has also the power to stir up a subtle emotion while it starts a train of thought — and what great force can be expected from human speech? But it is in naturalness that this declaration is perfectly delightful, for there is nothing more natural than for a grave

/ 73

City Father to forget what the books he has read once — long ago — in his giddy youth may be — were about.

And the books in question are novels, or, at any rate, were written as novels. I proceed thus cautiously (following my illustrious example) because being without fear and desiring to remain as far as possible without reproach, I confess at once that I have not read them.

I have not; and of the million persons or more who are said to have read them, I never met one yet with the talent of lucid exposition sufficiently developed to give me a connected account of what they are about. But they are books, part and parcel of humanity, and as such, in their ever-increasing, jostling multitude, they are worthy of regard, admiration, and compassion.

Especially of compassion. It has been said a long time ago that books have their fate. They have, and it is very much like the destiny of man. They share with us the great incertitude of ignominy or glory — of severe justice and senseless persecution — of calumny and misunderstanding — the shame of undeserved success. Of all the inanimate objects, of all men's creations, books are the nearest to us, for they contain our very thought, our ambitions, our indignations, our illusions, our fidelity to truth, and our persistent leaning towards error. But most of all they resemble us in their precarious hold on life. A bridge constructed according to the rules of the art of bridge-building is certain of a long, honourable and useful career. But a book as good in its way as the bridge may perish obscurely on the very day of its birth. The art of their creators is not sufficient to give them more than a moment of life. Of the books born from the restlessness, the inspiration, and the vanity of human minds those that the Muses would love best lie more than all others under the menace of an early death. Sometimes their defects will save them. Sometimes a book fair to see may — to use a lofty expression — have no individual soul. Obviously a book of that sort cannot die. It can only crumble into dust. But the best of books drawing sustenance from the sympathy and memory of men have lived on the brink of destruction, for men's memories are short, and their sympathy is, we must admit, a very fluctuating, unprincipled emotion.

No secret of eternal life for our books can be found amongst the formulas of art, any more than for our bodies in a prescribed combination of drugs. This is not because some books are not worthy of enduring life, but because the formulas of art are dependent on things variable, unstable and untrustworthy; on human sympathies, on prejudices, on likes and dislikes, on the sense of virtue and the sense of propriety, on beliefs and theories that, indestructible in themselves, always change their form—often in the lifetime of one fleeting generation.

II

Of all books, novels, which the Muses should love, make a serious claim on our compassion. The art of the novelist is simple. At the same time it is the most elusive of all creative arts, the most liable to be obscured by the scruples of its servants and votaries, the one pre-eminently destined to bring trouble to the mind and the heart of the artist. After all, the creation of a world is not a small undertaking except perhaps to the divinely gifted. In truth every novelist must begin by creating for himself a world, great or little, in which he can honestly believe. This world cannot be made otherwise than in his own image: it is fated to remain individual and a little mysterious, and yet it must resemble something already familiar to the experience, the thoughts and the sensations of his readers. At the heart of fiction, even the least worthy of the name, some sort of truth can be found—if only the truth of a childish theatrical ardour in the game of life, as in the novels of Dumas the father. But the fair truth of human delicacy can be found in Mr. Henry James's novels; and the comical, appalling truth of human rapacity let loose amongst the spoils of existence lives in the monstrous world created by Balzac. The pursuit of happiness by means lawful and unlawful, through resignation or revolt, by the clever manipulation of conventions or by solemn hanging on to the skirts of the latest scientific theory, is the only theme that can be legitimately developed by the novelist who is the chronicler of the adventures of mankind amongst the dangers of the kingdom of the earth. And the kingdom of this earth itself, the ground upon which his individualities stand, stumble, or die, must enter into his scheme of faithful record. To encompass all this in one harmonious conception is a great feat; and even to attempt it deliberately with serious intention, not from the senseless prompting of an ignorant heart, is an honourable ambition. For it requires some courage to step in calmly where fools may be eager to rush. As a distinguished and successful French novelist once observed of fiction, "C'est un art *trop* difficile."

It is natural that the novelist should doubt his ability to cope with his task. He imagines it more gigantic than it is. And yet literary creation being only one of the legitimate forms of human activity has no value but on the condition of not excluding the fullest recognition of all the more distinct forms of action. This condition is sometimes forgotten by the man of letters, who often, especially in his youth, is inclined to lay a claim of exclusive superiority for his own amongst all the other tasks of the human mind. The mass of verse and prose may glimmer here and there with the glow of a divine spark, but in the sum of human effort it has no special importance. There is no justificative formula for its existence any more than for any other artistic achievement. With the rest of them it is destined to be forgotten, without, perhaps, leaving the faintest trace. Where a novelist has an advantage over the workers in other fields of thought is in his privilege of freedom—the freedom of expression and the freedom of confessing his innermost beliefs—which should console him for the hard slavery of the pen.

III

Liberty of imagination should be the most precious possession of a novelist. To try voluntarily to discover the fettering dogmas of some romantic, realistic, or naturalistic creed in the free work of its own inspiration, is a trick worthy of human perverseness which, after inventing an absurdity, endeavours to find for it a pedigree of distinguished ancestors. It is a weakness of inferior minds when it is not the cunning device of those who, uncertain of their talent, would seek to add lustre to it by the authority of a school. Such, for instance, are the high priests who have proclaimed Stendhal for a prophet of Naturalism. But Stendhal himself would have accepted no limitation of his freedom. Stendhal's mind was of the first order. His spirit above must be raging with a peculiarly Stendhalesque scorn and indignation. For the truth is that more than one kind of intellectual cowardice hides behind the literary formulas. And Stendhal was preeminently courageous. He wrote his two great novels, which so few people have read, in a spirit of fearless liberty.

It must not be supposed that I claim for the artist in fiction the freedom of moral Nihilism. I would require from him many acts of faith of which the first would be the cherishing of an undying hope; and hope, it will not be contested, implies all the piety of effort and renunciation. It is the God-sent form of trust in the magic force and inspiration belonging to the life of this earth. We are inclined to forget that the way of excellence is in the intellectual, as distinguished from emotional, humility. What one feels so hopelessly barren in declared pessimism is just its arrogance. It seems as if the discovery made by many men at various times that there is much evil in the world were a source of proud and unholy joy unto some of the modern writers. That frame of mind is not the proper one in which to approach seriously the art of fiction. It gives an author—goodness only knows why—an elated sense of his own superiority. And there is nothing more dangerous than such an elation to that absolute loyalty towards his feelings and sensations an author should keep hold of in his most exalted moments of creation.

To be hopeful in an artistic sense it is not necessary to think that the world is good. It is enough to believe that there is no impossibility of its being made so. If the flight of imaginative thought may be allowed to rise superior to many moralities current amongst mankind, a novelist who would think himself of a superior essence to other men would miss the first condition of his calling. To have the gift of words is no such great matter. A man furnished with a long-range weapon does not become a hunter or a warrior by the mere possession of a fire-arm; many other qualities of character and temperament are necessary to make him either one or the other. Of him from whose armoury of phrases one in a hundred thousand may perhaps hit the far-distant and elusive mark of art I would ask that in his dealings with mankind he should be capable of giving a tender recognition to their obscure virtues. I would not have him impatient with their small failings and scornful of their errors. I would not have him expect too much gratitude from that humanity whose fate, as illustrated in individuals, it is open to him to depict as ridiculous or terrible. I would wish him to look with a large forgiveness at men's ideas and prejudices, which are by no means the outcome of malevolence, but depend on their education, their social status, even their professions. The good artist should expect no recognition of his toil and no admiration of his genius, because his toil can with difficulty be appraised and his genius cannot possibly mean anything to the illiterate who, even from the dreadful wisdom of their evoked dead, have, so far, culled nothing but inanities and platitudes. I would wish him to enlarge his sympathies by patient and loving observation while he grows in mental power. It is in the impartial practice of life, if anywhere, that the promise of perfection for his art can be found, rather than in the absurd formulas trying to prescribe this or that particular method of technique or conception. Let him mature the strength of his imagination amongst the things of this earth, which it is his business to cherish and know, and refrain from calling down his inspiration ready-made from some heaven of perfections of which he knows nothing. And I would not grudge him the proud illusion that will come sometimes to a writer: the illusion that his achievement has almost equalled the greatness of his dream. For what else could give him the serenity and the force to hug to his breast as a thing delightful and human, the virtue, the rectitude and sagacity of his own City, declaring with simple eloquence through the mouth of a Conscript Father: "I have not read this author's books, and if I have read them I have forgotten. . . ."

Josef Škvorecký

The Pleasures of the Freedom to Read

When I was a boy I lived in a society governed by rather strict and binding rules where disobedience was punished in the good old pre-Spockian way. One such rule: light in your bedroom must be switched off at nine sharp. Boys have to get up at seven and they need ten hours of sleep every night.

But there were all those books, and simply no time to read them. A boy's day, in that prepermissive society, was rigidly divided into school, homework (supervised), private tuition for slightly stupid urchins (I was one), a daily walk with Mother for sickly children (I was one), breakfast, supper, dinner and, finally, one hour of reading before bedtime in which to devour my *Tarzan*s or my *Captain Nemo*s. But they could be read only in short peeks: I had to hide them under volumes of some mandatory Czech classic deemed suitable for my age, more often than not Božena Němcová, the nineteenth-century Romantic concerning whose marital infidelities rumor went about at school, punishable, if somebody told on you, in the good, old pre-Spockian way. In his armchair on the other side of the coffee table, Father was brooding over his erotic novels by M. B. Böhnel (he had no idea I perused them also; they had beautiful titles— *The Immorals, Vice, Shame, Manhood, The Rejuvenated Man* etc.—but invariably proved disappointing, for this was in the lackluster preexplicit days); Mother was knitting under her lamp also within sight of my book, and so I mostly only dreamt about the Man of the Apes over blurred lines of the flirtatious Victorian lady.

The big time came after lights out! Cuddled in my bed, I covered myself, head inclusive, with a blanket, from under the mattress I fished out an electric torch, and then indulged in the pleasures of reading, reading, reading. Eventually, often after midnight, I fell asleep from very pleasurable exhaustion.

Since those ancient evenings in Náchod I have felt a similarly intense pleasure over the pages of books only twice. Not that I—in my undiscriminating way—would not enjoy reading books all my life: but I am not speaking about what in today's computerized language is called "reading experience" but about ecstasy.

In 1960 I had a four-month brush with death. I was withering away in the Motol Hospital in Prague with a bad case of hepatitis contracted during a hernia operation (pre-disposable-needle times). There was no TV in the hospital and no radio—being sick was considered a serious business, not an opportunity to enjoy yourself while avoiding work. Only two events pleasantly disturbed the anxiety-filled boredom of the long, severe days. First, Czechoslovakia, once again, went through the ritual known as "elections." Everybody voted. As so many things in the Communist states, casting a ballot is not a citizen's right, but a citizen's duty, and nobody is exempt. Not even the sick and dying in hospitals. One day an election committee of two entered our sickroom with its eighteen inmates, and for a brief time we had fun. Ours was naturally an *infectious* ward, and the brave committee members, as they hurried with their ballot box from bed to bed, displayed symptoms of mortal fear. One of the two constantly pressed his palm over his mouth and nose, while the other held out his box with his face averted from the yellow voters. Obviously, nobody had told them that one didn't catch the hepatitis bug from air.

We, the patients, on the other hand, knew the ways of the bug. We were told by a Chinese doctor (this happened in the pre-Sino-Soviet split days) who had it from an American medical lady. She apparently had lectured on the topic to students and staff of the Medical School of Charles University. The Chinese was a joker, so maybe he was pulling our legs; nevertheless the lady's discovery came about when a conspicuous thing happened in a U.S. Army unit and she, being a hepatitis specialist, was called in for consultation. Within three days, an entire company fell ill with hepatitis. Medical annals never registered such a case. Since, according to European consensus, such things can happen only in America, we expected some sort of science-fictional explanation, but it boiled down to a rather tasteless practical joke. The company, mostly rednecks from some southern region of the States, had insulted their black cook and he took his racial revenge by pissing into their soup. He certainly never dreamt what an effective revenge that would turn out to be. To his credit it must be said that he had no idea he suffered from hepatitis.

Apart from these two events there was nothing that would lighten the burden of gloom. Except, I hoped, the hospital library. But the library was a remnant of the puritanical Stalinist era, and it contained only three kinds of books: long rows of Collected Works by diverse Soviet and Czechoslovak statesmen (unopened); volumes of early Czech socialist realism (opened occasionally, and quickly shut); and finally Czech and Russian classics. I borrowed a copy of *Selected Shorter Works by L. N. Tolstoy* and, guided by Murphy's Law, opened it on a page which gave a detailed description of the last hours in the life of Ivan Ilyich. That put an end to my appetite for reading classics in the hospital, and I sent out word to friends to provide me with privately owned books.

My friends did not abandon me in my hour of need. Since books sent to the infectious ward could not be returned to senders (it was believed they would spread the bug), the only works my friends were willing to part with were of the light-reading category. Ninety-nine percent of them were detective novels.

In the shadow of death that made me indifferent to the duties awaiting me back at my working place, I embarked on the second literary pleasure trip of my life. How many whodunits I absorbed during my remaining three months in the hospital, I don't know. At least a hundred. Many Austin Freeman in atrocious prewar translations, a surrealistically titled novel by E. C. Bentley, *The Last Cabinet of Mr. Trent*, many Agatha Christies, Francis Ileses, J. D. Carrs, Rex Stouts and others in American paperbacks, Hammett's *The Maltese Falcon*, Chandler's *The Lady in the Lake* . . . Before my stint in the infectious ward I held such books in contempt, which probably had its origins with Father Melon, our saintly religion teacher. He considered reading detective stories sinful and specifically asked us in the confessional about whether we had committed that sin. The sin came under the heading "impure thoughts." Father Melon was blissfully unaware of the existence of one Father Brown and I repaid him his loving care for my soul by turning him into a character in some of my books, including, God forgive me, a few detective stories.

The third period of pleasure—you cannot even call it a period: just a few brief gratifying moments, often divided by years—came about in the following way. After two most unpleasant years in the army I landed a job with the State Publishing House of Fiction, Music and Art, as such establishments used to be lavishly called in the noncompetitive Stalinist years. I thought that, from then on, my life would be one continuous bliss, for I would be making a living just by reading books! What I did not realize was that the choice of those books would not be mine. But I soon found out. I spent the first couple of years skimming through East German socialist realists and writing reports on their *opera*. As for American literature, well, there *was* pleasure there. The publishing house brought out mostly classics, and since one of my duties was proofs, I did some very close reading of *Moby Dick, The Adventures of Huckleberry Finn, The House of the Seven Gables, The Narrative of Arthur Gordon Pym* and others. This was close reading in the sense of going through these, mostly long, works word by word, or more precisely, letter by letter; not in the sense of searching the texts for God knows what mysteries suitable for interpretation. And it was pleasure indeed. (What was presented to the customers as the cream of contemporary American literature offered less pleasure.) During those first years of my career as editor, the cream was thin. In fact, only four contemporaries got published: Howard Fast — but after various pronouncements he lost his status as a progressive and was banned — Albert Maltz, Philip Bonoski and V. J. Jerome. Maltz remains in my fond memory as one of those Americans who protested against the Soviet invasion of Czechoslovakia in 1968; Philip Bonoski as one who, after the same event, attacked Miloš Forman's Czech films more viciously than domestic Stalinists. V. J. Jerome? Well, I even joined in a little conspiracy with him. On assignment as his Prague interpreter, I did not know that he was the chief ideologue of the American Communist party — I found out years later from Lillian Hellman's *Scoundrel Time*. So I wasn't really that shocked when the first thing Jerome asked me about was whether I could take him to some underground writers' gatherings. I mistrusted him, for he was a damned Yankee Commie — that much I knew — but I soon dropped my reservations, for we discovered a point of mutual interest, and eventually I even used Jerome for my own ends. The time must have been the late fifties because I was launching an unsuccessful campaign to convince my editor in chief that we should publish Dashiell Hammett. The campaign, so far, had had no results because the view still prevailed that American detective fiction mostly wallowed in blood, therefore it was decadent, even though not necessarily outright reactionary. That Hammett had certainly been a fellow traveler and possibly a Party member would not prevent the harmful effects his gory writings would have on our new socialist man. I remember how one publisher's reader temporarily thwarted my efforts because he took the trouble and counted all the murders and killings in *The Red Harvest*. He came up with about 150 such atrocities — almost one corpse per page — and how could I argue against such a tangible proof of decadence?

Well, I trumped that diligent ass, and V. J. Jerome supplied the trump card. After we had become more chummy, I told him about my difficulties with Hammett. He brightened up and exclaimed as if he were recalling a particularly joyful event: "Why, I was in jail with Dashiell!" As it turned out, they both had displeased Senator Joe McCarthy and served several months together, mostly playing Ping-Pong. Suddenly, inspiration grabbed me. "Listen," I told Jerome, "would you be willing to write an introduction to the Czech edition of three of Hammett's novels? That might help because—" He interrupted me, blinking at me conspiratorily: "I know exactly what you mean. Never worry!" That day he left for New York, and some weeks later the mail brought me his introduction. He later printed the original in one of the last issues of *Masses & Mainstream*. In the Stalinist argot such texts were called "condoms": the political reliability of their authors—like a condom—protected the work under scrutiny against the bacilli of ideological accusations. Ideally, the author of the "condom" should have been Soviet—Karel Čapek (*R.U.R., The Life of the Insects*) was saved from drowning by Czech Stalinist zealots by a young Soviet literary scholar, Sergei Nikolski, who retouched his anti-Communism by stressing (quite truthfully) his antifascism. Ray Bradbury's *Fahrenheit 451* was made acceptable in Czechoslovakia by a Soviet eulogy and subsequent publication, and it was thanks to a Polish "condom" that we managed to publish Waugh's *The Loved One*. But in the case of Hammett, an American Communist sufficed. The editor in chief probably consulted the Interior Ministry anyway.

The Hammett affair, however, happened when socrealism was already on the decline and editors in publishing houses were beginning to receive more and more stuff that was quite pleasurable to read. Although Alexander Abusch, the East German Minister of Culture, still maintained that William Faulkner was a racist, a reactionary and an obscurantist (the Prussians have a stubborn tendency to orthodoxy), one could attach to one's report recommending Faulkner for Czech translation a "condom" printed in the "picture script" of the Russians, and that did the trick. Neither was it difficult anymore to explain that Hemingway's stint with the CIA hunting German submarines in World War II did not have to be necessarily considered too compromising, or that *The Mysterious Stranger* was not a testimony to Mark Twain's skepticism about the human race, but merely a token of his disillusionment with the capitalist man.

About that time I published my first novel *The Cowards* and lost my job. *The Cowards*, however, made me popular so that when the ban was lifted I was flooded with requests for articles, blurbs, reviews, interviews and even film scripts. Soon I had so much to write that I had no time left for reading. Literature as pleasure became something that I could dream about but that I was rarely able to afford.

The year 1968 came and went. My wife and I emigrated to Canada where, during the first few years, I again had too much to write — though for different reasons — and therefore didn't have time enough to read. Except for scholarly books which I *had* to study in order to prepare my lectures. For the first time in my adult life I lived in a country without censorship. All those things and stories and sentiments pushed by long years of press supervision and self-censorship into the remotest recesses of my mind erupted in the form of overlong novels that took an inordinately long time to write. The novels, eventually, brought me a certain notoriety even in North America, followed by requests for articles, reviews, blurbs, interviews, and even film scripts. On top of everything, my wife conceived of the ghastly idea to start a Czech-language publishing house so that all the hundreds of Czech and Slovak writers banned by the realsocialist government in Prague would have a chance to see their works in print. Without asking me whether I agreed or not (in true aggressive-feminist fashion), she made me her editor, and soon a flood of manuscripts, many of them tenth-generation carbon copies (try to read them!) littered my desk.

Hopelessly, I became one of the ever-increasing group of men and women who no longer read for pleasure. We are just caught in the reading trap.

But I still have my moments of the exquisite pleasure literature can bestow on a man. When I get the flu and develop a temperature, or when I have cleaned my desk of all reading and writing obligations and suffer from another attack of optimism — that from now on I shall turn down all requests for articles, and that, owing to Gorbachev's pressure, the gates of the Prague publishing houses will be opened to the Kunderas, Vaculíks, Havels and Kriseovás of the Czech underground, and the services of our publishing house in Toronto will no longer be needed — whenever I hypnotize myself into this kind of false consciousness, I reach for a book by Henry James. Over the pages of his serene, magnificently overwritten prose from whose cadences (and ideas) a word arises that no longer is and will never be again, I feel the old, intense delight that I used to feel as a boy under the blanket or as a candidate for death with only the duty to survive: that supreme bliss of reading for pleasure, and for no other reason in the world.

Stanislaw Baranczak

The Revenge of a Mortal Hand

1

It was in the late fall of 1982 when I first heard the news about the death of Grazyna Kuroń. She was the wife of my friend Jacek Kuroń, one of the most charismatic leaders of the human rights movement in Poland. I had been close to them during my years in Poland, particularly in the late seventies when the Kurońs (along with hundreds of their "dissident" friends) were working to make the regime's ways a little less inhuman. But in the fall of 1982 I was living peacefully in Cambridge, Massachusetts, where I had moved a year and a half before, while in Poland the first year of martial law (or "the state of war," as it was officially named there) was just coming to a close.

With a rather morbid sort of pride, the military regime claimed in those days that its imposition of martial law was actually bloodless: several dozen people shot by the police in street demonstrations, nothing to speak about. Grazyna was one of the indirect victims of the "state of war." Jailed in an internment camp, she developed a lung disease. She was released only when her situation was already hopeless: despite intensive treatment, she died in a hospital. Jacek, jailed too, was granted permission to leave the prison for a few days to attend the funeral.

The funeral elegy was one genre I had never tried before, but this time I felt that I simply could not help writing a poem on Grazyna's death. What happened to her was a stupefying blow not only to me but to anybody who had known her: it seemed unbelievable that this brave, strong-willed, good-natured woman who had so cheerfully coped with so much adversity in her life was suddenly gone, had ceased to exist. Why her? Why now and not later? Every death of a friend makes us ask such silly questions but this particular death was the hardest to accept and understand. Still, even though I sincerely wanted to bid farewell to Grazyna, I wasn't able to write a single word for quite a long time. I lived in agony for several weeks, immobilized, on the one hand, by the sense of the absurdity of that loss, and, on the other, by the sense of the exasperating conventionality of all the words, metaphors, rhetorical devices that the genre of the funeral elegy would have inevitably entailed.

In our illiterate times the classical "Eureka!" would be Greek to virtually everyone, so it is habitually replaced by an icon: a light bulb flashing above the head of a comic strip hero. Something like this flashed in my head one November evening when I suddenly found a solution. I realized that the only way to commemorate the death of someone like Grazyna—a death that was so blatantly undeserved, unjustified, unacceptable—was to write a poem which would be a total reversal of all the norms of the traditional funeral elegy; a poem which, instead of accepting the loss, would remain defiantly irreconciled with it; a poem which, instead of shedding tears over Grazyna's grave, would *talk to her* as if she were alive; a poem which, instead of bidding her good-bye forever, would try to fix and preserve her remembered presence.

To Grazyna

To remember about the cigarettes. So that they're always at hand,
ready to be slipped into his pocket, when they take him away once again.

To know by heart all the prison regulations about parcels and visits.
And how to force facial muscles into a smile.

To be able to extinguish a cop's threatening yell with one cold glance,
calmly making tea while they eviscerate the desk drawers.

To write letters from a cell or a clinic, saying that everything's O.K.

So many abilities, such perfection. No, I mean it.
If only in order not to waste those gifts,
you should have been rewarded with immortality
or at least with its defective version, life.

Death. No, this can't be serious, I can't accept this.

> There were many more difficult things that never brought you down.
> If I ever admired anybody, it was you.
> If anything was ever permanent, it was that admiration.
> How many times did I want to tell you. No way. I was too abashed
> by the gaps in my vocabulary and the microphone in your wall.
> Now I hear it's too late. No, I don't believe it.
>
> It's only nothingness, isn't it. How could a nothing like that
> possibly stand between us. I'll write down, word for word and forever,
> that small streak in the iris of your eye, that wrinkle at the corner of your mouth.
> All right, I know, you won't respond to the latest postcard I sent you.
> But if I'm to blame anything for that, it will be something real,
> the mail office, an air crash, the postal censor.
> Not nonexistence, something that doesn't exist, does it.*

I'm reminded of this poem whenever someone asks me if I find pleasure in writing. In this particular case, perhaps more than in any other, I'm unable to give a straight answer. The experience that led to my writing this poem was, needless to say, anything but pleasure. The several weeks of conceiving the poem's idea were one long wave of mental anguish. And yet I'll never forget the feeling which, in this mournful context, I'm a little ashamed to admit: the feeling of intense joy that flared up in me when, still in despair over the insoluble problem of Grazyna's death, I finally found a solution at least to my literary conundrum. It would seem that mourning and joy are two mutually exclusive states of mind. What, then, is there in literature (or maybe especially in poetry) that makes us simultaneously feel the deepest and sincerest pain and an equally deep and sincere joy flowing from the very writing out of that pain? Isn't this joy—let's put it a bit cynically—a *Schadenfreude* of revenge? Don't we find pleasure in writing because writing as such, even though it doesn't make the pain actually disappear, is nonetheless a way of retaliating against what causes the pain?

**Translated from the Polish by the author with Reginald Gibbons.*

2

The simplest definition of a graphomaniac holds that he is a person who likes to write. Should, then, the definition of a good poet hold that he is a person who doesn't like to write poems? If so, I would qualify for inclusion among the greatest. In more than the twenty years of my career I have written perhaps two hundred poems; I like some of them, but I didn't like *writing* any of them.

Am I, however, completely sincere in saying this? True, the process of writing, especially in its initial stages of groping in the dark in search of a convincing concept, can be real torture; and true, the chief difference between a good poet and a graphomaniac is that writing is easier for the latter since he lets himself be carried away, unabashed, on the plucked wings of literary conventions. Still, when after much aggravation the light bulb finally flashes in your head (sometimes accompanied by a huge exclamation mark), when you finally realize that a good poem has just been conceived, it is a feeling that can be compared with only a few other pleasures of life—perhaps with only one.

In other words, an outside observer has every right to treat the poets' complaints with utter suspicion. Logically speaking, if writing is really such a pain in the neck, it must be recompensed with some kind of pleasure—otherwise, who would bother to write poems at all? And, since there are apparently thousands of contemporary poets and none of them can seriously count today on any of the more tangible rewards (such as making money or winning a Maecenas' favor), the very joy of writing is most probably the only compensation for the pain of writing.

But wait a minute. Mixing pain with pleasure . . . Aren't we talking about masochism? Would writing poems amount to some kind of perversity?

Why, yes, of course, writing poems is a kind of perversity. And the joy of writing is, in fact, a very perverse kind of pleasure. Just as in every perversity, it results mainly from deliberate breaking of a taboo, from defiant resistance against a powerful rule or law, from rebellion against the commonly accepted foundations of existence. It's enough to put a verse line down on paper to scoff, in effect, at all the basic laws on which the world rests. For the very act of writing creates another world in which all those laws can be suspended—more, held in suspension interminably by the enduring power of conceit, rhyme, pun, metaphor, meter. No one, I think, has expressed it better than the contemporary

Polish poet Wislawa Szymborska in the conclusion of her poem "The Joy of Writing":

> Is there then such a world
> over whose fate I am an absolute ruler?
> A time I can bind with chains of signs?
> An existence made perpetual at my command?
>
> The joy of writing.
> The power of preserving.
> The revenge of a mortal hand.*

"The revenge of a mortal hand" that holds a pen is perhaps the only retaliation against the laws of Nature accessible to a human being. Since in the real, extratextual world I am unable to change or nullify any of the omnipresent laws of transience, decay, suffering, or death—in other words, since I can do nothing about the lurking presence of Nothingness in every atom of this world—the only solution is to create a separate world "bound with chains of signs," closed within lines and stanzas, subject to the absolute rule of my imagination. In such a world the flow of time can be magically stopped, suffering can be avoided, death can be rendered invalid, Nothingness can be scared away.

More important, this artificial world can seem more convincing than reality. After all, what makes poetry different from any other verbal description of the world is that a poem (only a very good poem, to be sure) strikes us with its determinateness, inner necessity, essential existence; to an even greater extent than "each mortal thing" in Hopkins' sonnet, it cries to us: "What I do is me: for that I came." To put it differently, a truly good poem, colloquial and seemingly spontaneous as it might be, differs from any form of extrapoetic speech in that it couldn't be possibly changed: even a single word replacement, even a slight shift of stresses, would disturb the balance. As a consequence, such a poem appears to be endowed with a certain special force of argument: it proves by itself not only the necessity of its own existence but also the

---

The entire text of this poem in a different translation can be found in Sounds, Feelings, Thoughts: Seventy Poems by Wislawa Szymborska, *transl. and introduced by Magnus J. Krynski and Robert A. Maguire (Princeton, N.J.: Princeton University Press, 1981).*

necessity of its own form. And this is an additional source of perverse pleasure for both the poet and his reader: an encounter with such a poem breaks another rule of our everyday experience, a rule according to which the world is based on randomness and chaotic unpredictability.

The joy of writing (and reading) poems, then, lies in the fact that poetry willfully spoils Nature's game; while fully realizing the power of Nothingness in the outside world, it questions and nullifies it within the inner world of a poem. But what is especially challenging for the twentieth-century poet is, I think, his awareness that the same can be done about the power of Nothingness revealed in modern History. Today's world is dominated by the seemingly inflexible laws of History even more than by the laws of Nature (some of which have been at least ameliorated by science). All the historical dimensions of this world conspire to overwhelm the individual with a sense of his insignificance and expendability; what counts is only the great numbers, statistical probabilities, historical processes.

And here again every good poem, by its sheer emergence and existence, appears to be, on its own miniature scale, History's spoilsport. History may compel us to think that the individual and his personal worldview do not count in the general picture; and yet poetry stubbornly employs and gives credence to the individual voice (moreover, as if to contradict the law of mimicry underlying modern society, the more inimitable and unique a poem is, the longer it survives in the memories of its readers). History may teach us abstract thinking; and yet poetry insists on seeing things in their specificity and concreteness, on viewing the world as an assemblage of Blake's "minute particulars." And finally, History may demonstrate by millions of examples the continuous triumph of Newspeak, a deliberate and systematic falsification of words' meanings; and yet a single good poem is enough to counterpoise all this tampering with language by making the reader aware of the word's hidden semantic possibilities. A poet who is offended by the course of modern History doesn't even have to write political poetry to find an appropriate response to it. It's enough that he writes his poems well.

3

All that may sound awfully optimistic and self-congratulatory. In fact, I am no exception among contemporary poets: just like the majority of them, I feel much more often helpless and desperate than victorious and elated in my private campaign against Nothingness. I do not stand on a sufficiently firm ground of positive belief to say with Donne: "And death shall be no more; Death thou shalt die," or even with Dylan Thomas: "And death shall have no dominion." Not even a poet (a representative of an otherwise rather presumptuous breed) can be as cocksure as to claim that his word can *really* stop the flow of time, invalidate suffering and death, put a stick in the spokes of History's wheel, make the earthly powers shrink and earthly injustices disappear.

In that sense, to return to my poem, I obviously have not managed to keep Grazyna among the living through my poem, nor have I wrestled her back from the dead. I have done only what I could have done, and that is to challenge the power of Nothingness by flinging my poem in its featureless face, by showing it that even though it engulfed Grazyna's life I am still there to remember how much her life meant to me—just as someone may be there after my death, just as something will always be there to exist in spite of Nonexistence (which, as its own name indicates, is "something that doesn't exist, does it"). To spite Nothingness—this is perhaps the essence of the perverse "joy of writing," "the revenge of a mortal hand."

III

Roy Blount, Jr.

Reading Appreciation

The first time I ever felt a girl inside her blouse was because of a book. A novel I bought in a drugstore. In it a sympathetic character of about my age felt a girl inside her blouse, something I had thought just wasn't done (or, more to the point, allowed) by a decent young person. The girl responded, literally, the same way the girl in the novel did, eagerly. So that's one thing I owe to reading.

On the other hand, recently I got to JFK's Pan Am International Terminal half an hour early, to make sure I was there when an extraordinary woman named Christabel arrived from London. I planted myself where I couldn't miss her when she emerged from customs, and as I waited I read Coleridge's *Christabel*, which is a *strange* damn poem. I got so wrapped up in it that I didn't see her go by, and it was forty-five minutes before we found each other.

But I can't help it, I love to read. I love the discretionary rhythm of it, so much more sustainable than that of eating or even drinking or even anything else: oh wait slow down mull that again go back again, never quite getting it all. The joy of text, cerebrolingual, aurilabial; the threads and knots and slippages; the weft of phoneme and notion. An intense rush may come from listening to speech, but speech, even if audiotaped, is not there in your hands to *peruse*, until it is set down in letters and becomes something else. Once I tuned in on the Joe Franklin television talk show at an inexplicable moment. I wish I had it on cassette, but it pleases me even more written down:

> First Guest: Is it Da-Da [pronounced as a baby might] like Da-Da art?
> Franklin: Yes. I think.
> Second Guest: D-A-H.
> Franklin: D-A-H. But the *H* is silent, like in the word *fish*.

There is so much margin for error in English! And personally I would not have it otherwise. To me a little minimalism goes a long way, for this reason: minimalism doesn't fool around enough. I want some (organic) *swash*. Robert Frost said, "I like to drag and break the intonation across the meter as waves first comb and then break stumbling on the shingle." But it doesn't even have to be that complicated. Here is a sentence I like, from *At Swim-Two-Birds:*

"It is my mission here this morning to introduce you to a wide variety of physical scourges, torments and piteous blood-sweats."

The Irish! More Flann O'Brien, from *The Third Policeman:*

"I put my hand in my pocket to see if my wallet was there. It was, smooth and warm like the hand of a good friend."

"Walking finely from the hips the two of us made our way home in the afternoon."

"We were in an entirely other field by this time and in the company of white-coloured brown-coloured cows."

I would not particularly like hearing any of those sentences read aloud. I love to hear people, or at any rate children (my daughter at six, to a friend: "I'll hit you so hard you won't be able to see straight except for the mean monster and the cruel thieves that beat you"), talk. But literature is what's lost aloud. Your tongue can't quite manage it, that's why there's a need for writing; but the most pleasant reading is that which your tongue can, and with relish does, *imagine* managing. The lines you leave most fondly behind are the ones that lead your tongue and lips and ear and palate in a dance in your mind. (Sense makes me want to say "in your head," but I yield to sound.) Kipling:

> The temper of chums, the love of your wife, and a new piano's
>   tune—
> Which of the three will you trust at the end of an Indian June?

A newspaper headline:

> NEW STUDY SEES LAG IN LAWS
> ON USE OF HUMAN TISSUES

The name of a television station:

KTPC-TV

Lives there a person with tongue so dead, he or she can regretlessly leave off repeating, silently, "KTPC-TV"?

But it's not all mouth, the pleasure of reading. Mental images are more or less integrally involved. Room for abuse as well as haplessness in that "more or less," but it is fascinating to come upon a trope in which you can't *tell* whether sound or image is taking undue advantage of the other. Discussing the current undervaluation of Dylan Thomas, Seamus Heaney mentions "the interface between the back of the throat and the back of the mind." I love to walk — as finely from the hips as may be — in big cities, where mannalike reading abounds. In New York I passed a deli with a sign outside that said:

SOUP TO-DAY
CALM CHOWDER

The life of letters. Consider *phlegm* and *phlegmatic* — the way that hard *g* comes out, from nowhere so to speak. (Speaking of phlegm, I told my daughter once, when she was little, that I felt bad. She said, "How?" I said I just, generally, felt bad. "Oh," she said; "my bottom teeth hurt and when I lie my head down my nose run goes into my mouth and when I sniff it back it just comes back.") It is a strange language, and yet I swear it is essentially phonetic, even onomatopoeic, because my mother taught me to "sound out the words" and to love reading. Written English dawned on me as she read me the Br'er Rabbit stories. We cannot abide it, anymore, when the author refers to the "venerable darky," but when Joel Chandler Harris and Uncle Remus get to narrating in concert, they cook. *Tooby sho. Bimeby.* Inventive oralists produced those elisions of *to be sure* and *by and by,* and the folklorist pulled them out of the air by means of spelling. I have never understood why so many readers are put off by the difficulty of written dialect. What is English, anyway? Take the word *bulb.* No one would call it dialect, nor would anyone say that it was authored. But *bulb* is a dialectic achievement. I have heard different people pronounce it "bub" and "bullub," but of course it is right in between — and so close to, yet so much more elegant than, *blub.* To pronounce *bulb* is to sketch a bulb in your mouth, with no waste motion. To spell it is to refine the process further.

Who dared first come out with *bulb*? How did that person know that other people would know what it meant — or *did* know what it meant, even when they nodded? Okay, maybe *bulb* was easy. An onion may have been the first bulb, and it may have been named in a synesthesial flash, the way people name a dog Woofy.

I don't want to get sticky, but children may come up with many words, the way they name their grandmothers. My mother was Mu-mu the last thirteen years of her life, compliments of my daughter. Once my son asked my daughter, "Why are there so many motorcycles around here?"

She answered, "All our friends are going for a rumpity ride."

"Rumpity?" I said too quickly.

"I didn't say that," she said. It could be that everyone begins linguistics poetically and then realizes it is not sociable to speak so directly from the interface of self and world.

Okay, *bulb*. But how about *would*? Who came up with the word *would*? Or the word *word*? How did those gristly neologists know how those words would be read?

I associate reading intimately — by no means entirely comfortably — with my mother, who couldn't breast-feed me but did infuse me with love and phonetics. She had a writerly gift herself, though she wouldn't admit it. Didn't want to deal with it. Had too many other things to deal with. (There would have been a great writer, who combined my mother's rich desperation with my bent toward publishability.) Here's something she wrote me in a letter:

> I had my first hospital duty. Of all people it was Julia Edwards. [She was a fat woman in our church.] She came in late, was hurrying down the hall. She still wears those high heels like we used to wear. She is big you know. We don't know what happened, but she fell. She hit on her seat rolled like a U down her spine and hit her head so hard it sounded like a water melon falling.

"Would you the undulation of one wave, its trick to me transfer" — Walt Whitman.

Lady Lovelace, Byron's daughter, said of Charles Babbage's Analytical Engine or Arithmometer, a protocomputer (this was back when the tongue still presumed that nothing could be fashioned that it could not describe): "The Analytical Engine weaves algebraic patterns just as the Jacquard loom weaves flowers and leaves."

The word *text* (also *architect* and *technology*) derives from the Indo-European root *teks-*, to weave. If you want to have some fun, dig down into the Indo-European–root appendix of the *American Heritage Dictionary*. *Threph-; wegw-; swombho-; bhergh-; regwos-; legwh-; gher-; ghengh-; ghrebh-* (to dig); *gheu-* (to pour); *aiw-* (vital force, life — whence *ever*, *aught, aye, nay, primeval, eternal, eon*). You can hear the language groaning to be born.

My children love reading but somewhat less than I do. That is probably just as well in many ways, for them and for their children. But what if the reading faculty atrophies in the culture? Back in 1980, I wrote something which derives from my mother's knee, but which no one would publish because it was too onerous to read. Another objection was that it sounded (presumably invidiously) black. Here it is, some of it:

Ah-yaaaah *read*in' craze. That's right: check it out y'yeh the *read*in' craze.

Get *back*, get *back*, with some olduhs 'n bettuhs, yehhh. . . . Abey-seedy, abey-seedy, eeeyef: *lettuhs*.

Hear me tell about it: little lettuhs on papuh, People: Right . . . *down* . . . there . . . in b'b'b'lack and white. Yehhh . . . uh, gimme that oooold software.

Sexy let me showya the big trend goin'. Lexy let me showya*bop* to what it's owin'. Bompy-daaaaahm . . . boomp. *Read*in' craze.

Sooooo . . . stay home, light a candle, dig out a volume. Left-a-right 'n' left-a-right, on . . . down . . . that colume. *Read*in' craze.

Let's scope out some histori-ori-orical *back*ground, Muchachas. *Read*in', yeah. Goes back to Sir Herbert Read, Poppuh, the Englandic philo-sopphuh. You ain't just thumbin' papuh, Jack 'n' Jenny, you swinging off into an *ancient rite*. Hmmm? *Got* to *love* it. Of old, there was a tribe, the Librarians. Who believed — get back — *read*in' transported you to faraway lands. Hey, don't look at me. Check it out. Ruh*read*in' craze.

You gonna plunge in. *Got* to, *got* to: I *knooowwwwww* you gonna plunge in. But first, let me do you this: a few tips, All Y'all, from the wooo-experts, man:

Uh-one. *Whoa!* Don't plunge too *fast*. Unh-uh, *hear* it: you can tome thy sweet self out. Brush up on y'Readin' Pro-gram three-four times, Patooties — I bet you ain't had that floppy hummin' since A&S Survey.

And uh-two. Read 'n' skim, for sure, yeah, read 'n' skim, Chickylickin'. But let's do the deal *right*, Folkses: keep repeatin', yehhhh, the *reader's mantra:* "What's Arthur *gettin'* at here, ummmm. What's Arthur *gettin'* at here, ummmm." *Arthur,* do you love it? Arthur was a god, Lovelies. Go on, *follow* him/her, he/she's dead.

And uh-three. Think lin-e-ar, Kids. Start with the Ishmael, get an easy r'rhythm goin', keep your sweet yinyang pluggin' toward they call it the Finis.

And uh-*four*. Don't dance, Brethren. You can't dance to readin', man. Talkin' *Gutenberg* reaction, physi-*depro* time. Ooo-chi-*hua*-hua.

And uh-five. Sexy just because you're *read*in', yeh, uhunh, don't mean . . . *you* know what I meannnn: Hey *aw*right, you can flash a little bicameral mmm-nos*tal*gia, Sweets, but don't, like, scramble them deeeeep-set precepts, hunnnh? *You* know. Don't hog consciousness. *You* know. Don't block will-o'-the-weal. *You* know.

Well, there was more of it. About hitting the Wall of Longueur, and so on. I'll tell you this: I am glad to have typed it up for the last time.

"The written word has its limits," said the Emperor K'ang-hsi (seventeenth century) of China, "for the primal sound in the whole word is that made by the human voice, and the likeness of this human voice must be rendered in dots and strokes." But the problem is deeper than that. I was trying to get at something deep-structural in that reading-craze piece, but I failed, bottom line, to please. A man named Philip Francis Little, according to Oliver St. John Gogarty, wrote:

The aim that all we poets have in writing is of pleasing
Ourselves, which is the object each one has when he is sneezing.

Which pleases, but doesn't suffice. I won't read anything without a contract. A contract endlessly deconstructible, to be sure (that goes — or I wish would go — without saying), but nonetheless phenomenal. Paul Valéry wrote: "A metaphor is *what happens* when one *looks in a certain way,* just as a sneeze is what happens when one looks at the sun."

You know why I cite that? Because *I* sneeze when I look at the sun. So did my father. And I used to assume everyone did. (But I find that most people are surprised to learn that anyone does.) And so, evidently, when he wrote that, did Valéry.

That's the chance writers take. *Appreciative* readers are tickled by that presumption.

Donald Hall

The Way to Say Pleasure

1

Poetry and pleasure. I think of a radio talk-show host who operates out of New York. When I did a new book of poems a publicist set me up to talk with him at noon live from a restaurant. The man was brisk, shrewd, attractive, funny, and mindless. Once he turned reflective. "I don't know, Don," he mused; "I didn't use to care about poetry and that sort of thing . . . Nothing but the almighty dollar . . . But last summer I bought a boat . . . I spent weekends just floating on the lake, doing nothing, and . . . you know what I mean?"

Thus was the art of Dante and Homer — not to mention Keats, "Casey at the Bat," and Dickinson — identified with doing nothing. (I remember a functional definition delivered by a professor of philosophy: "Your house burns down; they say: 'Be philosophical. Don't think about it.'") Of course poets themselves praise lethargy. The author of "Sleep and Poetry," as well as "Ode on Indolence," died at twenty-five: Jack Stillinger's newest edition of the *Poems* runs to 535 large pages while the *Letters* come in two volumes. Walt Whitman praised loafing; he also figured that *Leaves of Grass* was twice as long as the New Testament. We all agree, working like hell, that poetry reminds us of leisure which rhymes with pleasure if that's the way you pronounce it. What else does it remind us of?

a) Making love? b) Eating? c) Thinking? d) Playing games? e) June? f) Walking? g) Standing still? h) Listening to music? i) Looking at pictures? j) Touching sculpture? k) Smelling garlic? l) Goodness? m) Sin? n) Giving? o) Duplicate bridge? p) Receiving? q) Arguing? r) Dancing? s) Watching dancers? t) Watching athletes? u) Looking at flowers? v) Smelling flowers? w) Doing nothing? x) October? y) Suffering? z) Death?

2

"Poetry is the supreme result of the entire language," says Joseph Brodsky. Poetry is what language is for, what language exists to move toward. Language becomes poetry insofar as the poet employs the whole word: its vowels, consonants, characteristic pitches, volume, duration; its sequences as they connect with surrounding sequences, for prosody is always contextual; its history: etymological development back and forth across ideas often encompassing contradictions and swift alternations of feeling; each word's associations by sound and shape with other words of its own language and others, not to mention allusion potential and genuine; its syntactic moves within the sentence by which it walks, for syntax is sinew. At some point or other the poet must attend to the word's contemporary lexical reference.

Say that a short poem includes a hundred words. Say that each word includes a hundred edges and dimensions: The tiny poem flashes a potential ten thousand facets the poet must be aware of, wary of; the reader intent on pleasure must take in the ten thousand things.

Ordinary prose uses ten facets a word. Poetry is the supreme result of the entire language. Except as poetry, language is poorly used—and for that matter most poetry is language poorly used. As I write these paragraphs, how much of *paragraph* do I use? Insofar as translation can substitute for the original, so much is language not used for its supreme result; insofar as *paragraph* equals *caput* equals *Absatz* equals *párrafo*, so far is the word as nourishing as sawdust. What do we say when we say *pain? Emotion? Imagination?* Saying these words to each other, we nod our heads as if we agreed. We conspire to understand each other. But poetry — the supreme result—embodies or enforces a fierce nominalism. What does *pleasure* mean?

> And tear our pleasures with rough strife
> Thorough the iron gates of life.

This wholeness takes part of itself from the violence of "tear" (referring not only to maidenhead or peritoneum but to engines of warfare) rubbing against the lexical softness of *pleasures* and altering them; part derives from the double f-sounds in "rough" and "strife," part from the volume that rises four equal steps in the last four syllables of the first line. Word multiplied by word cuts a thousand facets in one couplet.

Poetry is not only the supreme result, it is the only possible result of language taken to extremity. And it is so particular, so contextual, and so historical that it will not suffer paraphrase or translation.

3

"If it ain't a pleasure it ain't a poem," said William Carlos Williams in a reading at Harvard. Between poems he talked about the vernacular, about poetry's sounds, about the vividness of direct impressions of experience. All art gives pleasure, he said; his asides enacted examples of his own.

But people take pleasure in all sorts of things. The critic's pleasure as she writes about Keats is clear, an attractive enthusiasm, as she imposes structures to make the Odes uniform. The Nietzscheans of deconstruction take pleasure in argument, in talking for victory. As for pleasures of sound, people find pleasure in Poe and Liberace; what do we accomplish by calling them wrong? More people take pleasure in the dramatic structure of a Miller Lite commercial, one Sunday afternoon, than enjoy Shakespeare and Chekhov in a decade. Art including poetry is pleasure if you are the sort of chap who likes that sort of thing.

Charles Baudelaire wrote the inscription carved on our boudoir-schoolroom: "Pleasure is a science, and the exercise of the five senses requires a special initiation, which is reached only through inclination and need."

4

The pleasure of sculpture happens first in hands that would touch: texture and shape; later in muscles that would lift: bulk, volume, heft. The eye seeing stone conducts to hand and muscle for response. Some sculpture uses shapes of lightness, flight, airiness (Calder) that require the imagination of weight in conflict with weightlessness.

We watch ballet with our legs.

For literature mouth is the receptor. Commonly we speak of ear but ear is less sensuous than mouth; it is halfway between the mouth which has no brains and the eye which is intellectual. For most critics, the reading eye drills straight back into the brain with no stop at the mouth or the muscles. For the whole-reader of literature, the eye is channel of entry, and the material that enters there is first tasted and chewed by the mouth, then distributed to muscles of the limbs. When we imbibe literature audibly, at a poetry reading, our ears funnel to our mouths. The thinking brain, an invaluable if late participant in this sequence, also attends life's feast; it sits below the salt.

Some mind-pleasures in poetry are literary, like allusion; others are psychological, like catharsis; there is a chess-playing pleasure in logic. All come long after we taste the work's verbal tangible (chewable) body. Many readers ignore (fear?) or remain senseless to primary body-pleasure. When critics write about poetry, usually they might be describing work translated from another language. If the level addressed is translatable, what gets left out? The notion that there is a noumenal poem underneath the flesh of linguistic circumstance denies the skin of literature. Brodsky who reads Auden magnificently would have us translate Russian poets keeping their meters intact, but Tsvetayeva's trochee brought into English sails us to the shore of Gitchi Gumee — or "The Raven" with caesuras. The spirit that resides in prosody dies in translation. It is false to think that we can encode and translate an essence: Platonism is antipoetic. Information gives pleasure but never so much as a head rub.

It is literature if, when you read it aloud, it gets better. Of course Marvell and Frost and Dryden and Hardy and Dickinson and Wordsworth read best aloud. So does great prose like the paragraphs of Henry James, Thoreau, Hume, and Gibbon. We must read literature with our bodies. A neurosis of the academy detaches head from body. Get drunk on weekends, screw a friend — but only for relaxation.

Literature is unseparable: Literature is coherent: Literature is not talking heads. We must not read Henry James with our eyes. We may read him with our toes maybe or our hair follicles but never never never never with our eyes. He made his greatest work walking up and down saying it aloud. We should read him aloud walking up and down.

5

Reading is maybe three thousand years old. For the first half of its life no one read in silence; reading in silence is not commonplace until after Gutenberg. Rich Romans paid slaves to read aloud while they dressed, bathed, and took walks; when they read in solitude they read aloud. When they heard a slave read they listened with their mouths. Even sixty years ago much of our culture connected the word with the mouth, and nobody set symposia about the pleasures of literature.

At school sixty years ago we learned by memorization and recitation, the famous rote-learning we affect to despise. We memorized not only *amo amas amat*, not only seven times seven, but also, "There is no joy in Mudville, mighty Casey has struck out." Nor is memorization the issue; the issue is performance. If father or mother did not read Scripture aloud they read Dickens. At school we listened to athletes of elocution compete on prize speaking day. After school we met at Lyceum or Oratorical Society or local Chautauqua, to sing songs and speak pieces. By 1930 this out-loud culture was mostly dead and there's no point in whining about it. But in the 1930s American poets forgot how to scan; *Understanding Poetry* is a gravestone over the corpse of meter. Connections between print and mouth are largely canceled.

Bodiless intellects tell us there's no author, and quite likely no text: In the ancient war between the poets and the philosophers — theorists are philosophers; none reads a poem except Harold Bloom — the removal of the author from the text is the intellectual's final solution. Plato finally expels the poets by a nifty expedient: Looking them in the eye he declares that they don't exist. Remember Richard Wilbur's couplet:

> We milk the cow of the world, and as we do
> We whisper in her ear, "You are not true."

6

When we bring the body back to the book, the book exists for the mind to receive, to mull over, to react to, to learn from. We must not be aesthetic airheads praising style over substance as if we cheered Democrats over Republicans. *Let it all in*: But its wholeness enters only through the body's door. Doubtless the alphabet was a mistake, but I suppose that silent reading was worse. Nonetheless if we are aware of absences inherent in silent reading we can recover the sensuous loss. After much practice in reading aloud, we can sense the physical words (in throat, mouth, and muscles) as we read in silence.

Thomas Henry Huxley once accused poets of "sensual caterwauling." I like that; I like also the primitive psychoanalyst A. A. Brill when he defines the poet as one who likes to chew and mouth beautiful words. (Serious people deplore mouthy frivolities.) I suppose that the most gorgeous sensuous lines in our language belong to John Keats in the odes, and among the odes "To Autumn" contains the most mouth juice. Everybody knows it, but let us swallow a couple of lines anyway:

> Then in a wailful choir the small gnats mourn
> Among the river sallows, borne aloft

> Or sinking as the light wind lives or dies . . .

Load every rift with béarnaise! Assonance is loud with *light* and *dies*, subtle with the short *o*'s, and the liquid consonance thrills the tongue: wailful, choir, mourn, river, sallows, borne, aloft . . . Leg-pleasures of rhythm, separate from meter and aided by meter, follow close behind mouth-pleasures. Of course it is too obvious for mention, this sensuous caterwauling, this chewing and mouthing, except that . . .

Maybe we *need* issues of magazines that assert pleasure in literature: When Helen Vendler wrote three hundred pages on Keats's odes, paraphrase and source hunting, she did not consider it worthy of remark that these poems occur in lines, in meter, in stanzas, with rhythm, assonance, and consonance — or that they make a noise when spoken aloud.

7

There are some pleasures without pain. These are closest to the surface of the skin. Take the word *pleasure* itself. The way to say *pleasure* is to take a long time in the saying: drag it out, and while you say it, lick it all over like a nipple. Hit the *p* lightly, then glide over the slippery *l*, touching it lightly with the tip of the tongue; slide languorously over the diphthong, curl around it the way a cat curls on top of the VCR, let it roll and ride on the long journey from its *a* to its *e*; let it spend a week in the sun while it makes the journey. When the chant of this diphthong regretfully concludes itself, next reach to the alternate and contrasting pleasure of the *zh* consonant: This noise wears white leather boots halfway up the thigh, a consonant as subtly attractive as a Dallas Cowgirl. Then, after a minivowel, there's the rolling conclusion of an *r*, *l*'s cousin making a fit coda. A coda is what you need by this time. *Pleasure* is a weekend of a word; you need a rest, after you learn the way to say *pleasure*.

BREAKFAST SERVED ANY TIME ALL DAY

Other pleasures without pain: keeping time with the foot, dancing while you sit in the chair. Otherwise, this pleasure is called rhythm, which includes expectation, disappointment, and fulfillment. We feel rhythm bodily in the shifting of weight (or the imagination of weight) and in the motion of muscles to shift it. The *bang bang bang* of "small gnats mourn" receives itself within ten syllables shaped swinging by pairs sorted out into relative volumes; the great lounging precise sentences of Henry James, or of Marianne Moore, his disciple, swing the leg also — to a tune longer in the interval, that locates itself first in muscle then in mind.

Like narrative, rhythm sets up and disappoints-fulfills. Because disappointment is not supposed to be pleasurable, I suppose that we have reached past the borders of pleasure-without-pain into the country of pleasure-pain. Like narrative, like metaphor, like any resolution involving two (or more) disparates coming together, rhythm is sexual. The development of story, like the development of line, sentence, paragraph, essay, poem, or metaphor, advances and recedes, separates and concludes, arcs and subsides. Is lovemaking a pleasure?

But the structure we ascribe to *Macbeth*, "To Autumn," *The Death of Ivan Ilyich*, copulation, and *Walden* may with equal justice be ascribed to a well-made fifteen-second TV commercial.

Once we go past the nerves on the skin's surface, pleasure and pain come together. We find no "sunny pleasure dome" without "caves of ice." "All the instances of pleasure have a sting in the tail." "Pleasure is the first good," pain is the second. In "Alexander's Feast" Dryden sings: "Rich the treasure, Sweet the pleasure;/ Sweet is pleasure after pain." Sweeter than it is before pain *or without it*. For all things are a flowing, sage Heraclitus says. Although we are bent on pleasure, we acknowledge that love has pitched his mansion in the place or even the palace of excrement; for nothing coheres that is not fragmented. When desire gets what it wants desire dies. Nothing proceeds except by the rhythm of opposites. We breathe out to breathe in to breathe out. No pleasure is profound that does not embrace pain: The progeny of this embrace is beauty.

8

The body's reading opens up bodily pleasures which leave us vulnerable to pain. Sensitivity to pleasure does not enlarge without at the same time an enlargement of the sensitivity to pain. Now the bodily pleasure of poetry is itself unmixed; it is there or it is not there. Ugly language is not painful but disgusting or boring: The mouth does not hurt reading bad poetry; the leg muscles do not ache. The whole poem, past its sensuous mouth- and leg connection, includes pain largely by reference.

Granted that there are some small poems, like Herrick on Julia's clothes, that carry no pain; the pleasures that they carry are neither profound nor long-lasting. The pure song of joy is brief, pleasing, and shallow: It is not "Lycidas," "The Garden," "Ode: on Intimations,"

"Among Schoolchildren," "Burnt Norton," or the five dozen best sonnets. Although the brief joy-song is fairly rare, it is what unliterary people call *poetry*—childlike, happy, brainless, dear, impractical, and pure: sunbathing on a boat.

Great poems in paraphrase sound like the mutterings of a depressive poised on the bridge: One of the many troubles with paraphrase is that the body's pleasure (like Tsvetayeva's trochee) will not translate. When Shakespeare's sonnet speaks of his own dying while he gazes at his youthful love, his joyous vowels sing along with the intricate resolutions of his metaphors: The one set of words brings ecstasy and despair together at once. At once everything is whole and rent—and *everything is neither if everything is not both.*

Walking with a set smile among children studying at school, our thoughts are desperate yet they sing forth in lines profound in pleasure. The King bows his head for the executioner's ax as on the silk sheets of a bed.

9

Literature is largely although not entirely the product of maniacs.

Any notion that connects genius with abnormal psychology is routinely dismissed with the epithet *romantic*. Conventional minds need to dismiss the notion of functional aberration. But discovery necessitates eccentricity because the center is already known. Of course it must be noted that neither mania nor anything else guarantees discovery.

The incidence of bipolar mood disorder in artists, especially in writers, rises high in proportion to the rest of the population. Bipolarity implies gross swings of mood, but not necessarily the madness of delusion or suicide. Some manic depressives—including Robert Lowell and Theodore Roethke—enter institutions for thought disorders not just mood disorders. In any case, bipolarity is painful and wasteful: Mania is self-deceptive and depression self-destructive: At extreme manic states one lacks judgment so thoroughly that one is unlikely to write well; in extreme depression one cannot lift a pencil. Recent pharmacological discovery allows many patients respite from these extremes.

But manic inspiration can make great art: The confidence and energy of a limited manic state are the divine afflatus, the sense of possession or transport. Mania characterizes not only poets but saints, mystics, mathematicians, and inventors. The poet's inspiration is a heightened ability to perceive and embody previously unrecognized identities. It reaches past pleasure to joy. Pleasure is the body's and allows the poem its entry. Joy is the spirit's and responds to what mania provides: the insight that recognizes and establishes connections and resemblances. Metaphor is the spirit's rhetoric as mania is its chemistry; the psyche which we experience as immaterial works through material means.

Mania is essential to the survival of the species, and to the large machine of civilization; it enhances not the individual but the collective. Manic depressives may kill themselves when they are down but when they are up they lay eggs which hatch and survive. Creation needs destruction. By inventing epics and wheels when they are inspired, manics provide for the whole machine. When they are low they provide nothing—but they do not break the machine. (They break themselves and people around them.) When they write books they write out of their experience much of which is hopeless. They report on loss and despair, which are endemic to all life, in the flesh and body of their art which is pleasure. This marriage of dark and light, this wedding of pain and pleasure, makes literature's bipolar wholeness. Poetry weds the unweddable and embodies the conditions we live under: nest of pleasure, twigs of dread.

Gail Godwin

What's Really Going On

"My wife and I were traveling in Europe," my lawyer said, after we had done our business about a mortgage and a will, "and she was reading *Middlemarch*. She finished it in Barcelona and couldn't talk about anything else. We were walking down the street outside our hotel and she was going on about how I had to read it. I can't recall my exact reply, but I wasn't too enthusiastic. I said something like, 'Look, I don't have *time* for things like that.' And she began to cry."

* * *

A young woman I have known since she was nine is sitting in my kitchen. The winter sun is pouring in through a south window and we are eating lasagna from the local deli and drinking wine and having a fine old time. Her one-year-old daughter, a child with an irresistible good temper, is transporting herself around the room in her Tot Wheels, an ingenious combination of walker, table, playpen and carryall. She has one of my dishtowels and is "dusting" the lower cabinet doors and humming a little one-note tune while her mother describes a novel she has just read, Iris Murdoch's *The Time of the Angels*. Seldom at a loss for words, she nevertheless forces herself to pause long enough to find just the right ones to express precisely why this book gave her pleasure. "It had something for all the shelves of my mind," she says. Satisfied with her tribute, she takes another sip of wine.

It is a rainy spring noon in Connecticut, and, following a late morning concert of chamber music, the patrons drift beneath their umbrellas to a carriage house which once belonged to a famous American writer. A buffet luncheon, with champagne, is laid out attractively on trestle tables covered with white linen, and on a small nearby table (also covered with a white cloth) are modest stacks of books, available for purchase, by a living writer who is on hand to autograph them. A guided tour of the dead writer's house is scheduled immediately after lunch, for this is Sunday, a day when the most desk-chained and schedule-ridden movers and shakers may be glimpsed taking time off for culture.

A woman of prepossessing size, wearing a red suit, bears down on me confidently, her pen already unsheathed. "I'll hold your plate," she says, "while you sign your book for me. I must confess I've never read you, but they said over at the cash box that this was your most popular one. I don't have time for fiction. With the kinds of responsibilities I have, there isn't time to escape to never-never land. I'm in charge of sixty-two branch banks. What reading I do has to focus on the contemporary issues. You know. What's really going on."

* * *

The lawyer, who was acute enough to read the message being sent to him by his wife's tears, began *Middlemarch* dutifully in Barcelona and came to the end of it regretfully three weeks later in his bed at home. He had lived in it, he told his wife, thanking her for the experience. A busy attorney in a growing village that bubbles and seethes with all the schemes and cross-purposes of its diversified populace, he is in a good position to know that Bulstrode is alive and flourishing, still exerting power openly in the community as well as behind the scenes, still cutting the same moral corners and making the same excuses to himself. And every day the same temptations—though decked out in modern dress — lie in wait to compromise dreams and ideals. The modern Lydgate will change his vote at a meeting and thus betray a friend. The new Dorothea will wonder how it has happened that all her passionate energies and zeal to change the world have been deflected into small acts of local kindness and civic responsibilities; yet our village will be a better place because of them.

Having allowed George Eliot's expansively imagined world to percolate through his own, the lawyer is conscious of moving in a richer social brew. He sees more patterns and associations. He compares, recognizes, reflects: updating the details when necessary. But, as far as old Human Nature goes, not much has changed. The novel he lived in for three weeks goes on living in him.

My young friend with all the shelves in her mind was not so long ago an unhappy little girl who lived up the road from me. Her parents were my friends first. They had just moved full-time to the country and had taken her out of her fancy private school in Manhattan. Her disquieting precocity, her quick tongue, and a rather stagy demeanor did not go down well with her new peers. Before long, she became the official pariah at her rural school. Each day on the bus, the other children devised new teasings and torments, snickering or whispering mysteriously behind her back, or pretending not to hear her when she spoke. Desperate to change her image *somehow*, she made her mother take her to the village beauty shop for the new "Wedge" cut which an ice skater had made the rage, but the hairdresser botched it and she emerged humiliated in looks as well as spirit. It was at this juncture that she began spending the occasional weeknight at my house. I don't remember how it got started. Perhaps her parents had to go out of town; or maybe her mother and I cooked it up to make her feel less of a social outcast. But I remember very well making up the bed in the guestroom that first time, with pastel-striped sheets and a reading pillow, and, with forethought and intent, placing a copy of *Jane Eyre* on the bedside table.

The next morning, over bacon and eggs, she asked if she could take it home and finish it.

"Oh God, I loved that book. I LOVED THAT BOOK! You know the part when Jane sneaks up to the room where Helen Burns is dying and gets in bed with her and Helen says, 'Are you warm, darling?' and then they say good night and the next thing that happens is that nice teacher comes in and finds Jane asleep with her arms around the dead girl? I cried and cried. I couldn't stop. I wanted to run to my parents' room and be comforted, but I couldn't, because it was three o'clock in the morning and I had been reading under my covers with a flashlight, which was forbidden. So I just lay there in the dark and sobbed, all by myself."

She is telling me this, laughing and drinking wine, twelve years later, as we lunch together in the winter sunshine and her daughter propels herself happily around my kitchen in her Tot Wheels. Yet we both know she is telling another story as well, one we enjoy reminding each other of from time to time, the story of how a precocious ten-year-old scapegoat rose from the ashes of her defeat and took her destiny into her own hands, the same way Jane Eyre did when she applied for a governess job away from Lowood School.

My friend told her father she wanted to start over again in a completely new setting, with new faces. She would like, she said, to go to boarding school . . . in England. England! Boarding school! What did she think he was, made of money? She held her ground for another fall and spring. Riding the hated school bus again, however, she held herself aloof: she was already in England. Her father was not made of money, but neither was he poor. And there was the reassuring presence of an actual godfather in England. A suitable boarding school was found — she helped write the letters — and off she went at twelve, determined to create herself henceforth as the heroine of her own story. Which, to the applause and occasional consternation of those of us who are following her through the low and high chapters of her life, she has been doing ever since.

And that leaves you, lady in the red suit, in charge of sixty-two branch banks.

My nose was already out of joint as I signed your book, a book that took me three years to write and a lifetime of perceptions about "what's really going on" to be able to write, and whose people and stories, because they came under the label of "fiction," you had just relegated summarily to never-never land. You would carry it home, your purchase attesting to a cultural excursion, and leave it lying around for a while, opening it perhaps only to show a friend the authentic signature inside: proof of a real event that had taken place in the real world of that rainy Sunday in the same state with all your banks.

Nevertheless, I hid my considerable pique behind my manners. Why waste my breath on such as you? How could I begin to expand your narrow conception of what was real? This was a buffet lunch with some books to sign, not an invitation to lecture. Let her impoverishment be her punishment, I thought spitefully, handing back the signed book and pen, and, as you showed no inclination to go away, I switched myself on automatic and, smiling insincerely, said: "Tell me, what are some of those responsibilities you have? I mean, what exactly does a person *do* when she is in charge of sixty-two branch banks out there in the real world?"

"Well, for a start," you plunged in, sailing right over my blockade of irony in perfect innocence, "one of those banks burned down last week. I am the person who has to find a new location, and get the people moved in, and the machines, and all that goes with that!" Then we talked mortgage rates, and points, and credit risks, and I asked you if you thought women had a harder time than men getting loans. You wiggled out of this one, saying only that, "What the bank wants, you see, is to make sure you are at just as much risk as it is. The bank can't have all the risk on its side."

By then more people had gathered nearby, they all had books to be signed, and you said magnanimously, "Well, I've taken enough of your time." "Not at all," I said, "it's been so interesting, all that about banks," and turned my back on you forever.

But I can't get you out of my mind. For weeks I have mentally lugged your solid red-suited image around, setting it up at different times of day, in different moods, and alternately haranguing and imploring it to include fiction in its reality.

Why? Why should I care whether you will ever discover a subtler world within your own through the lucent journey through *Middlemarch?* What is it to me if you've never died and wept for your old self in the dark and been born some new, stronger thing as a result of having been thoroughly shaken by a novel? Whose loss is it but yours if you go through life without profiting from the experiences of Jane Eyre and Dorothea Brooke and Emma Woodhouse and Isabel Archer Osmond* and Jude Fawley and Pip and Ivan Karamazov and Joseph K.?

And yet I feel I failed you by letting you walk away so complacently. You told me some things about your world; I told you nothing about mine. I used my manners that day as a cover-up for lack of sympathy and verbal laziness. I couldn't be expected to love you as the lawyer's wife loved him when she communicated her ultimatum on the street in Barcelona. You didn't give me any reason to *like* you very much. But maybe I would feel that I had failed *myself* less if I had been alert enough to seize my final opportunity with you. Why didn't I—oh, why didn't I, as you were turning to go—point to the book you were carrying away and challenge you good-humoredly in your own language: "I risked three years of my life to write that novel. Risk two weeks of yours to read it. I can't have all the risk on my side."

The figures would have been so clearly stacked in your favor that you might well have judged it impractical to turn such an offer down—especially since you'd already made the investment in the book. And your acceptance might have led to further investments of the same nature, which would have made you, eventually, an immeasurably richer woman.

Until a recent rereading of The Portrait of a Lady, *I would have gone on calling her by her maiden name, as most readers do; but because of what has been really going on between me and that novel for twenty-five years, I at last understand that Osmond is the shadow side of her moon. He completes her. She couldn't have married anyone else, being what she is, and she will never leave him. Auden once said that the real books read us, not we them, and that particular book has found me out.*

Jonathan Holden

Poetry, Baseball: The Pleasures of the Text

It was a warm, hazy day in mid-June, and I was driving from my home in Kansas north on K-177, a two-lane highway that wends through the desolate Flint Hills and eventually breaks into civilization again near Lincoln, Nebraska. K-177 is the kind of road described so poignantly in the book *Blue Highways*. Like everything in America that has become marginal, that is approaching extinction, the scenery along this road is beginning to acquire a precious quality, as if the scenes you're passing through are no longer real: you're in a painting.

The drive is a lonely one. The highway has an old-fashioned feel. Every now and then it makes a right-angled turn, the speed limit signs plunge from 55 to 25, and you find yourself proceeding very carefully through towns like Waterville, towns so tiny and quaint, so utterly lost, that they resemble the very scenes which Norman Rockwell enshrined on covers of *The Saturday Evening Post* back in the fifties. Tidy, white, clapboard houses, lush little lawns, a brick schoolhouse. As I drove through them, alert for speed traps, I wondered what it would be like to grow up in such a place. And then I remembered. I *had* grown up in such a place—a rural town in New Jersey, called New Vernon. Although New Vernon was only thirty miles west of the Holland Tunnel, it had seemed to me so backward, so totally out of it, that I've since come to realize that our feeling of "the action" as being always somewhere else, somewhere just over the horizon, must be endemically American. It doesn't matter where you live. The action's always somewhere else, over some rainbow. In such places, the only legal alternative to being bored is either to get out or to cultivate the resources of your imagination.

When you're a boy in America, virtually the only aesthetic activity available to you that isn't considered effeminate like piano lessons is sports. Tennis is an aesthetic sport, but its landscape is too specialized. Baseball is much handier. Like a book you carry around with you with its lightweight stage-sets, baseball can be imagined—can be opened and set up—anywhere. The poet Richard Hugo, in his personal reminiscence "The Anxious Fields of Play," described definitively, I think, the way in which baseball can provide, for an American boy with an aesthetic temperament, a vocabulary for the imagination:

> By the mid-'30s, when I was ten or eleven, baseball had become such an obsession that I imagined ball parks everywhere. In the country, I visualized games in progress on the real grass cattle were eating. In the city as I rode down Fourth Avenue on the bus, the walls of warehouses became outfield fences with dramatic doubles and triples booming off them. Hitting was important in my fantasies. Pitching meant little except as a service necessary for some long drive far beyond the outfielders. I kept the parks small in my mind so home runs wouldn't be too difficult to hit.

My baseball fantasies were as fully elaborated as this, but with one difference. Of the imaginary major-league teams I used to manage and travel with when I was fourteen, I remember best the pitchers. I wanted to be a pitcher, not a batter, like Hugo. But instead of imagining myself striking batters out, I imagined what it must be like to try to hit against the star pitching staff I had invented. Each starter had been outfitted with a distinctive repertoire of pitches and a style of delivery as individual as a signature. I had batted against all of them, usually in the late innings. I knew, intimately, the special strengths and weaknesses of each, as well as their personalities and the history of their careers, and I knew exactly what their stuff looked like.

The guy with the best stuff—impossible to hit when he was on—was Terry Farrell. A towering, crew-cut, thin-lipped, former college quarterback, with a prep-school education and a spoiled, imperious disposition, Farrell was the New York Yankees' stopper. Farrell's delivery came straight over the top, like Carl Erskine's. He had only two pitches. He only needed two. Farrell was always a threat to strike out fifteen batters in nine frames. He might, one day, break Feller's record of eighteen. Farrell's delivery was deceptive, because it was seamless and the effort behind it didn't show. He was so tall (6' 4") that his stride seemed slower, lazier, than it actually was. Instead of "rearing" back to throw, he'd lean back, almost indolently, as he launched into his surge, like a tennis player revolving away from you to start that top-spin serve which, when I was a boy, was known as "the American twist." As he threw straight down he'd seem to place the ball somewhere out in front of you. Farrell's bread-and-butter pitch was his fastball. It would take off.

He threw what baseball connoisseurs still refer to as a "light" (as opposed to a "heavy," bat-breaking) ball. It had a vertical rise of maybe six inches. It was strangely buoyant. It didn't "hop" or "tail." It bobbed up. Then it vanished in the catcher's mitt or else you'd popped it up. Farrell's fastball was most deceptive when it was low. He could actually start a pitch at an altitude well below your knees, and it would rise perversely like a Ping-Pong ball with backspin into the strike zone, leaving the batter almost paralyzed with astonishment. The batter could get so preoccupied, so fascinated with Farrell's fastball, that when Farrell threw his curve it would catch the poor batter with his pants completely down. Farrell would set the ball out in front of you, as usual, and . . . I never did find an adequate verbal formula for what I, as a batter, would behold. The pitch started out as fat as a grade-school softball, but then it would sink so suddenly, so drastically, it seemed to break all the laws of nature at once. And it was about half the speed of the hummer you'd been expecting.

It's necessary to spell out these details not because they are important in themselves, but because they're indicative of how completely and carefully I had imagined myself into the batter's box, and how important it was for me to find the right words—not pictures but words—that would enable me to do this. I became a severe and almost sophisticated literary critic of the words for baseball action. I studied models. There weren't many. The best was the Yankees' baseball announcer, Mel Allen. Allen invented what will probably remain the best English language verbal formula for the sublimity of a tremendous home run: "There's a *long* drive—/ *deep* to left field—/ Woodling—going back—back—/ to the *wall*—/ that ball is going, going, it is *gone*—/ a *home run!*" There is poetry here: rhyme, rhythm, mnemonic charm, and highly evocative verbal mimesis that captures a phenomenon whose beauty is a function of its elusiveness. "It is *gone*." Absence, or, as Wallace Stevens put it in "Sunday Morning," "Death" is "the mother of beauty."

Allen also invented what remains the single most beautiful verbal formula to evoke, in a catchy, concrete way, a pitcher's delivery. Most of the time he used obvious and rather prosaic formulas in different combinations: "Raschi rocks, fires." "The right-hander kicks, fires." "He kicks, delivers." "Round comes the arm, the pitch—." "Round comes the arm, the delivery—." But describing the great Allie ("The Chief") Reynolds, Allen broke into poetry: "The big right-hander wheels/ deals." For years, when Terry Farrell came up in my pitching rotation, I tried to come up with a formula that might be the equivalent of Allen's for Farrell's slightly more erect, stately delivery. I always failed. "The tall right-hander kicks/ flicks." No. "Flicks" is too lightweight. Worse, it's inaccurate. How about "kicks/ whips"? No, we need a perfect rhyme here, because the majesty of the pitch must mirror—be derived from—the majesty of the delivery. I tried working the problem backward: start with a verb. "The tall right-hander somethings/whips." "Hips/whips"? No, I needed a second verb. "Flips/whips"? No, he couldn't throw twice during the same delivery. There *is* no suitable twin for "whips." What if I changed the second verb? Was there a verb for throwing as vivid as "deals" or "whips"? "Throws" and "hurls" were too generic. The obvious candidates were "fires" and "blazes." Neither of them has a suitable twin.

Reading Claire Bee's series of sports books for boys, I searched hard for descriptions which would evoke the elusive charm of a pitcher's misdirection, but I was always disappointed. Every curve which the star pitcher Chip Hilton threw was a "darting" curve. Every slider was a "darting" slider. Every fastball went like an "arrow" or was "burning," "blazing" or "smoking." These last three terms I analyzed and rated. All were clichés. Each evoked a concrete image. A "burning" fastball "burned" your hand to catch: when somebody "burned it in" it would sting. A "blazing" fastball added to the notion of heat a visual image—the ball traveled so fast that like a rocket ship or a comet, like most fast-traveling missiles in a comic book, it trailed a little flamelike tail, a little "blaze." It was a blaze, a blur. Of the three clichés, I preferred "smoking" because of the texture and sound of the word "smoke," its feel on the palate—the way in which the whole word starts with sibilance, a hiss, and ends in a percussion, like "smack." I was around fifteen when I invented my own satisfactory verbal formula for the slow curve thrown by "Ted Gray," a seedy, aging southpaw I'd modeled on the Yankees' late-blooming Tommy Byrne. The ball "curled" away over the outside corner. Or it "curled" in to catch the corner. A fastball might "graze" the corner. Even then, I sensed that a simile such as "like a bullet" would somehow be too obvious, but that you could get around this problem if you assimilated the simile into a predicate: "graze" evoked bulletness with suitable tact, with suitable indirection. Although I did not know it then, as I studied these problems I was thinking like a poet. I was thinking about the minutiae of language—such questions as: which is more opaque, a "gray" fog with an *a* or a "grey" fog with an *e*. I was trying to come up with solutions to the very kind of verbal problems which absorb poets in much the same obsessive way that the derivation of a proof can fascinate a mathematician. I was looking for the words I needed—words for the most elusive and therefore tantalizing aspects of my experience. Once I had found these words, then I could memorize them or write them down and read them whenever I wished. I could possess—as much as anyone can possess—moments of value. I couldn't freeze them. I wouldn't want to ("Death" is, as Stevens truly says, "the mother of beauty"), but I could at least, by replaying some words—"the big right-hander wheels/deals"—review moments of mysterious beauty whenever I felt like it. More than that, I could *create* such moments.

When we read poetry, if that poetry is any good, we become creative ourselves. Consider, for example, the following passage from William Stafford's poem, "Bring the North":

> In split Heaven you see one sudden
> eye on yours, and yours in it,
> scared, falling, fallen.

This little passage is about the elusiveness of all human experience, which is sudden, like a shooting star. We never get a chance to observe it thoroughly enough. It's already in motion by the time we first become aware of it. Its speed—its brevity—is scary: it is time itself. By the time we notice it, it's gone, it has eluded us. Yet in the brilliant flourish of Stafford's language, "scared, falling, fallen," where the vowel sounds themselves flare, close up and fade, we can participate, silently, on our very own lips, in that shocking suddenness. Each time we read those words, we can create it.

Reading silently to myself the right words, either from memory or from a printed page, wasn't only a handy way to imagine the kinds of experience that I wanted more fully to witness as a spectator, more fully to possess. It was a way by which I could, somehow, actively participate in such experience—provided, that is, the verbal evocation were sufficiently artful. Whether we only imagine it or have actually done it, whether it be as insubstantial as a feeling—the great fantasy-ridden longing of being in love, say—or be as temporarily substantial as a fact—the desperately engrossing action of making love, of consummating it—there is a sense in which nothing that we do or that happens to us has taken place as fully as it might have (has, indeed, been realized or taken place at all) until we have found the adequate words for it—written words.

I was sixteen years old when I finally faced, as a batter, a curveball

Jonathan Holden / 119

realer than anything I'd ever imagined. We were playing Bernardsville, in a Pony League Game. The field was a mown, lime-lined cow-pasture in rural New Jersey. Thirty years later, describing this in a poem, I located once and for all what I felt was an adequate verbal formula for the curve. Because I was left-handed and because all the pitchers I had faced until that evening were right-handers, although I had seen curveballs "curl" in either on my hands or to catch the outside corner, I had never been scared by one. But for once I was facing a southpaw, a stocky Italian kid with black sideburns and a black, DA haircut as oil-slicked as the back of a starling, the kind of kid who in 1958 was known as a "greaser." He was fast, just wild enough to make a batter nervous, and his fastball had a nasty little tail on it. He had me 0 and 2 immediately on fastballs — two swinging strikes. What happened next is told in the following poem:

A Personal History of the Curveball

It came to us like sex.
Years before we ever faced the thing
we'd heard about the curve
and studied it. Aerial photos
snapped by night in *Life*, mapping
Ewell ("The Whip") Blackwell's sidearm hook,
made it look a fake, the dotted line
hardly swerved at all.
Such power had to be a gift
or else some trick, we didn't care which.
My hope was on technique.
In one mail-order course in hypnotism
that I took from the back cover
of a comic book, the hypnotist
like a ring master wore a suit,
sporting a black, Errol Flynn mustache
as he loomed, stern but benign
over a maiden.
Her eyes half closed, she gazed
upward at his eyes, ready
to obey, as the zigzag lightning strokes
of his hypnotic power, emanating

from his fingertips and eyes,
passed into her stilled, receptive face.
She could feel
the tingling force-field of his powers.
After school, not knowing
what to look for, only
that we'd know it when it came —
that it would be strange —
we'd practice curves, trying
through trial and error to pick up by luck
whatever secret knack a curveball took,
sighting down the trajectory
of each pitch we caught
for signs of magic.
Those throws spun in like drills
and just as straight,
every one the same.
In Ebbets Field I'd watch
Sal "The Barber" Maglie train
his batter with a hard one at the head
for the next pitch,
some dirty sleight-of-hand down and away
he'd picked up somewhere
in the Mexican League. Done,
he'd trudge in from the mound.
His tired, mangy face had no illusions.
But the first curve I ever threw
that worked astonished me
as much as the lefty cleanup man I faced.
He dropped, and when I grinned
smiled weakly back. What he'd seen
I couldn't even guess
until one tepid evening in the Pony League
I stepped in against a southpaw,
a kid with catfish lips
and greased-back hair,
who had to be too stupid
to know any magic tricks. He lunged,
smote one at my neck.

Jonathan Holden / 121

I ducked. Then, either
that ball's spin broke every law
I'd ever heard about or else
Morris County moved almost
a foot. I was out
by the cheapest trick the air
can pull—Bernoulli's Principle.
Like "magic," the common love songs
wail and are eager to repeat
it helplessly, *magic*, as if to say
what else can one say, it's *magic*,
which is the stupidest of words
because it stands for nothing,
there is no magic. And yet
what other word does the heartbroken
or the strikeout victim have
to mean what cannot be and means what is?

The pitch had started out behind me. I literally staggered backward out of the batter's box, but the ball was still in the air. It was slow and therefore, perhaps, it was hittable. Though I was reeling, as off-balance as a drunk, I fished after it with my bat. It was out of reach, far off the outside corner and almost in the dirt, and I could hear great mirth from the Bernardsville bleachers. As I found my way back to the bench, I could hear the Bernardsville girls maliciously tittering—the same girls who, when I was pitching, would shout in chorus, "Hey, skinny!" I *was* skinny, pathetically skinny. In high school it was like a curse. At swimming pools—any time I had to take my shirt off in public—I cringed inwardly at the cruel truth of the adage, "The only thing worse than being fat is being skinny." The curve had caught me with my pants completely down in front of the girls. I had nothing.

"Going, going, gone." "Wheels/deals." These little Ur-poems of boyhood were as fixed, for me, as, later, lines of poetry in print would be. They possessed an almost runic quality. One could summon them at will. For what purpose? Simply to recite them like a tiny prayer. To *dwell* on them. You didn't need a television. You didn't need any equipment at all.

It is this "dwelling" pleasure in reading, particularly reading poetry, which nonliterary people tend to underestimate. But even people who have not been initiated into the subtle resources of poetry may possibly agree that a good letter is ultimately more tantalizing than a long phone call, and that it has more staying power. A good letter is somehow more *meant* than a phone call. Why? Because there's no small talk, no wasted motion. As in a good poem, every word in a good letter has a force, a seriousness that is in direct proportion to the width of the margins. Whereas in a phone call there is apt to be flagrant inefficiency — long static-ridden gaps, mumbling about the weather, some tinkering around to locate the important topics — a good letter almost by definition will probably contain only things important enough that the writer spent some time trying to get them down right.

Some of the staying power of a letter, like that of a poem, is physical. The letter writer, the poet, is somehow *there* — tangible — in the written text. It is with more than a pang — it's with a shock, still — that I think about certain love letters I once received, how one goes back over them, tracing every word, even the salutation. What a fatal difference in consequence between "Dearest," "Darling," "My Love." Every written word in these letters is a sort of pledge uttered with the urgency of a drowning person. Both of you are in the middle of something so much bigger than you are that you can hardly keep your heads above water. You're signaling frantically to each other over the tops of the waves, blindly flinging notes in bottles — notes of encouragement pledging help, notes begging to be rescued, notes full of grim determination. Yet, even though each note is a jotted SOS, it is usually artful. Perhaps it is the most artful, shrewdly meant piece of writing which the average nonliterary person will ever do. It could be said of each note exactly what Robert Frost said of poetry, that it is "a momentary stay against confusion."

It is, above all, the way we *dwell* upon the text of a good letter, reread it as if to authenticate it again and again, that is poetic. Good love letters can, as the trite language of popular tunes would put it, "cast a spell." They have "magic." Even the handwriting has an energy of its own. The poet William Stafford investigates these very issues in his little poem "Report from a Far Place":

> Making these word things to
> step on across the world, I
> could call them snowshoes.
>
> They creak, sag, bend, but
> hold, over the great deep cold,
> and they turn up at the toes.

> In war or city or camp
> they could save your life;
> you can muse them by the fire.
>
> Be careful, though: they
> burn, or don't burn, in their own
> strange way, when you say them.

At first glance, this poem appears to be about poetic composition: making "word things" suggests writing poems. These "word things" are cunningly crafted out of local and natural materials—leather and wood and lore—and if we remember the orthogonal grid of a snowshoe's thongs, we imagine these word things as having an orderly structure. "Creak, sag, bend, but/ hold" describes pretty accurately Stafford's own prosody—a free verse which alludes strongly back to meter, a grid not unlike the strands composing the remembered net against which, Frost implied, all poets practice. These word things "hold" over the "cold." It's typical of Stafford's wit that he would complete the poem's only full rhyme with a rhyme as obvious as "cold." "Cold" is Stafford's recurring metaphor for the forbidding otherness of the natural world. The obviousness of the rhyme satirizes any comfort which such a pat, almost jingly rhyme might seem to hold out.

But "Report from a Far Place" is not as self-reflexive as it looks at first glance. The poem is more about reading than it is about writing. It is not, Stafford suggests, the *writing* of poems which, "In war or city or camp/ . . . could save your life." It is the reading of them, it is the summoning of words—"you can muse them by the fire"—which could be salvational. It is the way in which these "word things" "turn up at the toes." In Stafford's poems, casual asides are often the most telling moments. "And they turn up at the toes" evokes the way that the abstract nature of words allows us breathing room from a physical world in which, without their help, we might otherwise suffocate. Just as the curled-up tips of skis or snowshoes deflect the snow, so do words deflect the immediacy of the world, allowing us, albeit creakily, to walk on it, to slide forward, to remain precariously and tentatively on top of things, able to look out over our lives for a little way, able to keep things in some perspective.

As Stafford's poem would suggest, there is a sense by no means trivial in which every achieved poem is about the art of reading, in much that same way that, as I suggested at the outset, if you want to study the art of pitching you should be able to imagine what it might feel like to try to hit against your own repertoire. Another poem on this subject — perhaps the definitive poem — is Robert Francis's famous poem, "Pitcher":

> His art is eccentricity, his aim
> How not to hit the mark he seems to aim at,
>
> His passion how to avoid the obvious,
> His technique how to vary the avoidance.
>
> The others throw to be comprehended. He
> Throws to be a moment misunderstood.
>
> Yet not too much. Not errant, arrant, wild,
> But every seeming aberration willed.
>
> Not to, yet still, still to communicate
> Making the batter understand too late.

In the standard reading of this poem, pitcher is to batter as poet is to reader. The poem is therefore conspicuously self-reflexive: Francis, the poet, is pitching the poem to the reader who, if he is to get the point of Francis's wit, must (paradoxically) miss it in order to connect. Again, what may be less obvious but more significant, is that the poem is more about the experience of reading than it is about the art of writing, more about the experience of batting than about the art of pitching. "Making the batter understand too late" evokes with a wonderfully delayed surprise a *reader's* satisfaction at completing those connections that click when somebody else's good metaphor registers. Francis is giving us a lesson here. In order to render the most dazzling effects, a writer must inevitably recall his own best experiences as a reader. An effective poet will necessarily be an expert in what is now called "reader-response theory." He will be as alert and critical when reading his own words as I used to be when I was a boy studying sportscasters' descriptions of baseball.

Poets fall in love with writing poetry, initially, not from some urge to express themselves but from reading the poetry of other people, most of whom are dead, and admiring that poetry so much they would give anything to create such beauty too. Just as some people, hearing folk music or bluegrass, want to grab a guitar and begin to copy the chord changes and the picking, not satisfied until they can make such music themselves, with a bare minimum of means—memory, ear, fingertips, guitar—to summon it at will, so do poets, wounded by the beautiful verse of others, take up the lightest, most minimal instrument in the world—mere words—and begin practicing this seemingly marginal, seemingly anachronistic art of reading, this closely held form of prayer. The words have lost none of their old power. They "burn, or don't burn, in their own/ strange way, when you say them."

Madison Smartt Bell

Literature and Pleasure: Bridging the Gap

I like to read. Reading, say, the latest Elmore Leonard gives me pleasure. Reading Dostoevsky gives me pleasure too. Is there a qualitative difference between the two experiences? Could a polygraph, or an EEG, or some yet more subtle device to measure my responses detect a difference between them? And doesn't that sound like a stupid question? But stupid or not, it is a question which is asked, in one form or another, and is answered affirmatively by the partition of our literature today.

The average "pleasure reader," the one perusing the drugstore rack, is apt to think of "literature" as a scary word; this ideal and perhaps nonexistent subject will not associate "literature" with amusement. From this point of view it is unlikely to be perceived as pleasurable, but as a form of work, a school subject. Nowhere else than in poetry is this split between high art and entertainment more apparent; it's plain that the work of Robert Lowell or Elizabeth Bishop or John Ashbery or Henry Taylor is not on the same continuum with the verses on the greeting cards in that other drugstore rack, an aisle over from these glossy paperbacks. With fiction the distinction is not quite so absolute. It can be blurred, and often is. Works of wholly serious intent and great artistic merit, by Anne Tyler or Walker Percy or Louise Erdrich or a fair number of others, may against all the odds make it onto the best-seller lists and thence into the hands of the person who reads for fun.

But no one really expects that to happen, at least not very often. Several years ago I had a chance to hear a young editor at one of the leading trade publishing houses explain the rules of the game to a group of some sixty apprentice (i.e., unpublished) writers. As a quite genuine service to these novices, she listed what interested her professionally, what kinds of fiction she would be most likely to acquire, in her order of preference:

1. The "generational saga," along the general lines of *The Thorn Birds*.

2. The "occult" or "horror" novel, in the manner of Stephen King, et alia.
3. The "premise" novel ("premise" here meaning some conceit such as "man-eating shark terrorizes Long Island village").
4. The "serious and literary" novel, qualified in no other way.

Our bright and helpful young editor did not enunciate the words "serious and literary" out of the side of her mouth, not quite, but rather with a half-smile that might have suggested any number of things: sadness that circumstances prevented her from purchasing more "serious and literary" novels for her company, or regret that "serious and literary" novels cannot be conveniently stamped into some more marketable genre, or sorrow for the folly of those writers who perversely persist in writing more and more "serious and literary" (i.e., unamusing) novels. Certainly she had not created the situation she was talking about, nor did she necessarily approve of it. She was only describing it, as accurately as possible. Whether or not it could or should be changed did not seem to be much on her mind.

Her tacit assumption appeared to be that the books in the first three genres she identified would be devoured by a mass audience of pleasure readers, while those in the fourth category would be enjoyed by some unspecified elite — presumably too small a group to turn an interesting profit for the publisher. In this latter respect her attitude represented the group mind of contemporary trade publishing with almost perfect fidelity. Wherever the marketing of books is concerned, "serious and literary" novels fall at or near the bottom of almost anyone's list. The demand for such novels is comparatively small, and trade publishing wants to be responsive to the demands of its audience (though whether it merely supplies those demands or also creates them can be a perplexing question). Certainly the preponderance of sales of imaginative literature are made to people who are seeking amusement. It would seem to follow that if "serious and literary" novels do not sell, then they do not amuse. Elmore Leonard is fun; Dostoevsky (or Thomas Pynchon) is work.

It's an occasional fashion among "serious and literary" novelists, a class to which I like to think I belong, to bash the trade publishing business and blame it for all or most of their travails. If publishing is considered in aggregate, many persuasive arguments can be constructed along these lines, but they mostly fail to take account of the probability that the individuals involved in the business are in it for love. They have to be. Publishing is less profitable than any comparable form of ordinary business, less glamorous than any other form of show business. So a liking for some form of literature must be a motive factor in the trade, as little as it may sometimes appear. Perhaps the majority of trade house editors would swiftly declare that, were it not for a variety of vicious circumstances, "serious and literary" novels would be found at the top of their lists and not at the bottom.

Well then, why aren't they? Is it because the alleged general reader is stupid and tasteless? Doubtful—people are seldom as dumb as we think. Blaming the reader is too much like blaming the victim, in any case. At the moment it is quite tempting to shift the responsibility over to the distribution networks, which are indeed becoming increasingly monolithic, narrowing the range of their stock as they expand their number of outlets across the country. The big chains, as they verge on becoming a single big chain, are a handy target, though like the publishers they can plausibly claim that they are only trying to serve the expressed needs of their customers. To a pessimist it may seem that we do not have very far to look to a future where the Big Chain will offer only mass-market material, where serious and literary works will appear only in small serious and literary bookstores (always under threat of extinction from the more economically powerful Big Chain) and very likely only be published by serious and literary small presses. What is already the case for contemporary poetry could become the case for contemporary fiction too, and whose fault will that be? With so much goodwill and love of literature around, it's hard to say for sure. A share of the blame must belong to the book business, at both the production and distribution ends. The audience too must accept some share of it. And perhaps some of the responsibility belongs to the *writers*, injured and innocent as we may prefer to appear.

The book business tends to draw an absolute distinction between literature which pleases and so-called serious literature: here we have a few tons of pulp to be flung to the barbaric hordes, and there we have a solemn, unquantifiable something-or-other, published for prestige as much as for sales. This second class of literature is not very well served by the trade's implication that no one particularly wants to read it. As serious literature dwindles from the lists of the most commercial houses, "alternative" publishers and small presses leap into the breach, picking up some of the work which can find no outlet elsewhere. That's a creditable undertaking, but its final effect is to deepen the split between fun books and the other kind—by taking it all the way down to the level of production. If not for the small presses our literary culture would be a lot worse off; however, one of their inadvertent functions is to acknowledge and underline the point that serious literature is becoming almost irrevocably separate from literature which is thought to amuse.

The progressively embattled defenders of serious literature are apt to posit the mass-print culture as the adversary, forgetting that such an attitude does not offer a genuine escape from it. Indeed, no real exit exists. There is no stance possible which *ignores* mass culture; it is only possible to stand in some relation to it, even if in a relation of the most vehement denial and rejection. Seeking that nonexistent door out of the system, too many people, especially too many writers, can end up assuming the posture of the ostrich.

It's true that at the lowest common denominator of literacy, what is mainly consumed is genre fiction produced to a standard of quantity over quality, if not actually mass-produced. The rapidly assembled, shoddy work of armies of hacks has overwhelmed, at least in terms of numbers, all the categories that young editor mentioned, and a good many she didn't. The quite understandable response of a substantial number of more conscientious and serious-minded fiction writers has been to withdraw altogether from most of these genres. Deprived of an adequate stake in the game of mass-market publishing, serious literature takes its ball and goes home.

The efforts of serious literary authors to reject and stand over against the declining standards of a business which has already rejected them have produced a variety of compensations, most noticeably an apparently new school or style variously described as "postmodern fiction" or "superfiction." This school can be crudely characterized, in a lump, by extremes of self-conscious experimentalism and extremes of self-referentiality. Certainly it would be idiotic to claim that "superfiction" has evolved only as a response to market pressures and cultural philistinism in modern America, for in fact it belongs to an extremely respectable tradition which can be traced back at least as far as Laurence Sterne. The most successful works of superfiction may stand honorably alongside *Tristram Shandy*, earning this position both by their intrinsic artistic merit and by their capacity to amuse (the latter quality indicated by the reasonable share of the fiction market fairly won by writers like Barth, Donald Barthelme, and Pynchon). Superfiction is not solely a reactive trend, but as Charles Newman has persuasively suggested,* the

---

*Charles Newman, The Post-Modern Aura: The Act of Fiction in an Age of Inflation *(Evanston, Northwestern University Press, 1985).*

pressures of reaction have helped force it into a somewhat cramped corner.

The indubitably serious and literary works of the "postmodern" authors are highbrow fiction and no mistake. The pleasure offered by these books is delivered at the price of some fairly strenuous mental gymnastics, a price which excludes the "light reader" (i.e., riffraff) at the door. Fine, but in making mental work the key to its pleasures, superfiction in effect consents to its partitioning away from the mainstream of popular literature, accepting the limiting label which the book business is inclined to put on it. And in agreeing to address itself to an elite, the school risks a sort of terminal involution, a hardening into cryptograms which only critics and scholars will be willing or able to decode. It risks becoming what its enemies all over the industry already like to describe it as being: a puzzle exclusively for intellectuals. In this respect, it is by no means a successful evasion of the rigid categorization which the book business, wittingly or not, tends to impose on books, but only a specialized form of acquiescence to it.

A side effect of the literary occultism which superfiction can foster when pushed to the wall is a general discrediting of realistic fiction, so far as the supposed serious and literary reader is concerned. Mimesis is out, or at least downscale, having of course become the provenance of genre fiction: mysteries, thrillers, procedurals, romances, and so on. It's as if the proliferation of quasi-realistic mass-market fiction has precipitated a crisis in literature similar to the one photography caused in painting. The expropriation of the techniques of fictional realism by the genre hacks and their word-processing programs has effectively closed off about half the horizon of artistic possibility to a large number of writers who prefer to take themselves seriously. Nowadays, and certainly with a few important exceptions, realistic fiction is likely to reach the highbrow audience only in some apologetically stylized variation such as "minimalist" fiction (comically labeled "Dirty Realism" in England). The rest of the literary authors are left to experiment as they please; but note that experimentalism by default can produce only an illusion of the liberation it is meant to achieve.

As literary fiction is vigorously shunted off toward its obscurantist dead end, genre fiction suffers an equivalent devaluation, its lion's share of the market notwithstanding. In fact, genre fiction is as caught in its cul de sac as the literary books are in theirs. Book publishers, booksellers, and book buyers are all joining in a perhaps unconscious agreement that a book which proposes to entertain surrenders all claim to artistic merit thereby, whereas, on the other hand, a work of artistic merit offers mental labor rather than amusement. Thus for one faction the word "genre" becomes pejorative rather than descriptive, while for the other the word "literary" serves as a cue to move along to another shelf. There is nothing intrinsic to the nature of literature that justifies such a strict division, which is capable of nourishing all sorts of misinformation. For instance, only in this kind of atmosphere could Nabokov make a serious attempt to dismiss Dostoevsky as a glorified mystery writer. And when that sort of accusation becomes possible, the arbitrary split between literary and entertainment fiction reaches its last level and begins to divide the writers from themselves.

Probably there has always been a certain cachet to *un*popularity in literature and the arts generally; the lonely struggle in the garret is a persistently appealing romance. However, it used to be possible for writers to break through to a wide audience without experiencing any loss of their artistic respectability. Milton's fame reached the point that his corpse was torn apart for souvenirs, but no one thought to accuse him of pandering to the masses who ransacked his coffin. Dickens and Dostoevsky, both popular serial writers, were and are taken quite seriously in spite of it. Certainly in our own century there have been plenty of serious writers who lived and worked in complete obscurity, but also there were Hemingway and Fitzgerald, best-sellers and celebrities in their own time. Only comparatively recently does it happen that a popularly successful writer may be assumed to have *stooped* to entertain. What such an assumption implies is not necessarily anything intrinsic to the writer or the work, but an uncritical acceptance of categories imposed upon them from without.

In former times, when all imaginative literature was called poetry, there was not such a complicated compartmentalization of it as there is today. It was less often proposed that some kinds of poetry were to be taken seriously while others were merely amusing; you were more likely to hear that all poetry was either one or the other, depending on who you asked. Plato identified poetry as a potentially dangerous frivolity and his discussion of it pretty well ended there. Poetry's antique defenders liked to point to its instructive and exemplary functions, constructing a serviceable argument which unfortunately tends to travesty the essence of poetry by ignoring all its other qualities, including its capacity to induce pleasure in the reader. Horace, in the *Ars Poetica*, tried to compromise these two positions, saying, "He who combines the useful with the pleasant wins every vote." We have had no better compromise yet.

Nor is there any reason to think of it as a compromise in the pejorative sense of that word.

In his effort to straddle opposing views, Horace may make the proposed combination of use and enjoyment sound a little like a forced union of opposites. It's as if the writer is advised to put a sweet jacket of literary blandishments on a pill of less palatable instruction, as if the pleasurable incidentals of literature are to be assumed by its didactic purpose as a sort of disguise. However, it is probable that Horace does not mean to suggest that the union of pleasure and usefulness in literature is an artificially contrived hybrid, but that it is natural, intrinsic to the nature of the form.

An absolute definition or even a comprehensive description of the pleasure which the reader obtains from literature would probably be impossible to construe. There are too many different kinds of literary pleasure for that task to be a feasible one. But the most fundamental delight which literature can offer must have something to do with the perception or discovery of truth, not necessarily a profound or complex or earthshaking truth, but a particular truth of some order. So with Dostoevsky, so also with Elmore Leonard on a good day; the pleasure of insight is not restricted to highbrow literature, though it may turn that pleasure to best use. And "inscape" or "epiphany" or whatever term may be chosen for that near-indefinable peak of the reader's enjoyment and the writer's achievement, is finally a moment of recognition — the reader's experience reflected back, in however complex a chamber of mirrors.

The weakness of involuted forms of literature whose core subject is themselves is that they cannot easily deliver such moments of truth. The real and important pleasures they produce for the puzzle-solving, maze-unraveling intellect are likely to be too abstract for the legendary general reader to share in them fully. The primary joy of recognition is more likely to be derived from literature which sincerely attempts to maintain some rapport, however tenuous, with a real world outside its own text.

Recognition, the reprise of the reader's prior knowledge in some form on which another imagination has worked, is not the only literary pleasure which exists, but it is an important one. Certainly it is too important for serious writers to turn it over to an underclass of hacks. But in their retreat from the thousands of variations which mimetic literature affords, and in that slightly affected abhorrence of the official genres of fiction which the book business has established, the serious writers are doing just that.

Once ensconced in the categories which the book business has distinguished, writers have a regrettable tendency to behave very much as they have been described. In their effort to tunnel out of their different holes they often burrow in deeper instead. Recalling that the boundaries between genres and serious literary fiction are not only arbitrary but really imaginary might have a salutary effect. There is no reason why genre fiction cannot be recovered for serious literature. And in fact that process of retrieval is always ongoing in small but significant ways. With his two Elizabethan novels *Death of the Fox* and *The Succession*, George Garrett has reclaimed the historical novel with perfect authority. Denis Johnson's *Fiskadoro*, Margaret Atwood's *The Handmaid's Tale*, and Paul Theroux's *O-Zone* all make plausible attempts to do the same for science fiction. Cormac McCarthy's *Child of God* cannot easily be disregarded as a mere horror/atrocity novel, while his *Blood Meridian* is certainly something more than just another western. It's a list which one may hope will go on.

As the success of the aforementioned novels and a good many others suggests, a little dabbling in genre does not necessarily corrupt the serious, literary writer. On the contrary, it can offer technical, formal, even thematic challenges which can help produce work of renewed vigor and also of broad appeal. As we take back some of that territory abandoned to genre fiction, we may get back some of the audience too.

Among us serious and literary writers, whimpering about the lost audience can be almost as charming a pastime as whining about the publishers. The unasked question is, *Who lost it?* The readers are still out there somewhere, consuming literary pap by the ton—maybe because they don't know where to find anything better. No doubt they want to be entertained, but they don't want Valium-on-paper, and if they take it, it may be because it's most readily available. It would be genuinely helpful to these readers if some serious writers reminded themselves that a perfectly honorable obligation of the storyteller is to amuse. Fail in that, and the audience stops listening and begins to wander out of the room. There is no shame at all in a little seduction, a few wiles artfully practiced to soften the mind and render it receptive to all the more sophisticated pleasures that the finest literature can produce; in fact that is just what was always meant by the ancient formula of instruction by pleasing.

Charles Simic

Reading Philosophy at Night

It is night again around me; I feel as though there had been lightning—for a brief span of time I was entirely in my element and in my light.

—NIETZSCHE

The mind loves the unknown. It loves images whose meaning is unknown, since the meaning of the mind itself is unknown.

—MAGRITTE

I wore Buster Keaton's expression of exaggerated calm. I could have been sitting on the edge of a cliff with my back to the abyss trying to look normal.

* * *

Now I read philosophy in the morning. When I was younger and lived in the city it was always at night. "That's how you ruined your eyes," my mother keeps saying. I sat and read late into the night. The quieter it got, the more clearheaded I became—or so it seemed to me. In the sparsely furnished room above the Italian grocery, I would be struggling with some intricate epistemological argument which promised a magnificent insight at its conclusion. I could smell it, so to speak. I couldn't put the book away, and it was getting very late. I had to be at work in the morning. Even had I tried to sleep my head would have been full of Immanuel Kant. So, I wouldn't sleep. I remember well such moments of decision: The great city that had suddenly turned quiet, the open book, and my face reflected dimly in the darkened windowpane.

At such hours I thought I understood everything. The first time it happened I was twenty. It was six o'clock in the morning. It was winter. It was dark and very cold. I was in Chicago riding the El to work seated between two heavily bundled-up old women. The train was overheated, but each time the door opened at one of the elevated platforms, a blast of cold air would send shivers through us. The lights, too, kept flickering. As the train changed tracks, the lights would go out and I would stop reading the history of philosophy I had borrowed the previous day from the library. "Why is there something rather than nothing?" the book asked, quoting Parmenides. It was as if my eyes were opened. I could not stop looking at my fellow passengers. How incredible, I thought, being here, existing.

* * *

I have a recurring dream about the street where I was born. It is always night. I'm walking past vaguely familiar buildings trying to find our house, but somehow it is not there. I retrace my steps on that short block of only a few buildings, all of which are there except the one I want. The effort leaves me exhausted and saddened.

In another version of this same dream, I catch a glimpse of our house. There it is, at last, but for some reason I'm unable to get any closer to it. No lights are on. I look for our window, but it is even darker there on the third floor. The whole building seems abandoned. "It's not possible," I tell myself.

Once in one of these dreams, many years ago, I saw someone at my window, hunched over, watching the street intently. That's how my grandmother would wait late into the night for us to come home, except this was a stranger. Even without being able to make out his face, I was sure of that.

Most of the time, however, there's no one in sight during the dream. The facades of buildings still retain the pockmarks and other signs of the war. The streetlights are out and there's no moon in the sky so it's not clear to me how I am able to see all that in complete darkness.

* * *

Whoever reads philosophy reads himself as much as he reads the philosopher. I am in a dialogue with certain decisive events in my life as much as I am with the ideas on the page. Meaning is the matter of my existence. My effort to understand is a perpetual circling around a few obsessive images.

Like everyone else, I have my hunches. All my experiences make a kind of untaught ontology which precedes all my readings. What I am trying to conceptualize with the help of the philosopher is that which I have already intuited.

That's one way of looking at it.

* * *

The Meditation of yesterday filled my mind with so many doubts that it is no longer in my power to forget them. And yet, I do not see in what manner I can resolve them; and, just as if I had all of a sudden fallen into very deep water, I am so disconcerted that I can neither make certain of setting my feet on the bottom, nor can I swim and so support myself on the surface. I shall nevertheless make an effort and follow anew the same path as that on which I yesterday entered, i.e. I shall proceed by setting aside all that in which the least doubt could be supposed to exist, just as if I had discovered that it was absolutely false; and I shall ever follow in this road until I have met with something which is certain, or at least, if I can do nothing else, until I have learned for certain that there's nothing in the world that is certain. Archimedes, in order that he might draw the terrestrial globe out of its place, and transport it elsewhere, demanded only that one point should be fixed and immovable; in the same way I shall have the right to conceive high hopes if I am happy enough to discover one thing only which is certain and indubitable.

I love this passage of Descartes; his beginning again, his not wanting to be fooled. It describes the ambition of philosophy in all its nobility and desperation. I prefer this doubting Descartes to his famous later conclusions. Here everything is still unsettled. The poetry of the moment still casts its spell. Of course, he's greedy for the absolute, but so is his reader.

* * *

There's an Eastern European folk song which tells of a girl who tossed an apple higher and higher in the air until she tossed it as high as the clouds. To her surprise the apple didn't come down. The cloud got it. She waited with arms outstretched, but the apple stayed up there. All she could do is plead with the cloud to return her apple, but that's another story. I like the first part when the impossible happens.

I remember lying in a ditch and looking at some pebbles while German bombers were flying over our heads. That was long ago. I don't remember the face of my mother nor the faces of the people who were there with us, but I still see those perfectly ordinary pebbles.

"It is not *how* things are in the world that is mystical, but that it exists," says Wittgenstein. I had a feeling of great clarity. Time had stopped. I was watching myself watching the pebbles and trembling with fear. Then time moved on.

The pebbles stayed in their otherness, stayed forever as far as I am concerned. I'm talking about the experience of heightened consciousness. Can language do it justice? Speech is always less. When it comes to consciousness, one approximates, one speaks poorly. Competing phenomenologies are impoverishments, splendid poverties.

Wittgenstein puts it this way: "What finds its reflection in language, language cannot represent. What expresses *itself* in language, we cannot express by means of language." We are not, most certainly, thinking about the same thing, nor were he and his followers subsequently very happy with this early statement of his, but this has been my experience on a number of occasions.

* * *

I knew someone who once tried to persuade me otherwise. He considered himself a logical positivist. There are people who tell you, for example, that you can speak of a pencil's dimension, location, appearance, state of motion or rest but not of its intelligence and love of music. The moment I hear that the poet in me rebels and I want to write a poem about an intelligent pencil in love with music. In other words, what they regard as nonsense, I suspect to be full of unknown imaginative possibilities.

There's a wonderful story told about Wittgenstein and his Cambridge colleague, the Italian economist Piero Sraffa. Apparently they often discussed philosophy. "One day," as Justus Hartnack has it, "when Wittgenstein was defending his view that a proposition has the same logical form as the fact it depicts, Sraffa made a gesture used by Neapolitans to express contempt and asked Wittgenstein what the logical form of that was. According to Wittgenstein's own recollection, it was this question which made him realize that his belief that a fact could have a logical form was untenable."

As for my logical friend, we argued all night. "What cannot be said, cannot be thought." And then again, after I blurted out something about silence being the language of consciousness, "you're silent because you have nothing to say." It got to the point where we were calling each other "you dumb shit." We were drinking large quantities of red wine, misunderstanding each other liberally, and only stopped bickering when his disheveled wife came to the bedroom door and told us to shut up.

Then I told him a story.

* * *

One day in Yugoslavia, just after the war, we made a class trip to the town War Museum. At the entrance we found a battered German tank which delighted us. Inside the museum one could look at a few rifles, hand grenades and uniforms, but not much else. Most of the space was taken up by photographs. These we were urged to examine. One saw people hanged and people about to be hanged; people on tips of their toes. The executioners stood around smoking. There were piles of corpses everywhere. Some were naked. Men and women with their genitals showing. That made some kid laugh.

Then we saw a man having his throat cut. The killer sat on the man's chest with a knife in his hand. He seemed pleased to be photographed. The victim's eyes I don't remember. A few men stood around gawking. There were clouds in the sky.

There were always clouds, as well as blades of grass, tree stumps, bushes and rocks no one was paying any attention to. At times the earth was covered with snow. A miserable, teeth-chattering January morning and someone making someone's life even more miserable. Or the rain would be falling. A small hard rain that would wash the blood off the hands immediately, that would make one of the killers catch a bad cold. I imagined him sitting that same night with his feet in a bucket of hot water and sipping tea.

That occurred to me much later. Now that we had seen all there was to see, we were made to sit on the lawn outside the museum and eat our lunch. It was poor fare. Most of us had plum jam spread on slices of bread. A few had lard sprinkled with paprika. One kid had nothing but bread and scallions. Everybody thought that was funny. Someone threw his thick slice of black bread in the air and got it caught in a tree. The poor fellow tried to get it down by throwing pebbles at it. He kept missing. Then, he wanted to climb the tree. He kept sliding back. Even our teacher who came over to take a look thought it was hilarious.

As for the grass, there was plenty of it, each blade distinct and carefully sharpened, as it were. There were also clouds in the sky and many large flies of the kind one encounters at slaughterhouses that kept interrupting our thoughts and our laughter.

* * *

And here's what went through my head just the other night as I lay awake in the dark:

The story had nothing to do with what you were talking about.

The story had everything to do with what we were talking about.

I can think of a hundred objections.

Only idiots want something neat, something categorical . . . and I never talk unless I know!

Aha! You're mixing poetry and philosophy. Bertrand Russell wouldn't give you the time of day. . . .

"Everything looks very busy to me," says Jasper Johns, and that's the problem. I remember a strange cat, exceedingly emaciated, that scratched on my door the day I was scratching my head over Hegel's phenomenology.

Who said, "Whatever can be thought must be fictitious"?

You got me there! Error is my first love. I'm shouting her name from the rooftops.

Still and all! And nevertheless! And above all! Let's not forget "above all."

"The Only Humane Way to Catch a Metaphysical Mouse" is the name of the book I work on between three and four in the morning.

Here's what Nietzsche said to the ceiling: "The rank of the philosopher is determined by the rank of his laughter." But he couldn't really laugh. No matter how hard he tried he couldn't laugh.

I know because I'm a connoisseur of chaos. All the good looking oxymorons come to visit me in my bed. . . .

* * *

Wallace Stevens has several beautiful poems about solitary readers. "The House Was Quiet and the World Was Calm" is one. It speaks of a "truth in a calm world." It happens! The world and the mind being so calm that truth becomes visible.

It must be late night—"where shines the light that lets be the things that are"—which might be a good description of insomnia. The solitude of the reader and the solitude of the philosopher drawing together. The impression that one is on the verge of anticipating another man's next turn of thought. My own solitude doubled, tripled, as if I were the only one awake on the earth.

Understanding depends upon the relation of what I am to what I have been. The being of the moment, in other words. Consciousness waking up conscience — waking up history. Consciousness as clarity and history as the dark night of the soul.

The pleasures of philosophy are the pleasures of reduction — the epiphanies of saying in a few words what seems to be the gist of the matter. It pleases me, for instance, to think of both philosophy and poetry as concerned with Being. What is a lyric poem, one might say, but an acknowledgment of the Being of beings. The philosopher thinks Being; the poet in the lyric poem re-creates the experience of Being.

History, on the other hand, is antireductive. Nothing tidy about it. Chaos! Bedlam! Hopeless tangle! My history and the History of this century like a child and his blind mother on the street — and the blind mother leading the way! You'd think the sole purpose of history is to stand truth happily upon its head.

Poor poetry! For some reason I can't get Buster Keaton out of my mind. Poetry as imperturbable Keaton alone with the woman he loves on an ocean liner set adrift on the stormy sea. Or, poetry as that kid throwing stones at a tree to bring down his lunch. Wise enough to play the fool, perhaps?

And always the dialectic: I have Don Quixote and his windmills in my head and Sancho Panza and his mule in my heart.

That's a figure of speech — one figure among many other figures of speech. Who could live without them? Do they tell the truth? Do they conceal it? I don't know. That's why I keep going back to philosophy.

It is morning. It is night. The book is open. The text is difficult, the text is momentarily opaque. My mind is wandering. My mind is struggling to grasp the always elusive . . . the always hinting . . . What do you call it?

It, it, I keep calling it. An infinity of *it* without a single antecedent — like a hum in my ear.

Just then, about to give up, I find the following on a page of Heidegger:

> No thinker has ever entered into another
> thinker's solitude. Yet it is only from its
> solitude that all thinking, in a hidden mode,
> speaks to the thinking that comes after or
> that went before.

Charles Simic / 141

And it all comes together: poetry, philosophy, history. I see — in the sense of being able to picture and feel the human weight of another's solitude. So many of them. Seated with a book. Day breaking. Thought becoming image. Image becoming thought.

IV

James Laughlin

The Pleasures of Reading the Classics in Translation

One morning—perhaps it was forty years ago—I was riding downtown to the office on the Lexington Avenue subway. Across the aisle I noticed a well-dressed, well-groomed man of middle age reading a small vellum-bound book. I was curious and moved over beside him. It's not usual to see books of the Renaissance period on the subway. He was reading an italic Greek text of the poems of Callimachus, one of the great early Greek poets who was born in 310 B.C. I like now to imagine that I said to the gentleman: "He could sing well, that one, and laugh well over the wine." To which the gentleman's reply was my favorite line of that poet: "The dead do not rest but travel over the sea like gulls."

Nothing so romantic took place. He showed me his edition, a pocket-size Aldine printing of 1520, and introduced himself. It was John J. McCloy, the lawyer and banker, administrator of Germany for the Marshall Plan and adviser to several presidents. He told me the best way to get a calm start for a hard day at the office was to read a bit of Greek on the subway. We came to my stop and I never saw him again.

I was envious, of course, that McCloy could read Greek as easily as the *Times*. All my mentors told me that Greek was essential for poetry. Ezra Pound, with whom I studied in his "Ezuversity" in Rapallo, assured me that the sounds of Greek words were the most expressive for poetry of any language. So when the New Directions office moved from the country to Greenwich Village, I enrolled in a night-school course at New York University in Washington Square. Alas, after a day's work I was too tired to concentrate. The venerable instructor, who had to change his glasses when he went from book to blackboard, was a clod. He was chiefly interested in grammar, something I have always detested as an impediment to the flow of beautiful sounds. After a month I was able to write only: "The captain orders the soldiers to take the horses across the river" or "Who was leading the army into the city?" And what had that to do with Homer or Sappho whom I so longed to read? I gave up. I have remained fairly innocent of Greek to this day.

But does studying Greek really matter? To be sure, one cannot hear the magical sounds of the Greek words if one doesn't know them. Yet I want to argue that the sounds are only part of it, that there is a substance in the old texts, a wisdom about life, which can be had almost as well from translations, of which there are many good ones in modern idiom. This is equally true of Latin literature. Many of my friends are *afraid* of the Greek and Latin classics. Because they didn't study them in school, they fear there is something hopelessly difficult about them. For many of us the Greeks and Romans seem as distant as the inhabitants of Mars. Nonsense. The Greeks and Romans were as human as we are, perhaps more so because their lives had not been contaminated by space travel and computers. They were closer to the verities: love, death, the stuff of existence. There is more straight truth about the curious meanings of our earthly existence in ten pages of the epigrams and epitaphs of the *Greek Anthology* than you will find in a month of those so-cogent articles on the Op-Ed pages of *The New York Times*. Perhaps the greatest pleasure, and instruction, that I have had in my "declining" years is reading the classics in translation. Mr. McCloy knew what he was talking about. We can get a kind of calm, a perspective, a solace from our horrid world by communing with the ancients.

My first mentor was the Latin master at Choate, H. P. ("Hup") Arnold. A dear man but rather stuffy. He was most interested in construction, that we should get the syntax of the *Aeneid* right. He was convinced that Virgil was good for our morale. Virgil would make right-thinking men of us. Like the headmaster's sermons. He never introduced us to Catullus or Petronius or any of the Latin authors who are *fun*. To be sure, I profited from Hup. We were assigned to construe thirty lines of the *Aeneid* each day. Some of my classmates were idle fellows. They were as bored with Virgil as I. But they paid me twenty-five cents to explain to them what our lines were about. This bribery produced in me a dislike of Virgil (or guilt feelings) which did not leave me until 1983, when the dearest of all my friends, Robert Fitzgerald, published his magnificent version of the *Aeneid*. Robert finally convinced me that Virgil was acceptable. But oh those seven-line similes that Virgil loved, and which were such a pain to construe. Skip them. They're not poetry, they're verbiage. Fitzgerald's is certainly the most palatable translation. But where to dip in? Perhaps Book IV, the story of Aeneas's "thing" with Dido, or Book VI, the visit to the underworld. To read the whole poem would take great fortitude. Of Virgil, my own favorite is the fourth *Eclogue*, which I translated at Harvard, the prophecy poem about the marvelous child who will redeem the world. The medieval scholars took it to have foretold the coming of Christ:

> For thee, little boy, will the earth pour forth gifts
> All untilled, give thee gifts
> First the wandering ivy and foxglove,
> Then colocasias and the laughing acanthus
> Uncalled the goats will come home with their milk
> No longer need the herds fear the lion
> Thy cradle itself will bloom with sweet flowers
> The serpent will die
> The poison plant will wither
> Assyrian herbs will spring up everywhere

This translation and a good selection from Virgil's shorter poems can be found in the paperback, *Latin Poetry*, edited by L. R. Lind, Oxford.

If Hup Arnold was musty, Dudley Fitts, the star of the English department at Choate, was a spring breeze. My first confrontation with him as a fourth-former was dramatic—and classical. Fitts, dressed in his black cloak, was flying down the stairs of the dining hall, some great thought obscuring his attention to obstacles, and I was rushing up. We collided on a landing, and both fell down. Fitts reassembled himself with dignity and addressed me in stentorian Bostonese: "You young puppies who haven't even read Thucydides!" Later we became great friends. With his mastery of six languages he was the intellectual eminence of the school. It was physically accurate to call him "highbrow." There was an extra half inch between his eyes and his hairline. In the museum at Athens I saw the bust of an Attic scholar who had the same extension. His sixth-form honors English course was phenomenal for a school in those days. It began with readings from Roman *Poetics*, then the *Oedipus Rex*, next Chaucer whom we were taught to pronounce as written, *Coriolanus* rather than *Macbeth*. We skipped all the soggy English poets who have made students hate poetry, and finished with *Dubliners*, Eliot and Pound.

On condition that I keep silent while he was working, Fitts gave me the run of his classical library. He would toss me a book from his shelves and tell me, "Look at this." Translations, of course. All the lively texts that Hup Arnold wouldn't tell us about. When I came to Choate, Fitts was doing his remarkable adaptations of poems from the *Greek Anthology*. They are more paraphrases than literal translations. Of his method he wrote: "I find it impossible to equal the delicate balance of the elegiac couplet, and I have deliberately chosen a system of irregular cadence, assonance and the broken line. . . . I have simply tried to restate in my own idiom what the Greek verses have meant to me." The result is fine English poetry which is Greek in spirit, but tempered with contemporary wit.

The *Anthology* is a huge omnium gatherum of more than four thousand epigrams, both Pagan and Christian, beginning in Greece about 700 B.C., then ranging through all parts of the Mediterranean world where Greek remained an important literary language for seventeen hundred years. Many of the poems are dross, the work of hacks or pedants. But the best are among the glories of Greek literature and all poetry. Their compression has produced a crystallized lyricism—and profound wisdom about the joys and sorrows of the human condition.

Here are a few of Fitts' versions:

I am an apple tossed by one who loves you.
Yield to him therefore, dear Xanthippe:
                both you and I decay.

—Plato

You deny me: and to what end?
There are no lovers, dear, in the underworld,
No love but here: only the living know
The sweetness of Aphrodite—
                but below,
But in Acheron, careful virgin, dust and ashes
Will be our only lying down together.

—Asklepiades

My soul, when I kissed Agathôn, crept up to my lips
As though it wished (poor thing!) to cross over to him.

— Plato

Mouth to mouth joined we lie, her naked breasts
Curved to my fingers, my fury grazing deep
On the silver plain of her throat, and then, no more.
She denies me her bed. Half of her body to Love
She has given, half to Prudence:
                    I die between.

— Paulus Silentiarius

O lovely whiskers O inspirational Mop!
But if growing a beard, my friend, means acquiring wisdom,
Any old goat can be Plato.

— Lucian of Samosata

Stranger by the roadside, do not smile
When you see this grave, though it is only a dog's.
My master wept when I died, and his own hand
Laid me in earth and wrote these lines on my tomb.

— Anonymous

What text of the *Anthology* to recommend? Fitts is available in a New Directions paperback but his choice is not broad. Peter Jay's Penguin selection is good. Probably the best is J. W. Mackail's *Select Epigrams* of 1911, prose versions, but the translations are sensitive and faithful to the Greek spirit. Unfortunately, Mackail is not in print and must be found in a library. If the reader becomes hooked, there is the indispensable five-volume edition in the Loeb Classical Library, published by Harvard University Press. The prose translations by W. R. Paton smack a bit of 1911, when they were published, but are often quite beautiful.

When later Fitts came to Martial (A.D. 40-104), one of the greatest masters of satire and the ribald epigram, his penchant for kidding ran away with him. Anachronism is fun to do, but it can go too far. In X, lxviii, Martial is making fun of a promiscuous Roman lady named Laelia who tries to excite lovers by talking to them in bed in Greek. But when

Fitts makes Laelia French-speaking Abigail from near Boston it doesn't, for me, quite work, clever as it is.

>Abigail, you don't hail from La Ville
>Lumière, or Martinique, or even Québec, P.
>Q., but from plain old Essex County;
>Cape Ann, believe me, for ten
>generations. Accordingly, when
>you gallicize your transports, such as they are,
>and invoke me as *mon joujou! petit
>trésor!, vie de ma vie!*, I grow
>restive.
>   It's only bed-talk, I know,
>but not the kind of bed-talk you
>were designed for, darling.
>   Let's you and me
>go native. Damn your Berlitz. Please,
>woman, you're an Abigail,
>   not a *pièce exquise*.

Fitts is closer to Martial's biting directness when he keeps simple:

>Those are my poems you're reciting, Fidentinus,
>but the way you garble them
>   makes them all your own.

>You claim that all the pretties are panting for you:
>for you, Fitts,
>face of a drowned clown floating under water.

>D. Fitts is
>   the lewdest man!
>He'd wear full dress
>   in a nudist camp.
>   (that one about a noble Roman who wore his toga at orgies)

>You don't lay her, you lick her, you sick fraud,
>and you tell the whole damn town you're her lover.
>Gargilius, I swear to God,
>if I catch you at it you'll be tongue-tied for ever.

Fitts' true greatness as a translator will survive through his versions of the Greek plays. Collaborating with Robert Fitzgerald, he did the *Oedipus Rex* and *Antigone* of Sophocles and the *Alcestis* of Euripides. Later, on his own, he did *Lysistrata*, the *Frogs*, the *Birds* and the proto-feminist *Festival of Women* of Aristophanes. I shall have something to say about the Fitts-Fitzgerald achievement when I come to Fitzgerald.

I would not want to leave my beloved schoolmaster Dudley Fitts without a few lines of the hilarious poly-logodaedaly of which he was capable. These are from the story of "O'Byrne Redux," a Boston politician who ran off with his secretary, done in a macaronic of Fittsian Latin and "whooped up" slang.

> It vox calamitosa matronae ad astra whoopantis,
> it clamor et kiddorum, virumque patremque AWOLatum
> buhuando simul, nec est qui det bonum goddam:
> 'Quo usque tandem, O'Byrne, beddumque boardumque
>   skippabis?
> 'Redi, pater, redi, O'Byrne, marite, relinquere fleshpots . . .'

My next tutor in the classics was Ezra Pound. Dudley Fitts arranged for my enrollment in the "Ezuversity." Happy days. A lovely seaside resort on the Ligurian coast, no tuition, and a master who, except for his obsessions with Fascism and anti-Semitism, was unfailingly kind and always inspiring. Pound's critical standards were high. He had no esteem for most of the texts which were inflicted on students in the "beaneries." He looked only to the poets who had invented something new in poetry, not to the camp followers. Our syllabus was the canon given in Pound's *How to Read* (reprinted in the *Literary Essays*). For the Greeks: Homer, Sappho and Sophocles. In Latin, Catullus, the best of Ovid, Propertius and, grudgingly, Horace. We can best grasp what Pound felt and thought about Homer by reading his Canto I, which is a rescription from Book II of the *Odyssey*, the *nekvia* section in which Odysseus descends to the underworld to consult the prophet Tiresias. Typical of Pound, the mixmaster, he is not content with the story but styles the opening in the alliterative rhythms of the Anglo-Saxon *Seafarer*, which he had earlier translated.

> And then went down to the ship,
> Set keel to breakers, forth on the godly sea, and
> We set up mast and sail on that swart ship,

> Bore sheep aboard her, and our bodies also
> Heavy with weeping, and winds from sternward . . .

Equally typical of Pound, we didn't read Homer in a modern translation. We read him in the 1538 Latin version by Andreas Divus which he had picked up on a Paris quai bookstall about 1910. Pound thought it to be greatly superior to Chapman or Pope in giving the Homeric feeling. This discovery tells us something about Pound's much-disputed "scholarship." There was a lot of happenstance in it. He would chance on a book; if he liked it, it would become dear to him and he would search no further. At a deeper level it shows his passion for languages, his "interlinguality," or his conviction that languages must be interwoven. There are some sixteen different languages in the *Cantos*, including Chinese. Pound advised young aspirants that they should have some familiarity with at least three languages if they wished to be serious poets—not for the content of the foreign poetry so much as to learn metric and how the sounds of words can be put together.

Wyndham Lewis called Pound the *pantechnikon*;* Pound certainly knew how to get things done. He didn't care for any of the existing translations of Sappho so he recruited the young poet Mary Barnard to study Greek and translate Sappho under his direction. Barnard's unvarnished versions of Sappho (available in a University of California Press paperback) are first-rate. (No complete poems of Sappho survive in original texts. She comes down to us in fragments of papyri or in quotations in the writings of grammarians. Mary Barnard sometimes combines phrases from different sources to make a more substantial poem.)

> Thank you, my dear
>
> You came, and you did
> well to come: I needed
> you. You have made
>
> love blaze up in
> my breast—bless you!
> Bless you as often
>
> as the hours have

---

*"Ezra Pound—Demon pantechnikon driver, busy with removal of old world into new quarters." (Blast, *July 1915*)

> been endless to me
> while you were gone

Guy Davenport's Sappho is equally fine, and in his California paperback we get the bonus of some expertly turned Archilocus and Alkman. Willis Barnstone has also done well with Sappho, as has John Nims.

Another modern poet who had deep feeling for Sappho was William Carlos Williams. He knew little Greek but with help from a professor friend, he made a superb version of Sappho's best-known poem, the "phainetai moi kenos isos theoisin," which he embedded in Book V, Part II, of *Paterson*:

> Peer of the gods is that man, who
> face to face, sits listening
> to your sweet speech and lovely
> > laughter.
>
> It is this that rouses a tumult
> in my breast. At mere sight of you
> my voice falters, my tongue
> > is broken.
>
> Straightway, a delicate fire runs in
> my limbs: my eyes
> are blinded and my ears
> > thunder.
>
> Sweat pours out: a trembling hunts
> me down. I grow paler
> than dry grass and lack little
> > of dying.

This poem of Sappho's has attracted translators over the centuries, beginning with a Latin version by Catullus. Williams also adapted an Idyl of Theocritus for his last book, *Pictures from Brueghel*.

The story of Pound's connection with Sophocles is curious. In his early critical books he had little to say about him but when he was confined in St. Elizbeths Hospital for twelve years, "a guest of the government," as he put it, often bored, he turned, with his own special kind of ironic humor, to truncated adaptations of the *Elektra* and *The*

Women of Trachis. His theory was that if the dialogue were done mostly in slang but the choruses in verse he could interpret the plays in a new way, without losing the "Greekness" or the sense of tragedy. I have seen productions of both plays; I think they "work." The slang makes the audience laugh but, since all the rhetorical fustian of the old translations has been eliminated, the myths come through as realities which relate to contemporary situations. Pound said that translation is a form of criticism.

One of the snappiest Ezraisms in *The Women of Trachis* is the couplet which the Victorian Gilbert Murray rendered

> Set me a brake
> On stony lips, steel-hard and true . . .

and Pound comes out with

> And put some cement in your face,
> Reinforced concrete . . .

In the *Elektra* it is startling to jump from

> (*Orestes to his tutor*)
>
> All right, Old Handy,
> you sure have stuck with us
> like a good ole horse rarin' for battle,
> urgin' on and keepin' right forward
> up in front every time.
> This is what we're agoin' to do,
> listen sharp and check up if
> I miss any bullseyes.

to the elegant verse threnody, written in a meter like the Adonic, of Elektra's mourning for her brother whom she thinks to be dead:

> "All that is left me
> my hope was Orestes
> dust is returned to me
> in my hands nothing,
> dust that is all of him
> flower that went forth."

The contrast actually serves to expedite the dramatic action. Pound started me on Catullus (B.C. 87-54), a constant presence in my own work:

> Catullus is my master and I mix
> a little acid and a bit of honey
>   in his bowl . . .
>
> Catullus could rub words so hard
> together their friction burned a
>   heat that warms
>
> us now 2000 years away . . .

The gist of Catullus is clarity, simplicity, and a mix of sharp eye with soft feeling. An immediacy which puts him close to such modern poets as William Carlos Williams and Kenneth Rexroth. There is a wide range in Catullus; the love poems to Lesbia, the poems of jealousy when she is giving him a bad time; the satiric poems which ridicule profligate Roman society, mythological poems such as the one on Peleus and Thetis, and the superb epithalamium for the marriage of his friend Mallius.

    Pound translated only three poems of Catullus. With the famous "Odi et amo" he found what so many others have found, that its very brevity is defeating:

> I hate and love. Why? You may ask but
> It beats me. I feel it done to me, and ache.

In his version of the salutation to Formianus' girlfriend, he captures Catullus's bite though not the tightness of his metric:

> "All Hail; young lady with a nose
>   by no means too small,
> With a foot unbeautiful,
>   and with eyes that are not black,
> With fingers that are not long, and with a mouth undry,
> And with a tongue by no means too elegant,
> You are the friend of Formianus, the vendor of cosmetics,
> And they call you beautiful in the province,
> And you are even compared to Lesbia.
>
> O most unfortunate age!"

There are so many good modern translations of Catullus it's hard to choose among them. I think I'd vote for Peter Whigham in the Penguin paperback.

Pound called Arthur Golding's translation of Ovid's *Metamorphoses* (1567) "the most beautiful book in the language." So we read Ovid in that bubbling, delicious old text. Golding's humorous tone is perfect for Ovid's color and wit. The *Metamorphoses*—A. E. Watts's translation is exemplary—is one of the most entertaining books of ancient times and, taken in bedtime doses—the mythological stories do pile up—it's not to be missed. The Latin is so fine: Ovid was facile, he wrote a great deal, but line after line are marvels of lovely sound. He said that poetry flowed from him of its own accord. I suspect that he dreamed in hexameters. His *Art of Love* was suppressed by Augustus. He was married three times and wrote a few pages on cosmetics, the *Medicamina Faciei Femineae*.

Here, in Golding's fourteeners, we have the god Apollo lusting after chaste Daphne in the woodland:

> So into flames the God is gone and burneth in his brest
> And feedes his vaine and barraine love in hoping for the best.
> Hir haire unkembd about hir necke downe flairing did he see,
> O Lord and were they trimd (quoth he) how seemely would she bee?
> He sees hir eyes as bright as fire the starres to represent,
> He sees hir mouth which to have seene he holdes him not content.
> Hir lillie armes mid part and more above the elbow bare,
> Hir handes, hir fingers and hir wrystes, him thought of beautie rare.
> And sure he thought such other parts as garments then did hyde,
> Excelled greatly all the rest the which he had espyde.

Pound was never a Horace fan. Perhaps he blamed the British Empire on men who had been made to memorize the "Integer Vitae" as boys at Eton and Harrow. "Horace," he said, "is the perfect example of a man who acquires all that is acquirable without having the root." When as one of his diversions in the St. Elizabeths claustration he was assembling his *Confucius to Cummings* anthology (the Library of Congress provided the books he needed), he could find no translation of Horace he liked; he translated the "Exegi monumentum aere perennius" himself. The content, he explained, had considerable appeal for a poet locked up in a "bughouse."

This monument will outlast metal and I made it
More durable than the king's seat, higher than pyramids.
Gnaw of the wind and rain?
                        Impotent
The flow of the years to break it, however many

Bits of me, many bits, will dodge all funeral,
O Libitina Persephone and after that,
Sprout new praise. As long as
Pontifex and the quiet girl pace the Capitol
I shall be spoken where the wild flood Aufidus
Lashes, and Daunus ruled the parched farmland:

Power from lowliness: 'First brought Aeolic song to Italian
    fashion'—
Wear pride, work's gain! O Muse Melpomene,
By your will bind the laurel.
                      My hair, Delphic laurel.

A serviceable paperback of the *Odes of Horace* is the one translated by the English poet James Michie, published by Washington Square Press.

    The glory of Pound's *Homage to Sextus Propertius* (a rescription not a translation) is the language, the sheer beauty of the melopoeia. The English poet Basil Bunting told me that Yeats considered the *Homage*, especially Section VII, Propertius's *"Nox mihi candida,"* the finest free verse written in this century, because of the way Pound could modulate from line to line as in a sonata in music. For me this passage is one of the most wondrous erotic poems in any language.

Me, happy, night, night full of brightness:
Oh couch made happy by my long delectations;
How many words talked out with abundant candles;
Struggles when the lights were taken away;
How with bared breasts she wrestled against me,
      Tunic spread in delay;

And she then opening my eyelids fallen in sleep,
Her lips upon them; and it was her mouth saying:
     Sluggard!
. . .

> While our fates twine together, sate we our eyes with love;
> For long night comes upon you
> > and a day when no day returns.

Robert Lowell translated Propertius's "Arethusa to Lycotas," but it is stiff, it does not flow, because he put it into rhyming quatrains. This is a problem for translators of the classics. When quantitative Latin or Greek verse is forced into English accentual and rhymed meters something seems to go awry in the poetic tone. Pope's couplets are scintillating but they don't sound like Homer. Could this mean that sound is in many cases more essential than content?

Pound's *Homage to Sextus Propertius* will be found in his *Personae* volume. Since he collages from the original it would be well to read Propertius in J. P. McCulloch (California) or John Warden (Bobbs-Merrill).

In his essay, "Generations of Leaves," Robert Fitzgerald demonstrates how "the classical tradition is observed when art is wakeful to reality in the fullest possible sense, including the reality of previous works of art." *The reality of previous works of art.* That perception, and the skill to re-create the old poets in fresh, new language, was the clue to Fitzgerald's greatness. Pound had it too, but Fitzgerald was far more disciplined in his practice. He would work for a day, sometimes more, on one line of Homer or Virgil to get it absolutely right.

Dudley Fitts had long urged Fitzgerald to tackle the *Odyssey* but Robert doubted he could handle such a mammoth task. Then when Pound praised some passages he had done, and when he realized that most of the texts being used in schools were in prose—Lang, Butler, Palmer, Rouse, Rieu and T. E. Shaw (Lawrence of Arabia), he took up the challenge. There was, of course, Richmond Lattimore's great verse version of the *Iliad*, yet, much as he admired Lattimore's language he disputed the structure in which, for the most part, every Greek line is equated with an English line. This method is faithful but somewhat stiff. There is great fluidity in Homer. His Greek is formulaic because it was composed for oral performance. A reciter does not put in pauses at the end of every line. To get the "flow" of the original, Fitzgerald, after much experimentation, decided to let the lines run on, placing words where they sounded most natural as speech. His version is convincing to the modern reader, almost as if Homer had written in English. The set pieces are good English poems. "There should be," he said in an interview, "on every page a lyric quality that I believed was important, and that corresponded to the singing that the Homeric poet had in his tradition."

For his metric Fitzgerald worked out a blank verse, based on iambic pentameter, but subtly varied to avoid monotony. Like Marlowe, he exercised originality and freedom in stress and phrasing.

> Of mortal creatures, all that breathe and move,
> earth bears none frailer than mankind. What man
> believes in woe to come, so long as valor
> and tough knees are supplied him by the gods?
>
> (*Odysseus is speaking to Amphinomos*)
>
> But when the gods in bliss bring miseries on,
> then willy-nilly, blindly, he endures.
> Our minds are as the days are, dark or bright,
> blown over by the father of gods and men.

Here the first two lines scan iambic but then come the little variations of extra syllables that make irregular feet. That's the art.

Fitzgerald's *Odyssey* and *Iliad* are available in Anchor paperbacks, and the *Aeneid* in a Vintage paperback.

There is a simple way to demonstrate, by comparison, our debt to Fitzgerald and his cotranslator Dudley Fitts for modernizing the translation of the Greek plays. They did it almost alone. When in 1936 they began with the *Alcestis* of Euripides, the standard texts were by two English scholars: the Scotsman Sir Richard Claverhouse Jebb (1841-1905) and Gilbert Murray (1866-1957). Those books were in every library and taught in most colleges. No wonder readers thought the classics were boring.

Here is the last chorus from Murray's *Oedipus, King of Thebes*:

> Ye citizens of Thebes, behold; 'tis Oedipus that passeth here,
> Who read the riddle-word of Death, and mightiest stood of mortal men,
> And Fortune loved him, and the folk that saw him turned and looked again.
> Lo, he is fallen, and around great storms and the outreaching sea!

> Therefore, O Man, beware, and look toward the end of things that be,
> The last of sights, the last of days; and no man's life account as gain
> Ere the full tale be finished and the darkness find him without pain.

And here is the same from Fitts/Fitzgerald's *Oedipus Rex*:

> Men of Thebes: look upon Oedipus.
> This is the king who solved the famous riddle
> And towered up, most powerful of men.
> No mortal eyes but looked on him with envy,
> Yet in the end ruin swept over him.

Fitzgerald and Fitts, with the seven plays translated together or alone, proved that Greek drama could be made readable, and because readable, moving and exciting. Their pioneering led to superb new translations such as those of William Arrowsmith (*New Greek Tragedy in Modern Translation*, Oxford) and others. The monumental project has been the four-volume *Complete Greek Tragedies*, edited by David Grene and Richmond Lattimore for the University of Chicago Press, embracing the work of sixteen translators. More recently there is another impressive project, done by one man, Robert Fagles of Princeton, who is very good: one volume of Aeschylus's trilogy, the *Oresteia*, and one of Sophocles' *Three Theban Plays*, both published by Penguin. Fitzgerald: *The Oedipus Cycle*, Harcourt, Brace. Fitts: *Four Comedies of Aristophanes*, Harcourt, Brace. Fitts and Fitzgerald: *Four Greek Plays*, Harcourt, Brace.

Back in the forties when I was trying with utter ineptitude to run the Alta Ski Lodge in Utah — if the pipes didn't freeze they clogged up and some of our most profitable guests were either alcoholics or certifiable lunatics — it was a relief to drive down to San Francisco to visit with Kenneth Rexroth. Kenneth was the best talker I've ever heard next to Pound, but a better cook, and he read in fields which Pound never entered, remembering it all with a photographic memory. Books covered every wall in the old Victorian house on Potrero Hill.

Unemployed, Rexroth spent three hours every afternoon in the bathtub with a reading board, turning two pages a minute. His comments, shouted into the living room, kept me in stitches. All very literary or serious reading. Once he reproved me: "Jim, only children read novels." His other life, as we know from his great nature poems, was in the mountains. We made many trips into the Sierras, both in summer, when we packed in with a donkey, and in early spring, when we went on skis and slept in snow caves.

Rexroth made a lively (and lovely) little collection of translations from the *Greek Anthology*.

> Playing once with facile
> Hermione, I found she wore
> A flower embroidered girdle
> And on it, in letters of gold,
> "Love me, and never mind
> If others had me before you."

What interested me most was the way Rexroth would use a classic text as the springboard for one of his own poems. Often it was hard to tell where the ancient poet stopped and Rexroth began, so close was the approximation in tone. Here is one using Martial:

> This is your own lover, Kenneth, Marie,
> Who someday will be part of the earth
> Beneath your feet, who crowned you once with roses
> Of song; whose voice was no less famous
> Raised against the guilt of his generation.
> Sweetly in Hell he'll tell your story
> To the enraptured ears of Helen,
> Our joys and jealousies, our quarrels and journeys,
> That unlike hers, ended in kisses. . . .

Here is one from Sappho. The quatrain is Rexroth's adaptation of one of her fragments.

> . . . about the cool water
> the wind sounds through sprays
> of apple, and from the quivering leaves
> slumber pours down . . .
>
> We lie here in the bee filled, ruinous
> Orchard of a decayed New England farm,
> Summer in our hair, and the smell

Of summer in our twined bodies,
Summer in our mouths, and summer
In the luminous, fragmentary words
Of this dead Greek woman.
Stop reading. Lean back. Give me your mouth.
Your grace is as beautiful as sleep.
You move against me like a wave
That moves in sleep.
Your body spreads across my brain
Like a bird filled summer;
Not like a body, not like a separate thing,
But like a nimbus that hovers
Over every other thing in all the world.
Lean back. You are beautiful,
As beautiful as the folding
Of your hands in sleep. . . .

Rexroth identified with Sappho. In his *Classics Revisited*, a collection of thumbnails of the classics of all the world's literatures from *Gilgamesh* to *Huckleberry Finn*, he says of Sappho that she "shares with Homer and Sophocles their splendor, clarity, and impetuosity. She is . . . bright, swift, and sure. She surpasses all other Greek poets in immediacy of utterance and responsiveness of sensibility."

The historians. Among the ancients Herodotus has always been my favorite because he is often such a glorious liar. He meets a traveler from a distant region and puts down his hearsay tall tales as if they were gospel. Herodotus became my persona for some bizarre memories:

> *Herodotus reports*
>
> That the girls of Cimmeria
> rubbed olive oil on their
>
> bodies to make them slippery
> as fish for their lovers and
>
> Rexroth did the painting of
> the tunnies from two lines of

>   Amphylitos & in Zurich there
>   was beautiful crazy Birgitte
>
>   who liked to circle the Mat-
>   terhorn in her plane and lie
>
>   in her bathtub at the Dolder
>   Grand while her admirers intro-
>
>   duced forellen and the Schubert
>   was played on the gramophone in
>
>   the bedroom and Henry had to
>   drive Marcia up to the hospi-
>
>   tal in Carmel to get the snake
>   out and the list of these deli-
>
>   cate practices could go on but
>   remember that the historian &
>
>   the poet and I are notorious
>   for our wild confabulations.

But my ancient history has been mostly a matter of nipping and dipping when I needed to look up something. Plutarch has a rare passage on the Eleusinian Mysteries which so fascinated Pound. I looked into Dionysius of Halicarnassus for what I could find out about Sappho's "Ode to Aphrodite" which he had preserved in his treatise "On the arrangement of words." History was one of the glories of Graeco-Roman literature, but the list is long of those I have not had the chance to read. I can't say that I have really read Thucydides, Xenophon, Josephus or the secrets of the Byzantine Procopius among the Greeks, or Polybius, Caesar (except what was inflicted on me in school), Sallust, Livy or Suetonius gossiping about the Caesars among the Romans.

When it comes to the poets, I'm deficient in Hesiod (Richmond Lattimore, Michigan), Alcaeus and the poet-playwright Menander. The same to be said for Lucan's *Pharsalia* (that tedious epic row between Caesar and Pompey), Seneca, that stuffed-shirt Cicero, Statius (so much admired in the Middle Ages), and both the playwrights Plautus (all those mistaken identities) and Terence, who adapted everything from Menander. I have a fondness for "the father" of Latin poetry, Ennius, because I stole his famous tmesis to write about my little boy when he was five:

Saxo Cere

comminuit brum a rainy day
when he can't play outside

and Henry is cutting little
axes out of a piece of card-

board he bloodies them up
nicely with red crayon and

then very lovingly one after
another brings them to me

at my desk where I'm working as if they were flowers.

"Saxo cere comminuit brum." With a stone / the bra- / he splits / -in. Could this have been the beginning of Concrete Poetry?

The satires of Persius (A.D. 34-62) have an appealing conversational quality which the poet W. S. Merwin has caught very neatly (Indiana University Press). Persius ranges from homilies in a moral tone to humor and some rather "frank" passages about the life of Rome. His style is sometimes involved and obscure. My favorite is "Satire One" in which he ridicules the fashionable poetasters of the day.

It could be that little fiction survives from ancient times because the medieval monks who preserved the original texts were forbidden to copy such frivolity. That's only a guess. All we know about the lost Milesian Tales of the second century B.C. by Aristedes is that they were licentious stories of love and adventure. They are thought to have influenced Boccaccio. Historians speak of a school of "novelists" known as the "Greek Erotics," who wrote adventure-romances: two lovers are separated, they escape from perils as grave as those of Pauline, and then there is a happy ending. The most palatable Greek novella is Longus' *Daphnis*

164 / *James Laughlin*

and Chloe, a pastoral of the goatherd Daphnis and the shepherdess Chloe, which goes beyond adventure to charming descriptions of sentiments and scenery. The old translation by George Moore (Braziller) is still readable.

When we come to Latin fiction there are two real corkers which can stand with the modern product: Petronius Arbiter's *Satyricon* (first century A.D.), on which Fellini drew for his film, and *The Golden Ass* of Lucius Apuleius (second century A.D.). Fine translations exist of both works: for the *Satyricon* that of William Arrowsmith (a Mentor paperback) and for *The Golden Ass*, Robert Graves (Farrar, Straus) and Jack Lindsay (Indiana University Press).

Petronius was a refined voluptuary. His aka was *elegantiae arbiter*, the arbiter of elegance; he arranged Nero's best parties. One of them is satirized in the great "Trimalchio's Dinner" chapter of the *Satyricon*. He must have been a stoic as well as an epicurean. When he knew that Nero had turned against him and put him on the hit list, he held a going-away party. After dinner, he cut his wrists but let them drain very slowly while he wrote out a list of Nero's sexual misbehaviors and partners, chatted with his friends and joined them in frivolous songs. Petronius—and Fellini—drew details for the death party almost verbatim on Tacitus's account in the *Histories*. We have only fragments of the *Satyricon* but enough to make up a comprehensive work. They are written alternately in prose and verse; the tone is basically comic, but a comedy halfway between black humor and the belly laughs of Henry Miller. Trimalchio is like a character in Miller, a Falstaff, both gargantuan and pathetic. The *Satyricon* is picaresque and episodic, with a mélange of styles, darting from the realistic to the fantastic. It is a very postmodern novel. Seneca's *Apocolocyntosis*, "The Pumpkinification of [Emperor] Claudius the Clod" is in a similar vein.

Apuleius, who lived in Carthage, was fascinated by magic. His tales are full of magical events. The original title of his book was *Metamorphoses*. The important transformation comes when a seductive sorceress applies an ointment which changes Lucius, the rather Candide-like young hero, into a donkey. This, for the author, yields the advantage of giving the narrator two points of view in satirizing human foibles. Toward the end the goddess Isis changes Lucius back to a man and he is initiated into the old Egyptian Mysteries. The English poet Louis MacNeice was an admirer of the *Satyricon*; he said:

It is hard to find a writer who combines such dissimilar qualities—elegance and earthiness, euphuism and realism, sophistication and love of folk-lore, Rabelaisian humor and lyrical daintiness, Platonism and belief in witchcraft, mysticism and salty irony. . . . The *Golden Ass* is not a mixture but a blend.

Both Greek and Latin continued as literary languages after the decline of the Roman Empire, but Greek moved in the direction of humanistic studies while Latin remained very much alive as a vehicle for poetry. F. J. E. Raby's *History of Christian-Latin Poetry* is the authority for this period; unfortunately he does not give translations of his citations. Here we see how the Church Fathers, such as St. Ambrose and Prudentius, used Latin for hymns which had real poetic quality. For singing, no doubt, they abandoned the quantitative meters of classical Latin and went to an accentual, often rhymed, short line. The "Dies Irae" of the Requiem Mass (1250) is an example of the new rhythm:

> Dies irae, dies illa
> Solvet saeclum in favilla,
> Teste David cum Sibylla.

I've left for the last the Latin poem that means the most to me for romantic reasons, the *Pervigilium Veneris* ("The Vigil of Venus"), a chant in honor of the spring festival of the goddess, in praise of love and the rebirth of love. It was probably written in the fourth century by an unknown poet. There are many translations of the *Pervigilium*, but I respect most the one made by Allen Tate. Here are his versions of three of the twenty-two stanzas. The whole poem will be found in L. R. Lind's *Latin Poetry* anthology (an Oxford paperback).

> Tomorrow let loveless, let lover tomorrow make love:
> O spring, singing spring, spring of the world renew!
> In spring lovers consent and the birds marry
> When the grove receives in her hair the nuptial dew.
>
> Tomorrow may loveless, may lover tomorrow make love.
> . . .
> The blood of Venus enters her blood, Love's kiss
> Has made the drowsy virgin modestly bold;

Tomorrow the bride is not ashamed to take
The burning taper from its hidden fold.

  Tomorrow may loveless, may lover tomorrow make love.
  . . .
With spring the father-sky remakes the world:
The male shower has flowed into the bride,
Earth's body; then shifted through sky and sea and land
To touch the quickening child in her deep side.

  Tomorrow may loveless, may lover tomorrow make love.

That refrain has been in my mind for years:

  Cras amet qui nunquam amavit, quique amavit amavit cras amet.

In his preface to *Sylvae* Dryden wrote:

  Methinks I come like a Malefactor, to make a speech upon the Gallows, and to warn all poets, by my sad example, from the sacrilege of translating Virgil.

All I can answer is that I will ever pray for the translators who may have risked perdition to give me so much pleasure.

My thanks to four classicists who have given me much encouragement since the death of Robert Fitzgerald: Guy Davenport, John Frederick Nims, Willis Barnstone and Carey Perloff.

A. L. Rowse

Literature as Pleasure

The idea of literature, in the precise sense of the term, is associated from very early on with the idea of pleasure. Evidently this does not apply to very early writing as such: inscriptions on clay tablets in the Middle East or on stone in Western Europe were in their nature utilitarian, or for purposes of record, or memorial.

The *Oxford English Dictionary* speaks of literature as meaning "literary production as a whole—the body of writings produced in a particular country or period, or in the world in general." Now, it goes on to suggest, that it has the more restricted sense of writing of *quality*—as opposed, for example, to "light literature," which it described earlier this century as being of "very recent emergence in both England and France."

I don't suppose that there was any light literature among the original English; though the Anglo-Saxons were remarkable, among all Teutonic peoples, for their literature, far richer than any other. We may say still that, among English-speaking peoples, literature is their prime expression among the arts, where the plastic arts, such as painting and sculpture, make a much bigger show among Latins, especially French and Italians.

Literature gives one an immense variety of pleasures, responds to and satisfies a number of different and even contrasting moods. One should note at the outset that it provides the steadiest, most constant of pleasures. It is always there, ready to hand, to be taken up or dropped as the mood takes one.

Indeed, where should we be without it? Without the knowledge we gain from literature we should be restricted to what we learn from our own short span of life, or what has been handed down by word of mouth from parents or predecessors. But this thought trenches upon the utilitarian aspect of literature, rather than the pleasurable, though the two are intimately connected. For knowledge is a great pleasure: for some of us to *know* is a leading stimulus in life.

This was recognized very early. The greatest of Anglo-Saxon kings, Alfred of Wessex, wrote that *not* to know was the saddest thing in life. Significantly, after the devastation of Anglo-Saxon civilization by the Viking barbarians, he deliberately set himself to revive literature. He learned Latin in order to translate into English from it, for Latin of course was *the* literature, the standard literature throughout the Middle Ages.

As for not knowing, ignorance of literature, as an early sixteenth-century writer said, what we in these days of democratic humbug would hardly dare to: "The common people, which without literature and good information, be like to brute beasts." To put it more kindly, they are plain bores; and I hope it will emerge, in the course of this essay, why. Dean Inge, himself a brilliant scholar, said that "the true intellectual is never bored." One notes of people who do not read that they are often prey to boredom, the readiest victims, serve them right.

Wordsworth, who was not a bookish man, recognized how books constitute not only "pastime" but "happiness" — two aspects of pleasure, we may say.

> Dreams, books, are each a world; and books, we know
> Are a substantial world, both pure and good;
> Round these, with tendrils strong as flesh and blood
> Our pastime and our happiness will grow.

His friend Southey, who was a bookish man, particularizes on this:

> My days among the dead are passed;
>   Around me I behold,
> Where'ere these casual eyes are cast,
>   The mighty minds of old;
> My never-failing friends are they,
> With whom I converse day by day.

Southey was also a bookman, in the sense that he was a collector: he had a large library, and this also gave him subjects to write about. But his particular point at the moment is one that very much appeals, and applies, to me.

When I retired to my remote headland in Cornwall, where I am somewhat marooned, I naturally missed Oxford, where at All Souls in the old days were the best company and conversation one could ever hope for. Here in far Cornwall I lead a life some people would think solitary, for I see very few people. In fact, I have plenty of company. Who then are my companions? — William Shakespeare constantly, Dr. Johnson for a change; Jane Austen and Trollope regularly; sometimes Gibbon or Horace Walpole; often Henry James, or Edith Wharton, Willa Cather or Flannery O'Connor. When I want a change, I take to reading French, Proust or Colette, Sainte-Beuve, Montherlant (*not* Sartre), Balzac. And then there are all my contemporaries, many of them friends: Harold Acton, Connolly, Evelyn Waugh (*not* Alec or Auberon), Auden, David Cecil, Graham Greene, and my fellow Cornishman, Q. (Quiller-Couch). I dare say I read too much, for I am reading all the time I am not writing, gardening or sleeping. I don't count travel, for of course I read in trains, planes and hotels. In that, I suppose, like Charles Lamb: "When I am not walking, I am reading; I cannot sit and think." He then goes on to say, what does not speak for me: "Books think for me. . . . I can read anything which I call *a book*." I am more choosy than that. True, there are people whose favorite reading is Bradshaw's Railway Time Table; but that hardly comes under the heading of literature.

A most important point is made by the Victorian writer, Alexander Smith: "I go into my library, and all history unrolls before me." And not only history, though naturally I derive pleasure from reading those historians who can write, those who contribute to literature. Today people are apt to overlook what an important department of literature is constituted by history and historians. What would Greek literature be without Thucydides and Herodotus; or Roman without Livy and Tacitus? How much poorer Victorian literature would be without Macaulay, Carlyle and Froude; or nineteenth-century American without Parkman, Prescott, Henry Adams. In our time we have had Samuel Eliot Morison, a far better writer than the second-rate Steinbeck — Willa Cather, who knew and could judge, makes that point about those two in one of her letters; but it was Steinbeck, not Morison, who got the Nobel Prize.

Literature then is a *constant* source of pleasure; it is also an independent one. So many forms of pleasure depend on other people. In the addiction to literature one is one's own master, not dependent on any one else's whims and moods, tempers and tantrums, or even preferences. One can choose for oneself, and one can choose to suit one's own mood. The poet Young reminds us that in literature there is solace, comfort, refreshment: one can retire into it from the *cares* of the world.

A musical friend of mine, when faced with a problem, is vexed or irritated, takes to his piano. A piano is not always available, nor can we all perform on it. But we can all read — all who are worth considering (to go back to that early sixteenth-century writer). Literature is, as Wordsworth said, a substantial world: it is an extension of life, offering a further dimension to existence. A far safer one, I may add, in regard to some flesh-and-blood confrontations in pleasure — one can take and enjoy *them* vicariously.

I am amused by the story of an intellectual friend of mine serving in the U.S. Army during the war, who was not accustomed to the continual sex talk in the mess, the conversation of *l'homme moyen sensuel*. One can imagine the astonishment when one day he came up with: "Why *do* these things, when you can read about them?" Far safer, anyway, in a world of ubiquitous disease.

And what *varied* pleasures are at hand in literature, suitable to one's every mood, from some tragic experience to comic, from the consoling when one needs it to the bawdy when one feels like it. High-minded Victorians like the poet, Robert Bridges, and Quiller-Couch, deplored the bawdy element in Shakespeare. It is there on every page; and the more one knows of Elizabethan language and usage, the more innuendos and double-entendres appear — accentuated on the Elizabethan stage by gesture, of course. The bawdy is a salty, preservative element in literature, so I do not underrate it. High-minded people disapproved of it in Sterne in his day; but they have disappeared, he remains alive. And in this matter I am with the low-minded.

What, however, are the more continuous and regular pleasures that I derive from literature? For steady enjoyment I look to good novels, in fact, the best: the classics of Jane Austen and Trollope, Hardy and Henry James. It is only occasionally that such writers offer excitement — though there is an extraordinarily exciting chapter in Hardy's *A Pair of Blue Eyes*. The hero is in danger of slipping over the edge of one of those terrifying cliffs in North Cornwall; his girlfriend makes a kind of rope out of her underclothes to reach him and hold on to. I noticed the other day the excitement of that theme in a recent short story by James Sterne, in which the fellow goes over the edge onto the rocks below. (But that was in Ireland.)

Usually one finds excitement more in a short story than *à la longue haleine* — in Hemingway's "The Killers," or Flannery O'Connor's "A Good Man Is Hard to Find," one of the finest in any language in our time.

If one wants a tonic, a pick-me-up, or a good laugh, there are writers to supply it. I am always stimulated by Saki, brilliant writer that he was—he makes me laugh, at the same time as I admire his wit and envy his concise, caustic style. I can always resort to the Note Books of Samuel Butler, sure of finding fun, an odd sly irreverent humor unlike anybody else.

Then one is impelled by curiosity: satisfying that offers an acute pleasure. I suppose that that is a reason for probing into historic mysteries. How much one would like to know the true explanation of the Gowrie Conspiracy that endangered James VI's life in Scotland—or so he said: we shall never know now. Do we know the full inwardness of the Kennedy assassination, or the whole truth about the Hiss case?

I take it that this is the impulse that makes so many people take to thrillers. Myself, though an old friend and admirer of Agatha Christie, I am not a reader of detective stories or thrillers. I confess however to curiosity: Cornish folk are exceptionally inquisitive (and suspicious). If I had not been inquisitive, from boyhood on, I should never have discovered the identity of Shakespeare's Dark Lady. Agatha, who was a good Shakespearean, realized perfectly that I had. Dullards didn't. She wrote me a charming letter, "from the mistress of low-brow detection to the master of high-brow detection."

Perhaps something of the pleasure that ordinary folk get from thrillers, I get from biographies, and particularly from autobiographies, a much rarer genre. Gibbon's autobiography gives recurring pleasure—one can read it again and again. I would much rather read John Stuart Mill's *Autobiography* than his theorizing about Liberty, or his boring *Political Economy*. I have always loved Newman's *Apologia*. Would that my friend T. S. Eliot had written an autobiography!—what a wonderful book that could have been, with his double life in the United States and Britain, keeping the cultural (not only the Atlantic) bridges going.

Of course one's taste changes, and not only as one gets older, but in the course of life. When one was young one could read anything, as Charles Lamb said he could. I loved reading the Brontës, but could not take Jane Austen; I loved Nathaniel Hawthorne, but it was a long time before I graduated to Henry James.

Strangely enough, as a mere boy I *made* myself read Carlyle, quite a lot of him. I would find my attention slipping over a paragraph and make myself go over it again to grasp its meaning. Now, I have long grown out of him; there is no doubt about his genius, but I find his style—even apart from other things, his Teutonism, his pro-German mania, his shocking attitude to blacks, his Philistinism and antiaestheticism—all alike intolerable. It is curious, and very interesting why the Victorians set him on such a pinnacle, and the influence he had on other men of genius, Dickens and Ruskin. Today I agree with Graham Greene in finding only his biography of John Sterling tolerable.

He was a vivid letter writer, with a sharp eye for character, especially other people's defects. So too his wife: I gather that she was one of the best of all letter writers. This, now almost a lost art, is another department of literature that gives me pleasure. I never tire of reading the Letters of Horace Walpole—none equal to him, except, I take it, those of Madame de Sévigné. Dr. Johnson's Letters are a grand ornament of Boswell's unsurpassed biography.

Here again I would rather read Boswell's Journals than most novels—they give one pleasure on various counts, including the bawdy. I prefer Scott's noble Journals to his novels, Kilvert's Diaries to almost any Victorian novel, and certainly Pepys' *Diary* to any Restoration plays. Similarly with Swift: the *Journal to Stella* and his *Letters* are unsurpassed of their kind, and more readable than *The Tale of a Tub*, if not than *Gulliver's Travels*.

Journal to Stella, a wonderful work, which operates both on the level of a children's fairy tale and a savage satire on mankind, reminds us that there is a whole literature for children as well as for mature, or old, age. Nor is this the only work with that double appeal: Lewis Carroll has it, so has Edward Lear. So have the children's stories of Kipling, and also—though few notice it—Kenneth Grahame's *The Wind in the Willows*.

It is the lost books of autobiography I most regret: Byron's Memoirs, which the conventional John Murray and the squeamish Hobhouse burned; and Dr. Johnson's fragment of autobiography which he destroyed shortly before his death.

People may not recognize, though they know it from experience, that a good cry can be a pleasure. Mrs. Carlyle cried for two whole hours after finishing Madame de Staël's *Corinne*, and she enjoyed it so much that she urged her old curmudgeon of a husband, who hadn't, to read it again. I know this to be true of fans of mine who have read my book about my Cornish Cats. The sad thing about our love for animals is that we have a different life-span: we love them, then they die, and it gives one heartache. Thomas Hardy has a most touching poem about that; and though my stories about each of my cats end sadly—and I have cried over them—everybody who reads them seems to like them.

What about even more serious sorrows in life? What is there for consolation? In the Dark Ages, Boethius wrote one of the most famous of all Western books on the consolation of philosophy. I am afraid that I do not find consolation in philosophy. A most admired modern philosopher, Wittgenstein, held that, of that of which nothing can be said, nothing is to be said. He found his consolation in religion. I know of others who, approaching their end, have taken to reading the Bible. Myself, when in trouble and need consolation, I read the Prayer Book. I was brought up as an Anglican and find the purity of the language at its best, the rhythms of the familiar prayers and phrases, touching and strangely consoling.

A philosopher friend of mine at Oxford found this in Shakespeare. He and his wife went through shattering experiences in the second German war, their only son killed, their daughter killed by a kick from her horse. He turned to Shakespeare: it is all there, he would say; that is true, the whole of life is there, set out there.

This need not surprise, for Dryden, who was on a level with him — unlike most academic commentators — wrote of Shakespeare: "He was the man who of all modern, and perhaps ancient poets, had the largest and most comprehensive soul."

For the inexhaustible variety of pleasures to be derived from literature we have a pretty early indication in a well-known passage from a contemporary of Shakespeare, Richard Carew's "Epistle on the Excellency of the English Tongue": "Will you have Plato's vein? read Sir Thomas Smith. The Ionic? — Sir Thomas More. Cicero's? — Ascham. Varro? — Chaucer. Demosthenes? — Sir John Cheke. Will you read Virgil? — take the Earl of Surrey. Catullus? — Shakespeare, and Marlowe's fragment." Carew was not thinking of plays, but of their love poems; in the Elizabethan Age, Shakespeare was more often compared with Ovid, his chief love among the Latin poets. Carew goes on to compare the charming poet, Samuel Daniel, with Ovid. "Lucan? — Spenser." Actually, Spenser was much better than Lucan; one might compare him more with Virgil, writing the epic of the Elizabethan, as Virgil wrote that of the Augustan, Age. "Martial? — Sir John Davies, and others. Will you have all in all for prose and verse? — take the miracle of our age, Sir Philip Sidney." Very well: there was a sense in which he began it all.

The historian Seeley, a disciple of German scholarship, said rather unkindly, "those who cannot have recourse to foreign literatures are forced to put up with their ignorance." But they are not wholly: there is such a thing as translation. The Elizabethans brought into being a whole literature of translation, from both classics and modern languages, to widen their horizons, deepen their knowledge, and give them pleasure.

Some translations gave them inspiration—think of the use Shakespeare made of Golding's Ovid and North's Plutarch. Some have become classics in their own right—Florio's Montaigne, Urquhart's Rabelais, Shelton's Cervantes, or Harington's Ariosto and Fairfax's Tasso, both good poetry in their English dress.

Today our horizons have become worldwide. Arthur Waley's beautiful translations have opened the world of Chinese poetry to us; years ago I derived much pleasure from the Japanese Court Lady Murasaki's novel, *The Tale of Genji*—such refinement and sophistication when we were still barbarians. We can now appreciate the fact that the Arabic Ibn Kaldun was one of the greatest of historians. One of the results of British rule in India was the opening of the treasures of Persian and Hindu literature, translations of lyric poetry as well as epic and drama. In effect the whole of the Russian classics may be read in translation—and even such bright blooms of approved Soviet literature as Gladkov's *Cement* or *Diary of a Communist Schoolboy*, if we ever feel inclined to.

In the dangers and shattering disillusion of the contemporary world, the separate histories, if not the identities, of English-speaking peoples are tending to merge into one mighty stream. Certainly this is true of the literature in our language, of which the largest volume naturally comes from the United States, with rivulets from Canada, Australia, New Zealand, South Africa. And not only from our various stocks but from those who use the language, some of them masters in its use, like Naipaul, from the West Indies or India itself. Nehru, a founder of modern India, wrote his autobiography in English.

A Russian exile from the tyranny of the tsars—so much less inhuman and cruel than that of today—wrote that he regarded Russian literature as his home country. Edmund Wilson, after the disappointment of his earlier liberal illusions, wrote that he regarded himself as an internal exile. From contemporary society, for which I feel little but apprehension and contempt, I too regard myself as an internal exile, withdrawn from it all. And I can regard as my country the marvelous literature in our language from all round the world.

Mary Kinzie

Nocturnal Habit: On Literary Addiction

Although I am not a great or ambitious reader, I am a compulsive rereader. Those in my acquaintance to whom I might give the former title do not, as a rule, reread quite so chronically. Their addiction is rather to the whole of fiction. They are also addicted to reading, plunge in everywhere, ambitious, generous, reading much and fast, while I read slowly and, as a rule, haltingly. Except for my addictions. These I read slowly by design. In either case, I am frugal. I do not finish a long novel in less than three weeks (the only exceptions of the past few years have been *The Philosopher's Pupil* and *The Good Apprentice*).

Poetry, I should say at the outset, is not a good kind of literature for addiction because it is so conscious-making; it marshals too many of the intellectual and deliberative faculties, even if its springs are far deeper than those of prose; and it cannot hold the attention when one is supine, the very lightness of the volumes will not suffice to moor them in the arms. The heavier the tome, the more true this is. An avuncular and prolific poet like Wallace Stevens must be read in daylight, the closer to awakening the better: He wraps you in your own emerging consciousness. Most other poetry is at once too thin and too severe for the nocturnal habit. The reason for the severity in my case may be that the poetry-reading technique, like several second languages, has been taken up too late to be unwitting.

Splendid exceptions to the nonaddiction clause for poets will happen, but usually in the form of writers who wrote much else as well. Louise Bogan is one. Every sentence of hers is touched with enchantment and the unstudied eccentricity that comes of solitude, independence, and indefatigable devotion to art, literature, reading, correspondence, and travel, all purchased at the cost of a career in literary journalism—although even here Bogan managed to make the inimical and the exigent her servants. For she taught herself how to say the particular truth down to the bone about almost any writer in fifty words. Indeed, she taught herself everything she knew. But in saying this one also acknowledges that she chose to know only what was hard and had to be many times forgotten then relearned. She writes a prose of such passionate clarity and torque, it is, like her poetry, the formal emblem of prophetic insight:

> Just afterward, a mood of pity descends on the freshly punished spirit. Everything in the world becomes piteous, and not a sound or sight can escape from the love wrapped in fog and obscurity: secret to itself. Those nearest the heart drain off the first pity. How lovely they are, and how vulnerable! Their flesh, their very being, draws out the misty love like a thread: over and over it wraps them round. Today they live; their hair seems exquisitely clean and lies bright on their foreheads. They are young. Their bodies and their wishes will come to nothing. It is our purpose to love them; yet the thread continues to wrap them round until they live inside a cocoon of this soft emotion which is part dread.

She has been talking about sexual love. How many novelists have been able to lift their eyes long enough from the erotic pleasures even of characters ostensibly quite different from themselves, to entertain such visionary remorse, such outpourings of forgiveness? And here Bogan has done it — the "it" embracing not only her sketching in of the upwelling affection, but also her half-conscious hints about a doom and a dread that are born of chronic subjection, recent elation, and the serious indifference of the old to the young — she has done all this in her journal, in a paragraph, at the age of sixty-two.

Louise Bogan is also exemplary in distinguishing the highest poetry from the lesser literary *jeux*, in the end to her own detriment as a poet, because she became convinced, only halfway through her life, that she was no longer a poet who produced poems. And yet she did not become either of the things no-longer-practicing-poets become in this country, an academic or a hack. She did what Yeats enjoined on others and never managed himself, "Be secret and exult." She was categorically reticent, diffident of power, utterly dignified, ever a tactful, persuasive, and frequently great writer whose soul and tongue were given to poetry. What addicts one in the writings of Louise Bogan is above all this consciousness, without ego, without apology, without bravado, that even in abandonment she was one of the chosen of the muse.

To the rule that the addiction to literary works and attitudes involves the spinning of plots and telling of stories, then, exception will be made in the case of the works of those who have, in a manner of speaking — a very elevated and inspired manner — made of themselves the stories, often veiled and mysterious, that their lives were meant to tell. Thus the belletristic prose of certain writers of great complication and scruple, like Henry James, can also be excepted, whose travel sketches are intoxicating—far more so than the travelogues of self-proclaimed "intoxicants" like D. H. Lawrence. I would also except the pure brookwater of Edwin Muir's books about Scotland and the Orkneys.

Some great works, like Homer's or Shakespeare's or Goethe's, are for me too distant from the familiarities and immediacies that make for compulsion. And while I can imagine being addicted (although I am not so fortunate) to the plays of Shakespeare, Ibsen seems likelier to obsess someone faintly repelled by the stupefaction of actors and the obtuse machinery of the theatrical stage.

But addictions cannot be forced, coming or going. It is as fruitless to try to rid oneself of an attachment to a book like *The Plague*, all of whose characters are crass and lusterless, and which is written in a style almost willfully inexpressive, as it is foolhardy to insist too boldly on a book one is *supposed* to like. Henry James's oeuvre abounds in such texts, and certain friends are apt to be relentless in their fondness for *The Bostonians* or *The Princess Casamassima*, from which I retreat to the more humane minor charms of *The Awkward Age* or the hilarious ravishments of *The Sacred Fount*.

James himself is, however, the most addictable of novelists, and *The Portrait of a Lady* a splendid romance with which to begin one's experiment. For although one cannot force, one must try things on. Fellow addicts will recognize the low-grade suffering that accompanies a long hiatus between just having finished a tenth reading of one beloved volume, and the strictly postponed inauguration of the seasonal ritual of rereading another,* when one entertains with dread the pious resolve to see whether *this* year might be the one when George Eliot or Doris Lessing will finally kindle some warmth in the heart. Then one is frantic for a new author who might ravish from the very first sentence.

But I would not bother with most of the famous writers touted nowadays, still less would I subject myself to reading papers and magazines. What point can there be in scanning book reviews by people who cannot read and can barely write? who have never been addicts? The best course is to keep listening to the promptings of many and various friends, until you believe you detect, in the corroboration of one friend's taste by

---

*Summer is the hallowed period for Anna Karenina, The Bell, Buddenbrooks, The Memoirs of Hadrian, and A World of Love. All except the Thomas Mann would feel wrong, I think, and even a bit sour at Christmas.

that of his least favorite associate or of a total stranger, the settling down of true worth, the filtering through of reliable enchantment. So it was that I came to read the marvelous Paula Fox, whose fiction seems profoundly urban and grim, even while she avoids the "tropes" of crowds and of victims (although these are, in a hidden sense, her themes). After looking at a recent reissue of a twenty-year-old novella of hers, I have a strong and happy confidence that the work of Gina Berriault will also draw me from book to book, and back again, for a long time to come.

Nor would I recommend to the fellow addict aching through a dry period that the short story be attempted. Short-story writers simply do not do. When you put down Eudora Welty or V. S. Pritchett, two of the finest *short* story authors, you will only feel cheated, abandoned, misled. It is deflating to invest so much of one's credulity in a schema that will not be sustained for any period (although Welty's stories go on four pages longer, as a matter of course, than you think they ought, while Pritchett's always end, to one's ambiguous relief at being spared further evidence of his abrasive genius, a page sooner, which adds to the effect of being dismissed in a slightly bruised state).

To the proviso that authors of short stories are poor candidates for addiction one might make an exception for Franz Kafka, who is too stubborn for, and more profound than, this somewhat pejorative genre term. But Kafka, vast as are his genius and his guile, is too chastening to be addictive. Isak Dinesen might also be construed as an exception, inasmuch as her long tales come close to enciphering an entire world — a world in which, owing to the tales' narcotic aimlessness, one can almost relinquish one's sense of reading lines of print. She makes you think you are at Norderney or Elsinore, listening to the cardinal or the old nursemaid. While with Katherine Anne Porter one never forgets that one is reading; indeed, one is troubled by a whiff of the arch and synthetic. Even if her long story "Holiday" repays many a repetition, I find that most of the elegant and "feeling" Ms. Porter I read with one eye on the door.

Yet another rule of thumb is that the author who will addict you had better have an oeuvre large enough to feed your addiction. An exception might be the relatively parsimonious Marguerite Yourcenar, who nevertheless gives the impression of enormity, because of the unstinting philosophical passion with which her two "historical" characters, Zeno and Hadrian, survey the empire of knowledge surrounded by psychological and imaginative darkness — a darkness that is, in part, the darkness of past time.

A corollary to the large-oeuvre proviso is that addiction to an author invariably drives you to read everything your beloved author has written. Occasionally, this means that you will need to subject yourself to the puzzling biography of John Knox by someone who also finds him antithetical, or to the treatise on tea brewing, or the book on Sartre, the youthful political feuilleton, or often oversweet books for the young. These one reads as one pets the fretful child, out of motives of overarching love.

Lest one glut oneself on the loved objects, however, one must not wrongly or too frequently indulge them. The rereading of novels by an addicting author must be aboveboard: No skipping, no touchstone- or favorite-chapter reading. You will sicken yourself on the dainties and eventually lose touch with the culinary variety and graduation of appetite that attracted you to novels instead of effete prose-poems or pithy *essais*. Addictions must be rationed. Do not too often return to your books, even when you can hardly forebear to begin them again once you have finished. If this advice is not followed, disgust may replace delight at meeting for the ninth time characters out of a grade-B intrigue-romance, as in Elizabeth Bowen's novels. Bowen herself is, by the way, a writer I exclude from another general stricture—against indistinct characters, and a paucity of them, because her narrative style is so conscious, so tearless and dry, sails along with so much snap, that one reads hungrily on, well beyond the point of judgment. And Bowen's short stories are peculiarly satisfying. Like Henry James's, they have a kind of deepness that shimmers up to the surface like the cone of purple in the center of an isolated natural pool.

Still, the writer who is strong enough to addict a reader should not be overwhelmingly trashy or formulaic. If I make an exception here for the subclass (short for subterranean class) of crime writers, among whom, I am ashamed to say, I have found only Ngaio Marsh to be readable,* although I recognize and deplore—and soon forget—Marsh's slick automatism and wooden characterization, it is not because I am able to detect the least merit in the breed as a whole. The classier exemplars, like Dorothy Sayers and, more recently, P. D. James, fairly prove the rule here, because for all their striving to blend the pleasant prurience of crime writing with the more serious architecture of moral fiction, they are both unbearably "worked up," plotted and plodded through.

She is not for a minute rereadable. The molecules break down as soon as the end of one of her books is first reached.

But the potentially addicting writer must not be too sublime, nor given to discourses more properly contained in volumes of history or semiotics. To the first stricture, Tolstoy is, in my experience, an exception, while Henry Fielding is not. To the second, Umberto Eco is *not* an exception, although Jorge Luis Borges is — he being another "short-fiction" writer who breaks one's resolve in that direction as well, that is, he never disappoints merely by reason of brevity. I am not yet willing to say, however, that Borges is addicting. Like Kafka, he is deeper, and at the same time less fleshly, than the kind of writer for whom one can suspend one's disbelief, which is to say, for whom one can acquiesce even when the author fails to satisfy the appetites for sensation and for boredom so perfectly conjoined in the greatest popular literary form, the novel.

The best novel will convincingly render the unmemorable longueurs of life, but punctuate them with illuminations, passionate excursions, and embodiments of thought, which rivet the mind and assuage the will. The balance is hard to achieve. Muriel Spark is dazzlingly overpunctuated, while Ivy Compton-Burnett is willfully drab and unmemorable, though her books are fueled by almost endless malice. Larger sympathy is needed in her case, as is greater disguise of the daedal pleasure in Spark, although the latter is also genuinely addictive, and provides the sense, which is so necessary to the novel's working, of layer shifting under layer of meaning. In the background there must always be this inexorably massive but only half-visible "thing" of spiritual truth, like a huge house approached through a thick storm of fog. At times, one feels the reverse, that the novel's deepest significance is not "under" but "without," raking the house like a beacon: Large novels absorb one in surfaces of portrayal crosshatched by intermittent philosophical design. Borges and Kafka provide the intermittence of such designs without the surfaces of person and accident and mysterious randomness against which, in fictional literature, we are repeatedly thrown, as if they were the stuff of greatest heaviness in existence.

This is, finally, what one craves, as a reader, to be schooled in the relative accuracy of the impression of density ascribed to experience, and of porousness ascribed to truth. Spiritual exercise and discourse alone cannot (and should not) thicken the latter; frivolous or ignorant literature cannot render the former properly faint, like brief dewfall on a morning of baking heat. Experience must fall, yes, and truth must rise, and yet there must also be that mild nocturnal terror that begins when we seem to see *through* it all — all the day's pursuits, the alert routines, so tiring to the hands, the meandering of dialogue, the thousand bright glances exchanged with the child, the silent movement of the pencil, the unsavory telephone, until experience becomes impalpable, like a series of perforations in the atmosphere—like rain falling at a great distance from us until it vanishes as if it had never been. It is then that we can catch a glimpse, sidewise, evasive, with its weird sighing, of the spirit extinguishing above its candle, or pouring like mist down from its stone wall-niche—suggesting the least density and yet the most worth and the sharpest spur to yearning, so that even in a world where the temples have been broken and the spiritual realm abandoned, one knows absolutely that it is the only realm that is ponderable.

Writers like Iris Murdoch understand the requirement that the architectonics of the novel cohere with a vision of spiritual truth. At the same time that, like Tolstoy, she has a firm base in the medley or *satura* version of the form, Murdoch also devises moments during which the characters and their social order disintegrate. She charts a progress from light to dark. Murdoch almost always starts with a jumble of interdependent characters and families in a world touched by alternate waves of freshness and decay. Then she moves on to the solitary wastes where the self is broken and the spirit flayed. Nor is suffering a mere mechanism for reaching other ends. Pain is not a station on life's way but the harshest possible result of hubris, a precondition for self-knowledge but also a terminus from which self-knowledge can never rescue one—precisely because *its* horrors are what one must suffer. Her comic endings merely flare out against the nagging gloom of human vanity.

This view has been clarified in Murdoch's work during the evolution of her twenty-two novels, all but the first three of which and the Irish novel (*The Red and the Green*) I reread as often as I dare, compelling myself to brake the momentum that goads me along, tearing somewhat haphazardly at the familiar surprises. Nor can I read her critically (this may be a corollary to any true addiction). She seems to enchant the very faculty that might otherwise reach for a pencil to make notes in the margin. Surely, I think each time I am rereading one of her books—surely, this is how literature was meant to be enjoyed, in full foreknowledge of the plot yet gripped by equally potent indifference to the eventual severing of the threads that are being spun, and so cleverly knotted, as one moves. But this experience is also like taking a drug with which your body is already familiar: Because you are addicted, you are always a bit high, even before you break the bottle's seal, or reread the introductory paragraph. You return to Murdoch's familiar adjectives like "muddled" and "rebarbative" and the uncanny aptness with male protagonists and the carnival episodes and the hints of the inevitable violent stripping-away, with a fatalistic shudder. For the drug only pleases by poisoning.

Paul Valéry claimed that one only reads well "with some quite personal goal in mind. It may be to acquire some power. It can be out of hatred of the author." I believe that anyone who seriously rereads Iris Murdoch does so, a little, out of hatred, resentment, struggle. Her cast of characters is too replete with types of the self-satisfied intellectual, the balmy artist, the lonely apostate, with clever — but entirely sympathetic — incarnations of cowardice and arrogance and greed: One repeatedly sees one's weaknesses appallingly exposed in each novel. There are usually at least three characters with whom one cannot help, to one's shame, identifying. These creations are mirrors into which one peers, more startled by the glancing resemblances in moral being than by the patent disparities in life history.

I know no other novelist who is so hard on her people while succeeding in making them appealing. Or to state the case in reverse, no other novelist makes so thoroughly clear the flaws and insufficiencies and lethargies and "muddle" from which emanate harm and wrong. And yet the plot outcomes are arbitrary: artful, changeable. What stays the same, at the still center of her melee, is the image of the shrunken soul, maimed by impulse and indulgence. Murdoch's handling of circumstance is brilliantly free and persuasive, even — or especially — when it crowds the scene chaotically full of accidents. But events are finally the least substantial of her constructs: she shows how flimsy a fabric experience is, not as something lived, but as something valued.

But the personal goal with which one reads may also be love. This, too, is a means of acquiring merit, if not power. Moreover, to reread with affection a literary universe construed as essentially affectionate is to increase one's merit in a pure and lasting way. Such are the delights, moral, aesthetic, and creatural, of rereading Marcel Proust and Gabriel García Marquez. Both are writers outside the novel's pale who draw the boundaries differently around experience than do works of literary realism. Both are at once meticulous and extravagant in portraying imaginary worlds whose guiding law is sympathy — whether sympathy between the narrative consciousness and the emanations of past love, as in Proust, or the sympathy that binds plot and character to landscape in a compact that is literally magical, as in García Marquez. Both succeed in loosening the distinctions between works of the spirit and the productions of time, so fusing thought to world that the one is comforted and the other ennobled. As are we when we reread.

I once heard a very distinguished scholar, introducing a seminar that would be devoted to *Remembrance of Things Past*, say that he would like nothing more than to spend the remainder of his life rereading Proust. His seminar room was kept unusually dusky—I have always known it had nothing to do with his eyes—and the other students, all remarkably small, had heads I see in retrospect as remarkably similar: very black hair and doll-like skin, white and almost polished. This period was Borgesian in more ways than one. When I have had the energy to read Proust in the intervening years, I have wondered how many of us reverent readers he has "created," so like one another in our predilections if not our appearance. I have wondered how many times that scholar has reread *Remembrance of Things Past*, how many times he has puzzled over the anomaly of Swann's self-defeating "taste" for Odette, how frequently he has held his breath when the steeple of St. Hilaire was sighted, how often he has pondered the little musical phrase of M. Vinteuil, whether he can remember the several prehistoric occasions when he lost the threads of the periodic sentences, threads he now holds without anxiety in his hands, whether he has conducted pilgrimages to Proust's Combray and Balbec. Does he understand why Proust says the face of a mother is like an apostle's? I wonder how different from mine his Proust is, and almost envy him his, so much more rarefied and authentic. At a certain point in some new rereading, he will have acquired enough merit, established enough general belief in it, to cross over into that realm, that languorous and encyclopedic memory, that suspended and unattainable past time. And isn't this every true lover's goal, every literary addict's desire?—to blend with one's dependence, subside against the body, mercurial yet unchanging, of its language, a "text" so entertaining as to seem the very essence of happy self yet so subtle and illustrious as to slough the machinery of its own transformation into soul, until it resembles something strenuously sublimated, like a dense planet surrounded by spent flame?

Calvin Bedient

Sensible Ecstasies

1. PLEASURE AND PASSION

In "Coole and Ballylee, 1931," a passionate elegy for aristocratic pleasures, William Butler Yeats limns a nature "Now all dry sticks under a wintry sun," then writes that

> At sudden thunder of the mounting swan
> I turned about and looked where branches break
> The glittering reaches of the flooded lake.

Yeats glosses the swan as an "emblem" of the soul: the soul being, here, the most aristocratic of things, an equation of passion with beauty, hence the highest pleasure. The soul, like the aristocracy to which it gave birth, is all breathstopping transiency: it "sails into the sight/ And in the morning's gone, no man knows why." But what always arrests me in these lines, as it arrested Yeats, is a different sight — the bleak and glorious image of bare branches against the glittering flood. For isn't this another emblem of passion, at once a truer and more surprising one than that of the swan — in fact, its obverse? For me, the image pinpoints how passion introduces asceticism into pleasure, riddles beauty with severity. An obsession, passion at once impoverishes and enriches — impoverishes the near, makes glorious by contrast the far, the infinite. Its defoliations bare a further reach of bliss. Passion: a drive in painful excess of any satisfaction it might pluck from the wet flames of its own intensity.

Andrei Tarkovsky's final film, *The Sacrifice* (1986), dares to end with an almost identical image, throwing, as it were, the whole weight of the film upon it. Here the camera glides raptly round bare tree limbs that all but dance and even blossom with the background glitter of the adjacent sea. Again the suggestion of an impossible synthesis between denial and promise. The image redeems the personal holocaust caused, and suffered, by the hero, Alexander, a Swedish literary critic who has set fire to his seaside home and even his sanity, in an effort to satisfy his sense of guilt, the guilt of modern man himself (the not very coherent story includes the outbreak of a limited nuclear war). The family home, where the infinite sealight had gathered so gaily and sacredly in the white curtains and felt the folds of the white bed sheets in which Alexander's little son lay sleeping, is gone, and Alexander has been carted off by white-coated ambulance drivers after a cruelly comic scene of repeated chase and capture. What is left? The tree Alexander had lingered under with his son, as if outside history, in the opening shots. A sacrificial passion that does not burst into flames.

Tarkovsky's own passion for purity is saved from destructiveness by his need for beauty. Art is by nature a corrective to the extremism that denudes. Piercing as it is, the pleasure that Alexander himself takes in the piquant austerities of medieval painting or Japanese music, or even in the prostrate seashore, fails to satisfy his lust to see life humbled. By contrast, the choreographic flow of the actors and of Sven Nykvist's camera, the sealight gleaming on the dark hardwood floors of the doomed house, the beauty of the women there, the vulnerability of the likable child—all this argues that the true humility of life lies in the love of what appears, of what stands forth, impurely, out of nothingness.

In art, pleasure is the love—the love, not the forgiveness—of surfaces. It is an easiness there. It countermands the ferocity of sexual passion, which tears; the rage for purity in religious passion, which burns; and the murderous thirst for justice in social passion, which rebels. Aesthetic particulars break (as the branches in Yeats's image break) the arrogance of remorseless "essence." To convert purity itself into an object of pleasure, art interrupts it with an inky forest of branches.

It is precisely particulars that the artist must be passionate about. The artist turns passion—with its extremism, its essentialism—inside out, subduing it to a lining, a canvas for needlepoint. In art, intricacy, not a bleaching sweep, is the focus of intensity.

Take Yeats's lines on the mounting swan. As if in helpless tropism, the poet turns to look at a thunderous mounting. *There* is where the soul is; in that sound is its fury. So feels the man of polite words. Yes, *of course* the soul would mount; for what is life itself but a "darkening flood"? (By the end of the poem, Yeats's nihilism—his very, very bad mood, brought on by history—will prove even more extreme: there the swan itself will drift on the darkening flood.) The instinctiveness of the turn registers in the blurring play of sound between "turned" and "thunder," even if the first is comparatively moderate in resonance—as it were, in training. But what is turning compared to mounting? Almost nothing.

Looking is no approach, either. What escapes the breaking line-end after "break" is an ungatherable glitter, one that seems the freer thanks to the reach-extending anapest heard dancing precisely at the point of "glittering" — "The GLITtering REACHes": a rhythm liquid and loose after the constrained iambs in "I TURNED aBOUT and LOOKED where BRANCHes BREAK." Yet if the bunching *br*'s in "branches break" are escaped by "reaches," they are remembered, too, just as "lake" remembers what breaks it, "break," and "flooded" remembers the "sudden thunder" of what surmounts it, and so on. The interconnection of opposites is an audible pleasure of the text. The meanings, here, are not least passionately present in the impure physical registers of the sounds.

To be passionate about (of all things) pleasurable particulars — this is not what convinces the poet Geoffrey Hill that to write poetry is to risk, indeed dip into, sin. Rather, "error," for him, lies in dark swerves from a hypothetical purity of form. Purity of form? A contradiction in terms, a logical absurdity that is the only logic poets know. Where it coincides with a religious love of purity, as it does in Hill, flaws are doubly to be shunned, as at once artistic and spiritual. They are witnessed with a knowing horror.

But if purity is what one loves, why write poetry at all? No, in poetry the sin, if sin there is, lies in wanting a purity provocatively inked in by particulars. The poetry itself is the sin.

The twenty-third hymn in Hill's flawless *Mercian Hymns* (1971) virtually confesses the poet's desire to have both purity and particularity at once; to know passion through pleasure, and pleasure through passion. That art is the sanity of passion and the wholesomeness of pleasure — this it illustrates with a voluptuous severity.

The poem is about the menacing dichotomy between arrogant and humble things. Religious passion and physical pleasure appear to be ruthlessly parceled out by its two-part analytical structure. First, a characteristically exquisite verse-paragraph on the needling torment of a metaphysical passion:

In tapestries, in dreams, they gathered, as it was enacted, the return, the re-entry of transcendence into this sublunary world. *Opus Anglicanum*, their stringent mystery riddled by needles: the silver veining, the gold leaf, voluted grape-vine, masterworks of treacherous thread.

Then a second, breathtakingly "closing" paragraph on gross physical necessities and comforts:

> They trudged out of the dark, scraping their boots free from lime-splodges and phlegm. They munched cold bacon. The lamps grew plump with oily reliable light.

In the one realm, then, artwork and eschatology: a miraculous return embroidered in a practice-magic of ensurance, and of summons; in the other, an actual trudging return home after a day of hard labor. Darkness; a sublunary world fought off in the first by a dream of (implicit) descending and rescuing radiance and in the second, from below, by reliable animal lights. First, man the aesthetic animal with a formidably artful will, daemonically disburdening himself in the form of "higher" pleasures; second, man the physical brute. And that is it—a terse and exhaustive structure, intractably discordant, with running through it a thrilling rumor of the dark and the wild.

Yet the poem coheres even more than it needed to (as one of a number of mutually extending hymns). Tacitly, the two parts hinge on the narrative image of a medieval cathedral, with its work for both women (tapestries) and men (construction, as witnessed by "lime-splodges"). And common to the two domains is the animal hum of pleasure. Terrified though the women may be of the "treacherous thread" (and the second word must carefully extricate itself from the first), following the author himself in identifying craft with virtue, still they choose to work, as he does, in materials rich in nature (for instance, gold leaf, a sensuous correlative of glory) and even to copy natural forms ("voluted grape-vine"). And what gratification they must feel in enacting, through caressing duplications, the return: glad and envious, the verse, too, patterns a few repetitions: "In tapestries, in dreams . . . the return, the re-entry." As they reneedle the (in all senses) merely putative body of Christ (that riddle), perhaps they feel a touch vindictive (that pleasure), even as and because they follow Christ in ordering the viny riot of desire.

In the second paragraph, pleasure is more vulgar and overt, in proportion to its want of dignifying passion. Gone is the aesthetic edification—and editing—of our darkness and abjection, except in the reverberant power of the writing itself. What speaks here is, I think, a delicate child's awe of the mysteriously burly, self-sufficient world of coarse, grown-up men. (In *King Log* Hill writes: "At nightfall/ My father scuffed clay into the house./ He set his boots on the bleak iron/ of the hearth; ate, drank, unbuckled, slept"—another glimpse of gritty and grimy manhood, free of the postponed satisfactions of silver-veined dreams.) Appalling? As the primordial always is. But the verbal enactments of weariness and hard-earned comforts suggest sympathy, even complicity. And the men are, after all, makers and builders, not malefactors, much as they trail darkness into the house.

How pick a favorite from among the phrases: "free from lime-splodges and phlegm"? "They munched cold bacon"? "The lamps grew plump with oily reliable light"? Yet what anneals the frank auditory pleasure, and appeases what used to be called the soul, is the passion implicit in the virtuosity, as in the bold structure, with its elided connections and large compass in small space—a structure as stark as the writing itself is sensual. This passion is in part aesthetic—kin to that of the tapestry weavers—and in part a Western secular passion for the truth, however uncomfortable. When this last is fused with an equal passion for beauty, as it is here, it is less destructive than other passions. It is a rebuke to both the Dionysiac tendencies of the flesh and the peremptory and piercing demands of the spirit.

In another configuration, Louise Glück's poem "Night Song" marks the moment of a startling conversion of passion into pleasure (it is as if a cloud had turned into grass and hill, air into a path). Although Glück's poetry is sometimes scary with utterness (whether that of death alone or of the compact between sexuality and death), here it proves unexpectedly passionate about surfaces, sociality (discourse, sharing), the sidereal cycles, the moment. Ceasing to be nape-of-the-neck frightening, it attacks the earth itself, somewhat less frighteningly, with affirmation.

What has brought about this transformation? Ironically, a burst of passion. "We've been apart too long, too painfully separated." And later:

> You're tired; I can see that.
> We're both tired, we have acted a great drama.
> Even our hands are cold, that were like kindling.
> Our clothes are scattered on the sand; strangely enough,
> they never turned to ashes.

"A great drama"? Since Sylvia Plath, few poets writing in English could risk such a phrase. Glück, I suppose, gets away with it partly because, while the language is immodest, the tone is distracted: the event feels already distanced, a matter of legend. Besides, the speaker must mean the drama not of the stage but of Dionysus, from whose torn side the stage once slipped, radical passion already drying on its boards. Sexual passion is—as Ted Hughes has it in *River*—a "miracle-play:/ Masked, archaic," and its actors are sacrificial victims, appointed from the remotest beginnings to die.

Directly opposed to this is what William Carlos Williams called "that eternal moment in which we alone live." It is in such a moment that Glück's speaker happily finds herself, in the calm aftermath of passion:

> Tonight I'm not afraid
> to feel the revolutions. How can you want sleep
> when passion gives you that peace?
> You're like me tonight, one of the lucky ones.
> You'll get what you want. You'll get your oblivion.

So, in an elation that feels like a choice and is adopted as one, the speaker is released from prehistory and the future into the almost reckless freedom of the instant, her tone all but harsh with excitement. Immortality through sexuality? An immortality that is always for someone else, the immortality of and for by-blows. Better an individual, open-eyed relation to immediate reality ("Look up into the light of the lantern," the speaker exhorts at the beginning: "Don't you see? The calm of darkness/ is the horror of heaven"). Electrified into a fresh knowledge (a Paterian knowledge) of the induplicability of each moment, this speaker *will* not vegetate like the seabirds asleep on the jetty "in mounds, in vegetal clusters," or like the man nodding beside her, practicing the oblivion that sexual passion wants. The object of life ("I have to tell you what I've learned") is a passionate wakefulness: "I know now/ what happens to the dreamers./ They don't feel it when they change. One day/ they wake, they dress, they are old." The object is always to feel the revolutions, to exult in time as a paradoxical absolute, "opaque, rocklike," like the sea at this moment (the sea "cleansed of its superfluous life"). Wakefulness is truth, and truth is evolution, everything that has strained to come awake, to rise from nothingness.

The verse tells you how it is. Calmly the iambs feel the revolutions in "Tonight I'm not afraid/ to feel the revolutions." "Oblivion," by contrast, rushes into accentual indistinctness. It lacks the tingling spine of "revolutions." It loses the plausible duration of "passion" and even swallows the forthright sound of "one" ("one of the lucky ones"). It also pours by and flattens the *b* it contains, a last echo of the passionate, cut plosives that chisel, as on a tombstone, "You'll get what you want." Passion seeks out these pleasurable embodiments of its realizations; it wants to feel them, to dig its hands into the sand of an expressive medium. Further, it seeks out the one tone that will suffice—clamant, peremptory—and the right movement of thought, a remorseless compression: a manner compared to which ordinary styles of discourse would be, like dreamers, like the sleeping terns at the jetty, "assassins."

The intensity that marks Michel Tournier's novel *The Ogre* (1970) requires a somewhat different description: perverse, angelic. Joy, here, is the vertiginous inversion of power: the humbling of the strong to the weak, an ogreish adult back to a frail boy's frame, after the example set by St. Christopher (whose name means Christ-bearer). The cult of the child—here in part a reaction both to adult sexual characteristics and to history—has perhaps never before been so radically politicized or so defiantly, if discreetly, erotic:

> Love, while advocated in the abstract, is fiercely persecuted as soon as it takes on concrete form and calls itself sexuality or eroticism. This fount of joy and creation, this supreme good, this raison d'etre of everything that breathes, is hunted with diabolical resentment by the whole right-thinking rabble, both lay and ecclesiastic. . . .
> . . . Purity is the malign inversion of innocence. Innocence is love of being, smiling acceptance of both celestial and earthly sustenance. . . . Purity is horror of life, hatred of man, morbid passion for the void.

Here, then, as in art generally, passion attempts to become (against its grain) healthy, a sensible ecstasy. Even though "man is the creature of nothingness," earthly innocence is exalted above unearthly purity; earthly service (the Baptist) over the divine pride of election (here instilled in the Nazis); earthly appearances over the void.

Heavy, anal creature though and because he is, Abel Tiffauges, the self-styled ogre, is fated (so he believes) to be the bearer of lightness— and he is literally so in the final scene, where he carries on his shoulders, through marshes, a Jewish boy escaped from Auschwitz ("the Anus Mundi, the great metropolis of degradation, suffering and death"). In Tournier's grotesque and beautiful fable, imagination (Tiffauges believes he was also put on earth to read signs) is the child carried in and by the man, the angel borne by the ogre man also is. Only imagination escapes the "genital dungeon"; a "winged joy," a "divine inversion," it is a "sort of levitation caused by an increase in weight."

Before taken prisoner by the Nazis, Tiffauges, a French garage mechanic, breaks away into the streets, when he can, to thieve images of children with his camera. Bearing and preserving, a photographic negative is, like the ogre himself, a porter; it raises "the real object to a new power—the *imaginary power*." An emanation of reality via a "divine inversion," the photographic image is at the same time "consubstantial," Tiffauges says, "with my fantasies and on a level with my imaginary universe . . . Photography promotes reality to the plane of dream; it metamorphoses a real object into its own myth, . . . [conferring] on it a certain generality." "Equipped with a huge leather-clad sex," Tiffauges (in fact microgenital) is freed from "the obscure task of perpetuating the species"; freed from the obscurations of time. At least, *his* sex is "secretly lined [with] an immense blind retina, which will see and be dazzled only once, but will never forget." Art: not only a "phoric" abstraction from the particular, but deathless reproduction.

From children at recess Tiffauges hears rising a long cry:

> It was a sustained guttural note of extraordinary purity, like an appeal welling up from the depths of the body, and it ended in a series of modulations at once joyous and moving. It gave an astonishing impression of simultaneous rigor and plenitude, balance and excess.

A metaphor, this, of the interplay of passion and pleasure in art. Other to life, art is the way passion puts up with itself—its levitation into pleasure. In art, passion does not so much go back on itself as rise above its appetites, its instinct for power. Incarnate as it is in aesthetic particulars, it is practically out in the open. It looks about. It takes a deep breath. It seems to like what it sees and hears. Perhaps it even starts to like itself.

2. PLEASURE AND EMPATHY

Through empathy, the body feels its way into the artistic medium—into not only its representations but its materials and their arrangements—as a special form of intelligence. Outside of art, physical knowledge is diffuse, distracted. As a subknowledge, it grows restive, it wants to know itself more fully. That is one reason we have art. In art, the intelligence of the body—an analogical intelligence—becomes concentrated in delight.

When Nietzsche spoke of "the most comprehensive soul, . . . which flees itself and catches up with itself in the widest circle, . . . which loves itself most, in which all things have their sweep and countersweep," he described—in its optimal form—the soul of empathy, the physical imagination. Instinct as it is with both rejections and receptions, contractions and expansions, slowings and quickenings, the body is the keyboard of universal knowing. Kinesthesia—basic knowledge is all in that mold. The senses pool their impressions (Goethe: "the hands want to see, the eyes want to caress"). The ear? Not a cave or shell, as so easily supposed, but a live creature, primordial, swallowing—small, but an epic organ.

Extravagant as the physical imagination is—it seems to exist not only to safeguard life, to "read" the movements of other things, but as a ludic luxury—it is yet not passion. Empathy becomes passion only in the hysteric. The hysteric's compulsion—basically that of what Freud called the "immortal germ" of reproduction—is to become a host of others. Every reader is tempted to become a hysteric. But it is more comfortable, freer, just to be a reader.

In English literature, the great modern hysteric is D. H. Lawrence —the successor, in this regard, to Dickens. The latter's hysteria exploded as animism in description; Lawrence, both lucky and unlucky in coming later, when sex could be evoked, turned to the demonic physical intelligence of his characters, and exploded there. In Lawrence, the physical imagination seems intent on something—some fury or peace— that is really beyond the body's reach. Hence the occasional hectoring note of rhetoric.

Empathy is healthiest when it is self-activation for its own sake—a prodigality, not an errand. Of course, aggrandizement is a normal part of its range—as when a scrawny kitten suddenly performs a hundred-and-eighty-degree turn in the air and comes to earth again a bristling king of beasts, at least an inch taller as it faces down absolutely nothing at all. Reading can be like that. It is all closet adventure. Only, it is not so much the "ego" that swells as the plexus of the senses. Empathy—a concept now seldom evoked—is not exhausted by suspect "identification" or even suspect compassion. Its field is the entire work. The latter, even, has no existence apart from it. Empathy is the ingress, the medium of flotation, the muscle of realization, the aesthetic intelligence.

Empathy: a genius for removing the space between oneself and other things, using only the imagination for appropriation. To be other and yet oneself, that is what challenges it. T. S. Eliot is not usually credited with possessing it, but what William Carlos Williams called his hypersensitivity was, I think, just that. Here it is, in bold form, in a late work, "Burnt Norton":

> Garlic and sapphires in the mud
> Clot the bedded axle-tree.
> The trilling wire in the blood
> Sings below inveterate scars
> And reconciles forgotten wars.
> The dance along the artery
> The circulation of the lymph
> Are figured in the drift of stars
> Ascend to summer in the tree
> We move above the moving tree
> In light upon the figured leaf
> And hear upon the sodden floor
> Below, the boarhound and the boar
> Pursue their pattern as before
> But reconciled among the stars.

It is spring, with its rains and mud, its wild garlic and blue puddles in the road, its carts all but sexually bedded in mire (carts—for this 1935 lyric, with its boarhound and boar, is primal England revisited). The body so thrills to the moment that it forgives and forgets the past. How outward is its joy, a pure spring joy. Its correspondence with other systems of circulations—trees, stars—strikes like a revelation and feels like a justification. Here, where even punctuation begins to forget itself in ecstasy (beginning with "Ascend"), how easy the leap from one system to another—for instance, into the tree, as its sap. Yes, ascend thus into summer, then change into the light on the very leaves you have fed. For what is light if not the most busily gregarious, most empathic and generous of physical things?

Through empathy, we become—as Wallace Stevens said—at once more strangely and truly ourselves. In part, ours is a nature that is created in what it imagines; it is always other to what it just now failed to convince itself it was. Empathy—in multiplying us, does it true us or scatter us? Following Lipps, Wilhelm Worringer stressed that self-alienation is the reverse side of its self-activation:

194 / Calvin Bedient

> We feel . . . our individuality flow into fixed boundaries, in contrast to the boundless differentiation of the individual consciousness. . . . This affirmation of our need for activity represents, simultaneously, a curtailment of its illimitable potentialities, a negation of its ununifiable differentiations. In empathy, therefore, I am not the real I, but am inwardly liberated from the latter, i.e. I am liberated from everything which I am apart from contemplation of the form. I am only this ideal, this contemplating "I."

An "I" constituted, that is, by mental suggestion, by the union of the physical imagination and the work.

3. PLEASURE AND TRUTH

In aesthetic contemplation, thought takes on a rhythmic body. It is no longer thought, exactly; and the body is no longer body, exactly.

Art does not divide into painful truths and beautiful forms: it is beautiful (it puts on an emotional body) throughout. True, at moments the sense of affliction overwhelms every other feeling—particularly in movies, which can represent human suffering so graphically. Even so, this affliction is, at some level, loved, partly because it is mediated by form and partly because it scours us, as only truth can.

Joseph Brodsky speaks of "one's suspicion that to like a work of art is to recognize the truth, or the degree of it, that art expresses." That, at least, is one reason to like art, a reason consisting in gratitude to the truth itself. Why? Because it orients us. Discovers us. Brings us to our senses. Gets the bad taste of falsehoods out of our mouth.

William Carlos Williams' poem "The Last Words of My English Grandmother" is, for a poem, a tour de force of naturalistic mortification. The old lady it portrays so vividly is at once feeble and feisty, demanding and past being satisfied. What a handful! She is dying, yet you want to wring her neck. Pushed out of life against her will, she is understandably furious. On the other hand, the long struggle has wearied her, and her "last words" dismiss life pitilessly. She is lifted into an ambulance:

> Then we started.
> On the way
> we passed a long row
> of elms. She looked at them

> awhile out of
> the ambulance window and said,
>
> What are all those
> fuzzy-looking things out there?
> Trees? Well, I'm tired
> of them and rolled her head away.

Yet the poem saves even so grim an end for pleasure, not least by perceiving its comedy — the old lady's ridiculous incongruities create a ruckus even here, as the habit of looking, the inability to see, and the bitter refusal to see knock against one another. "Fuzzy-looking things" is, we can't help noticing, funny. How free the poem is of dulling sentiment. And how adroitly, with what daring speed (the tempo of helplessness), the poet has handled the subject — how right, for instance, the indifferent omission of a comma before "and rolled her head away." Talent and truth — here neither is compromised.

Even when it disappoints us, which is most of the time, the possession of truth feels like mastery (like knowing that the next step will be on a stone, even if the one after that is over a waterfall). However ambiguous it may be, it sends amorphousness packing like a vapor. Something fit for contemplation stands forth and stands firm. "Yes," we might think in looking at Eva Hesse's *Hang-Up* (1966): at the big, variously gray, cloth-bound rectangular "picture" frame stuck against the museum wall without any painting in it — a frame minus a function except to support the long, also variously gray cable that juts out of it from one side, high up, into the spectator's own usually sacrosanct space before falling limp, lying on the floor, then looping back, where it proves secured, down low, near the other side. "Yes, needing freedom and security at the same time is like that. Being a woman bound to a man is like that. Possessing both reason and emotion: like that. Wanting to be at once the observed and the observer, to challenge and to hide, like that. Requiring an audience yet resenting one — like that. Being disenchanted with painting but unable to leave it behind, as Hesse was, much like that." And so on. The work is at once startlingly simple and potently universal; an elegant theorem rich in applications.

Because form — as we tiresomely repeat — is inseparable from content, "truth" in art is always, in contradiction of its nature, unique or, as we also tiresomely say, "inimitable." It is Dostoyevsky's truth, Tolstoy's truth, Joyce's truth; if it is Faulkner's truth, can it also be Fitzgerald's truth? Listen to what the writers whisper: "the others are not telling the truth; it's not shaped like that, it doesn't feel like that; *here* is the truth."

Wallace Stevens' poem "Bantams in Pine-Woods" is spiritedly—yes, inimitably—about this very thing. Goethe asked how he could be alive if others were. Stevens' poem opens by hailing a magnificent bantam whose very appearance and bearing ask: how can you, all you others, be alive if I'm alive?

> Chieftain Iffucan of Azcan in caftan
> Of tan with henna hackles, halt!

Imitate me, if you can! cries the chief bantam through his gorgeous raiment and fine strutting. Intimidate me, if you can! answers the speaker, a lesser bantam, through the mocking, imitative flourish of his words. Who is this chieftain, this "ten-foot poet among inchlings," this "damned universal cock" who behaves "as if the sun/ Was blackamoor to bear [his] blazing tail"? No one definite. Anyone who fits the bill. The rhetoric (e.g., "blackamoor") suggests Shakespeare, that "universal" genius, but Whitman does almost as well; indeed Whitman better suits the American setting. Swellingly all-American though Whitman was, he did leave something for even "inchling" poets to do among the Appalachian pines—namely, point "their Appalachian tangs," mark local qualities. (But Williams, not Stevens, was the poet to insist on this.) Let the "universal" poet identify the world with himself; the poet of the particular will, conversely, identify with the world:

> Fat! Fat! Fat! Fat! I am the personal.
> Your world is you. I am my world.
>
> You ten-foot poet among inchlings. Fat!
> Begone! An inchling bristles in these pines,
>
> Bristles, and points their Appalachian tangs,
> And fears not portly Azcan nor his hoos.

Two shoemakers—as Milan Kundera says—can work together amicably until each writes a book; then they find themselves in mutually exclusive universes. The strong writer challenges others with a "whose"?

To find this truth worked out so pointedly, so originally, as Stevens works it out is a pleasure. To empathize with his cocky inchling bantam—that American independent—is a pleasure, too.

4. PLEASURE AND MASTERY

To want to create, Nietzsche argued, is to want to explode the will to become—to want to "speak of oneself through a hundred . . . media." This activity is useless, of course, unless it becomes masterful, a true making. "The artist's victorious energy"—even what is "ugly" in the work must communicate this.

The purpose of originality in art is to effect "the freshness of transformations"—which means: to discover "the freshness of ourselves" (Wallace Stevens). And this freshness coincides with a sensation of human prowess—something a random renovation of experience, say the proprietary stillness of a blue-spotted butterfly on the blue towel you go out to retrieve from the clothesline, does not supply. Art, as Yeats said, is "a victory as well as a creation." To stand above the subject, to bestow "beauty of shape, the organic quality," is to make of style "a continual deliberate self-delighting happiness." Style, with what the dance critic Edwin Denby called its "risk," its "nerve," its "now-or-never edge and thrill."

The artist's work says: follow and be transformed. But his mastery says: admire. The latter, though secondary, is essential, for we need to admire what the species can do—which means, I suppose, to admire ourselves, however circuitously. Human faculties? Their breakthroughs soon turn into limits. The wind dies, the sails slump—then another "victory" and it's all a breeze. To be a serious artist is to press at our confinement and to be a serious audience is to wait to be off again. The sober, the weary, the dried-up—these, as Nietzsche said, "can receive . . . nothing from art, because they do not possess the primary artistic force, the pressure of riches." "Whoever cannot give," he summarized, "also receives nothing." Art creates the feeling—"follow!"—that what one receives is what one somehow already had. As we experience a work of art, we ourselves are art, mastery on the convex side, power at the re-created end.

This is a pleasure to which the audience to art becomes addicted. An antidote to the quarter-truth—here stated by Paul de Man—that "invented fiction . . . asserts itself as pure nothing, *our* nothingness." Just as consciousness of the inevitable, facilitating, and constitutive role of empathy in our experience of art would qualify the new critical dogma that a work is merely a "text," an absence, so a recognition that art showcases human powers would squelch the new political idea that all works of literature are equal to one another, members of a pathetic democracy of symptomatic texts. We read literature because it expands us and we admire its achievements because each is rare and difficult, a victory.

William S. Wilson

loving / reading

I don't know what he means. A white house rises in front of me above its own gray-and-black reflection in a puddle—a sheet of dark water. It makes me tremble, the phenomenon: the dreamlike screen, the flattened and foreshortened mimicry; and then the true and shadowed, to me somewhat tilted, wooden house, with all the parallel lines of its cupboards rising up up and looming over me in the mist. I tremble in my ignorance. I cannot tell you how much I loved the actual house when I looked at it. I love it as much as I hate its reflection. There is no one inside the reflection. I was afraid it had stolen the real house. I step in the puddle and disorder it, while the real house sails unheedingly loomingly, as if tiltedly across a piece of wet lawn inside brackets of the mist.

—HAROLD BRODKEY
"S.L."

We are born reading. The infant reads the breast. Or the bottle. The first art of infancy is to find the mind's construction in the breast, and the face. The breast, whatever is doing the mothering, fits into an imaginative space that is prepared for it: ". . . the breast is created by the infant over and over again out of the infant's capacity to love or . . . out of need. A subjective phenomenon develops in the baby, which we call the mother's breast. The mother places the actual breast just there where the infant is ready to create, and at the right moment. From birth, therefore, the human being is concerned with the problem of the relationship between what is objectively perceived and what is subjectively conceived of." D. W. Winnicott, *Playing and Reality*, which I take gratefully from Robert T. Eberwein, "Reflections on the Breast," *Wide Angle* 4:3 (1980), and I thank Darrell Taylor for sharing his photocopy. I wrote about dolls and screens and breasts in an essay, "Dolls in Art," for C. W. Post College. As I get up to look for a copy of the catalog, I put my eyes on automatic pilot, and they scan the shelves until the external book coincides with the internal image, until the "objectively perceived" coincides with the "subjectively conceived of," which sounds to me like the primal quest for love as a longing for exteriorities that correspond with our vast interiorities. Breast-feeding is our first seduction by the world, and here is where glorious imaginative confusions can begin, where the literal need to seduce—the infant's lips and gums imply a nipple—meets the seduction by the other—the logic of the nipple is the implication of gums and lips—and then the reciprocities need to be worked out, although they never do work out perfectly. The "seduction" of the mother by the baby is actual and literal. The "seduction" of the baby by the mother is symbolic or imaginary (I am misappropriating Claude Lévi-Strauss, *From Honey to Ashes*, II.1. "First Variation"). Sartre describes the shaping of Flaubert's imagination: "An imperceptible abruptness in the way he is handled encloses him; he nurses to the last drop, of course, but if he persists in sucking a dry breast two irresistible hands will, without violence, firmly remove him" (*The Family Idiot: Gustave Flaubert*). That the way experience is for the infant, and the way it is for the mother, cannot be the same, and can't be mutually understood, is a way of saying that the subjective will never be fully married to the objective.

You cannot read but of the breast. And probably can't go to the movies, or look at a painting either. Or dream. An image appears on a plane, the dream screen, ". . . the surface onto which a dream appears to be projected. It is the blank background, present in the dream though not necessarily seen, and the visually perceived action in ordinary manifest dream contents takes place on it or before it": Bertram Lewin, "Sleep, the Mouth, and the Dream Screen," in Eberwein. Ideas like this interpretation have been in circulation, as when Hans Bellmer, who used dolls disturbingly in his visual art, wrote, "One would like to believe that there is a kind of screen between the self and the outside world, on which the unconscious can project the image of the predominating cause of its excitation. This would be visible to the conscious (and communicable in objective form) only if the outside world projected the same image at the same time and if the two images corresponded and were superimposed." He wanted experience to be like reading dreamily, as Surrealism tries to read existence as the dream of an objective consciousness that is congruent with one's own dreams. Much of Surrealism feels to me the work of Romance-language Mama's Boys, while the recollection of "true beauty," Plato tells us, through Socrates, makes the soul feel in a state "of ebullition and effervescence, — which may be compared to the irritation and uneasiness at the gums at the time of cutting teeth" (*Phaedrus* 251c): time to be weaned to objectivity.

The dream screen can be the visual image of the feeling of being full or satisfied: "The dream screen of the adult appears to be a representation of the most archaic human pleasure experience" (René Spitz, *No and Yes*, in Eberwein). And the screen, representing the feelings of pleasure, can itself be represented by anything that substitutes for the breast: "The dream screen, or the dream as a whole, may be represented by solid articles like the finger, rubber, or glass that were experienced during or later than the sucking period, in connection with oral satisfaction" (Bertram Lewin, "Reconsideration of the Dream Screen," in Eberwein). I am using "authorities" here to save time, but I did research for this essay. After typing out that quotation, I dreamed a bottle of wine on a table, then two bottles of wine, and drinking wine with a friend from two ordinary glass tumblers while looking at photographs of paintings of a woman that gradually read, to both of us, as portraits of my mother. I had helped the tiny old Jamaican aide pull the body of my dying mastectomied mother to the angle at which she could breathe, and amidst so many disclosures of futility there at the end, I dreamed that night the amputation of my hands.

The screen or the page or the blank canvas — just about anything that will hold an image — can be interpreted as the mothering breast, once so immediate, and never to be so available again: "For just as we begin our lives as mere babes with the imprint of nothing in our heads, except lingering traces of previous existence which grow fainter and fainter as we progress until we have forgotten them entirely, only by this time other notions have imposed themselves so that our infant minds are never a complete *tabula rasa*, but there is always something fading out or just coming into focus, and this whatever-it-is is always projecting itself on us . . . ." So John Ashbery, in *Three Poems*. This "whatever-it-is" can be a variation on the unnamed floating signifier, the maternal thingamabob, which has been neglected in reflections on the paternal thingamajig.

Now, as you read this sentence, your eyes going back and forth, playing over the page, and perhaps suspicious of a play on words, you might think of the pleasures of reading playfully: "Already in the first play of the nursing infant and in all later variants of this play with elastic, swinging objects, there is a condition of being moved while moving oneself and of moving oneself while being moved . . . . . . that is, we do something, reach out to the other in a grasping gesture, and surrender ourselves in such a way that something can be done to us—we choose activity and at the same time passivity . . . Thus we already meet the ambiguous structure of genuine encounter, in a shadowy and elementary form, in the first erotic play of the moving, touching lips, tongue and hands of the nursing infant" (F. J. J. Buytendijk in M. Grene, *Approaches to a Philosophical Biology*). Buytendijk does not mention the play of the eyes, but his description sounds like protoreading to me. The eye movements of babies have been much studied, and their heartbeats respond to frustrations in their visual fields: see "Variation du rhythme cardiaque en concomitance avec un spectacle visuel chez le nouveau-né," and "Activité oculomotrice chez le bébé en présence d'objets stables et en mouvement," both by André Bullinger, cited in *Infancy and Epistemology*, edited by George Butterworth.

We arise in the midst of reading, looking at a text, looking for a text, and looking, in Wallace Stevens's inexhaustible line, for "The poem of the mind in the act of finding/ What will suffice . . ." Looking is reading, and rather critical reading at that, to find what will suffice. Or more than suffice. I don't think that to speak of "reading existence" is a metaphor. Reading is what we are always already doing, and reading a text is a special case, as when Gloucester puts on eyeglasses to read the forged letter written by the son he misreads so badly. He misread existence, and so will read no more: "The dark and vicious place where thee he got/ Cost him his eyes." Whoever invented the reading of literal writing had already been reading, and misreading. Huck Finn catches the idea of interpretation as reading in an image: "I don't want no better book that what your face is. A body can set down and read it off like coarse print." "Coarse" is the word. After I had learned to read letters and words, I had as an adult to try to learn not to read, which was not to be ironic, not to defer sensations, not to annihilate experience by focusing beyond it. Reading infuses the immediate with indeterminacies. Ordinary experience is immediately consumed, but what is put up in writing to be read later is consumed amidst preservative postponements. More misreading of Lévi-Strauss . . .

The breast and the penis are both elastic, both hang, both can swell up, and both can emit a white liquid. I am aware of the imagery of pen-penis, of the phallocentric and phallogocentric. I note that the old patriarch in a novel by Anne Tyler *typewrites* the salutation, "Dear Caleb, I take *pen* in hand . . ." Emphasis mine. I cannot speak for or about those phallocratic writers, not too full of the milk of human kindness, some of them. I am writing on about writing; the page is held within the visual oval before me, and I read on with hope, browsing, wishing for something, I suppose, sure that "what will suffice" or even fulfill is somewhere, even if not here, not yet. In my experience the hands of the writer are breasts, the hands of the writer reach toward the breasts they (enviously) long to be, the hands reach toward paper, to screens, to other white plains or planes. Those American writers—even at sea, like Melville—they nuzzle the prairie. I hear Thoreau: "A sentence should read as if its author, had he held a plow instead of a pen, could have drawn a furrow deep and straight to the end." But what is that field he is plowing over, and what do I read through the palimpsests?

I try to read existence as carefully as I read a book. A writer of fiction, and of poems, renders a reading of existence, for the way that the author's "reading" is to be read is a model or example or lesson in how existence is to be read. The meaning of writing is the style of reading that it teaches. The meaning is: the way you have to read this poem is the way you should read existence. But to live is also to revise experience so that it reads the way we want it to. James Joyce writes to Nora Barnacle, "Do you remember the three adjectives I have used in *The Dead* in speaking of your body. They are these: 'musical and strange and perfumed'." He read her, he wrote her, and he sought to rewrite her so that she would read differently: "I hope you take that cocoa every day and I hope that little body of you[rs] (or rather *certain* parts of it) are getting a little fuller. I am laughing at this moment as I think of those little girl's breasts of yours . . ." Reading is always from a perspective, from a point of view, and in a scale that is a measure of some emotions. So Gulliver sees (reads) the breast under the magnifications of Brobdingnag: "I must confess no object ever disgusted me so much as the sight of her monstrous breast, which I cannot tell what to compare with, so as to give the curious reader an idea of its bulk, shape and colour."

The oddest text I have read about writing and the bodies of women is by Herman Melville: "The Tartarus of Maids." The narrator claims a celibate masculine creativity which has no parallel in mothering: ". . . my seeds were distributed through all the Eastern and Northern States and even fell into the far soil of Missouri and the Carolinas." He visits a papermill to buy paper to wrap his seeds in. The paper begins its manufacture as pulp that resembles semen: ". . . two great round vats . . . , full of a white, wet, woolly-looking stuff, not unlike the albuminous part of an egg, soft-boiled." From this pulp unmarried "girls" produce paper which retains the image of their faces: "I seemed to see, glued to the pallid incipience of the pulp, the yet more pallid faces of all the pallid girls I had eyed that heavy day." The faces of the laborers become lined like the paper: ". . . where had stood the young, fair brow, now stood the ruled and wrinkled one." Rosy notepaper is made by girls with no roses in their cheeks. The paper emerges from the machine into the arms of a nurse-midwife who for lack of employment in her profession labors at birthing paper: ". . . handling the piles of moist, warm sheets, which continually were being delivered into the woman's waiting hands." The eeriness of this story is that the women are speechless—not one speaks a word—and that they have dry chests, breathing into their lungs the "fine, poisonous particles," and "So, through consumptive pallors of this blank, raggy life, go these white girls to death." The power of this story, which requires that one read the paper on which Melville wrote and published as depriving women of their chests, their faces, and their speech, is that Melville regrets the denial of sexuality and of motherhood to these "female operatives," although he doesn't seem to want any of their sexuality for himself. He wants them to have the possibility of reproduction that is precluded by their laboring at production of paper. Melville is saying to read the paper you are reading as your relationship to impoverished lives. His writerly-readerly regret for the pale virgins is that they have nothing that can be part of the pleasures of reading and of being read. They are the ineligible condemned to illegibility: "At rows of blank-looking counters sat rows of blank-looking girls, with blank, white folders in their blank hands, all blankly folding blank paper." I last quoted this sentence in *Antæus* 21, Spring, 1976. Once a decade doesn't seem too often.

Freud defines mental life, as it is available to psychoanalysis, as "the interplay of urging and checking forces," in an essay about eyes, "Psychogenic Visual Disturbance." The pleasures of reading are the pleasures of *urging and checking* under conscious control, however accompanied by the unconscious accompanist of our activities. I feel (conscious) pleasures of reading in the drive, and the repression of the drive, and in the overcoming of the repression of the drive, to identify the literal with the figurative, and the figurative with the literal. With every phrase, my comprehension recomposes a plane, and tilts now toward the literal, now toward the figurative, a rather wobbly theory. As I read on, loving reading, I feel the weak initial comprehensions interacting and strengthening each other until reading constructs a foundation under its foundationless self. As I continue with weak analogies between nursing and reading, nothing anyone would remember, I am ready to raise the structure higher in order to secure its foundations. By breast I must mean tenderness. When the woman says to Jesus, "Blessed is the womb that bare thee, and the paps which thou hast sucked," Luke 11:27, Jesus replies, "Yea rather, blessed are they that hear the word of God." Richard Crashaw writes a poem on Luke 11, turning the wounds of Christ into breasts which the mother can feed on:

> He'll have his Teat ere long (a bloody one)
> The Mother then must suck the son.

The images or analogies can be added to, as long as they share a family resemblance: tenderness.

A story by Kay Boyle goes like this: a motherless and fatherless little boy is lying down in the dark next to a cow: "He could hear the soft humming of her belly as it greeted and returned the food from her fruitful jaws. On the ground he could feel the feast of white violets and clover heads that had been spread there before her. As he lay against her he thought of the great full sack of milk that was hanging between her legs."

The boy starts walking home, and comes to the stream and to the disenchantment with the image on the plane: "In the middle of the stream lay a little broken moon, rippling back and forth. He knelt down and put his two hands about its moving edges and tried to lift it up. In a moment the little moon was rippling back and forth again and his hands were wet and cold." The narrative problem, after this futility, is to bring tenderness to light. He continues to the house where he meets for the first time the brother of his dead father. In this story, "His Idea of a Mother," as in an extraordinary quantity of fiction I could cite, the figure of (motherly) tenderness is male. The little boy all but asks his uncle to thrash him. "'Hold on, sir,' said Uncle Dan. The little boy stood staring at him in silence. Uncle Dan glanced over his shoulder. 'I say,' he remarked in a lower tone, 'shall we walk down the road a bit so we shan't be disturbed?'"

If men can be motherly, and if breasts can be represented by something else, then we are exposed to the frustrations and disappointments that accompany substitutions, displacements, and representations. But then we are anyway. I feel a bewitchment among surrogacies, but bewitchment can be transformed into enchantment if I can keep my eyes open. The problem of representations and signs already exists. When I was a student of literature, and reading for irony and finding it without knowing why I was looking for it, or knowing what purposes not my own were being served, I was at the same time studying *signs*, a theme that was going to get more complicated, until I would read Freud on the repression that checked his urge to name Signorelli—he said "Botticelli" instead—and would read Lacan on Freud—and would feel the associations with death, not only with the paintings of Signorelli, but with the *sign* in *sign*orelli, and I would belatedly touch the feeling that all signs are ironic in their effect because all signs however momentarily annihilate immediacy in behalf of something beyond immediate experience, as the physical experience of the sign is subsidiary to the focal plane beyond it onto which it throws attention. The sign leads to something other than itself, except in some reversals of Pop Art. Not merely "signs" for the breast, but other signs, repeat the conflict between annihilation and tenderness. I would like to think that hands, in representing breasts, are not less hands for that, and that hands, in reading and writing, can subsume other images in reciprocal enhancement, and not suffer annihilation or depletion.

Hands bring us back to writing. "I take pen in *hand*," my emphasis. The tragic letter in the poem is signed, "Yours, in the darkness,/ Virginia." It begins, "Dear Galway,/ I have no one to turn to because God is my enemy. He gave me lust and joy and cut off my hands." The hands, when they are tender and nurturing, are breasts. I see reading as a special case of that primitive and prior and continuous reading of existence that begins with the *primarium manuale*, the "breast" as whatever first nourishes. I am as interested in the phallus as any man, but the pen-penis identity feels secondhand, while breast as a plane of reciprocating tendernesses (and frustrations) feels firsthand. Galway Kinnell writes in the poem I have been quoting, "Dear Stranger . . . ,"

> a face materializes into your hands,
> on the absolute whiteness of pages
> a poem writes itself out: its title—the dream
> of all poems and the text
> of all loves—"Tenderness toward Existence."

Kinnell dropped this poem from his *Selected Poems*, and I guess I see why. I bring it back because increasingly in my reading I look for moments of equality that make tenderness possible, and increasingly I see women characters choosing husbands or lovers who have "Tenderness toward existence." See how Lady Chatterly reads her lover:

"Shall I tell you what you have that other men don't have, and that will make the future? Shall I tell you?"

"Tell me, then," he replied.

"It's the courage of your own tenderness, that is what it is . . ."

I have to focus on this rather diffuse idea of tenderness because no one can stay at the literal maternal breast: "The view, smell and touch of the breast that the adult experiences is infinitely more organized and less intense than the infant's experience. It becomes part of other, more encompassing and more complex experiences and thereby loses the immediacy of primitive sensations." So Edrita Fried, "The Aims of Visual Curiosity," in *The Ego in Love and Sexuality*, a book that opened my eyes, and that women, and men, against pornography, or anyone interested in the erotics of eyesight, should read. I have to consider that whole chapter quoted here, and then I can return to the point, which is reading and tenderness.

Now that so many acts and images are read as castration, the question arises how castration is to be read. Here Jean-Paul Sartre, in an inspired revision, reads in Genet's fellatio his hostility to the patriarchal law, as he castrates the patriarch: "fellatio is castration." "Tenderness is then born, a quiet, triumphant maternal superiority." The tenderness is reciprocal: "The sacrifice of the Male puts an end to the Old Testament. His great passion on the scaffold is only the heroic symbol of the little bedroom passion which he renews each day. With the law dead and the archangel disarmed, the murdered child comes to life again in Genet. Delivered from adults, he can love like a child, he can love the child in the young tough who has been reduced to impotence. That little penis is a childhood figure, a rag doll. Genet's tenderness goes from childhood to childhood, and it is his own childhood that he finds in the beloved" (*Saint-Genet*, "The Eternal Couple"). Genet is the castrating mother in order to transfigure the criminal into tenderness. And by the way, after writing this passage, I dreamed of a man holding a knife at my groin, and tenderness didn't seem to be the point, unless one recalls the rooster, hog, calf, or lamb made tender by castration. Genet is not representative.

Amidst transfigurations, the breast can become the dreamscreen, the doll, a puddle, even a parasol. For Wallace Stevens, the imagination is *between* the mind and reality, and so the imagination is represented by anything that comes between the head and the sun. These fictions protect our minds from raw reality like parasols that protect the head:

> Eulalia, I lounged on the hospital porch,
> On the east, sister and nun, and opened wide
> A parasol, which I had found, against
> The sun. The interior of a parasol,
> It is a kind of blank in which one sees.

The contrast to the parasol is the hat that protects a man's eyes from moonlight. This man is thinking about mothering—". . . he imagined humming sounds and sleep." But in the night he wears a hat down over his eyes, his cynical shaping of his imagination as he refuses moonlight:

> Night nursed not him in whose dark mind
> The clambering wings of birds of black revolved,
> Making harsh torment of the solitude.
>
> The walker in the moonlight walked alone,
> And in his heart his disbelief lay cold.
> His broad-brimmed hat came close upon his eyes.

Not for him, the tight-lipped American man, to please himself in the land of the living. These images of hats and parasols: reading is that which we have always not yet begun to do, as with *Huckleberry Finn*'s mysterious line, ". . . and every lady's rose-leafy dress flapping soft and silky around her hips, and she looking like the most loveliest parasol."

I began this essay quoting a description of a child looking at reflections in a puddle, the "dreamlike screen, the flattened and foreshortened mimicry." The literal, I am following Lévi-Strauss, is meaning that is to be consumed immediately. The figurative is meaning that is put up for later. That experience at the "breast" described by Winnicott seems to me pivotal: ". . . the problem of the relationship between what is objectively perceived and that which is subjectively conceived of." I read among pivoting recombinations of literal and figurative—the mother is a house, the house is a mother—and I return to that child who is learning to read his experience, to share, in this essay that so many writers have had a hand in, the pleasures of reading prose so conscientious and responsible that it brings me to the highest pleasures in reading, as I learn the style in which experience must be read (not cleverly) from the style in which this writing must be read, that is, conscientiously, responsibly, in all its contentious dimensionality:

I move on, I come to the next puddle, and in it I see another reflection: leaves of a tree, part of a tree, and me looking down, me curly-haired, and the gables and two chimneys of another house. It is easier to see all these things — part of the house, part of a tree and its branches and wet leaves — in the puddle, where they are flattened and stilled and close to one another, than in the trembling air in all their mysterious separations and densities and differences. Are Daddy and I married yet? It is half symbolic and half real, us at the moment. I am not symbolic and I am not real to myself, not in the part of myself that I know. Nor is this affection familiar. Perhaps I have grown into it. I understand only what I can understand. This other house has wooden siding, too, and twisted and partially gleaming windows when shadowy fans of wind ruffle the surface in the duller but shiny light of the puddle. This is insofar as I can read what I see. Much of the world is a disorderly scribble to me, green and brown and silver chaos. The windows are framed, silled, corniced in a house that has a lot of parts. Here is the tilted head of the doubled and peering child. The reflection seems to be of leaves and of me and of part of a house. It is not habitable, but it is true. And it is legible.

Contributors

STANISLAW BARANCZAK is a Polish poet and critic who came to the U.S.A. in the spring of 1981 to become Harvard's Alfred Jurzykowski Professor of Polish Language and Literature. He is the author of, most recently, *A Fugitive from Utopia: The Poetry of Zbigniew Herbert* (Harvard University Press).

CALVIN BEDIENT's most recent books are *In the Heart's Last Kingdom: Robert Penn Warren's Major Poetry* and *He Do the Police in Different Voices: The Waste Land and its Protagonist.* He teaches at the University of California, Los Angeles.

MADISON SMARTT BELL's first novel, *The Washington Square Ensemble*, was published by Viking/Penguin in 1983. Born in Tennessee, he now lives in Brooklyn and currently teaches a fiction workshop at the YMHA.

ROY BLOUNT, JR. is the author of several books. His most recent book is *Soupsongs/Webster's Ark: A Double Book of Verse.*

GUY DAVENPORT was born in Anderson, South Carolina. A poet, fiction writer, critic, and essayist, he has received, among other honors, the Zabel Fiction Prize, a Rhodes Scholarship, and the Flexner Award for Writing. His story collections include *Eclogues* and *Apples and Pears*.

RICHARD FORD is the author of the novel *The Sportswriter* and of a story collection, *Rock Springs,* published this autumn.

GAIL GODWIN's latest novel, *A Southern Family*, will be published this October by William Morrow.

DONALD HALL's most recent volume of poetry is *The Happy Man*. In 1987, he published his first book of short stories, *The Ideal Bakery*, with North Point, a verse play called *The Bone Ring*, with Story Line, and a book of essays, *Seasons at Eagle Pond*, with Ticknor & Fields.

JONATHAN HOLDEN's first book, *Design for a House* (1972), won the Devins Award and was published by the University of Missouri Press. *Leverage* (1982) won the AWP Award Series for Poetry. He teaches at Kansas State University.

MARY KINZIE is a poet and critic who teaches at Northwestern University. She won the Devins Award for her first volume of verse, *The Threshold of the Year*. She was the recipient of a Guggenheim Fellowship in Poetry for 1986.

JAMES LAUGHLIN is both poet and publisher. Born in Pittsburgh, he attended Harvard University and founded New Directions, which he continues to run. His latest book of poetry is entitled *Selected Poems 1935-1985*, published by City Lights Books.

DAVID LONG lives in Kalispell, Montana, and is the author of *Home Fires*, a collection of short stories that was awarded the 1983 St. Lawrence Award for Fiction. Most recently another collection of his stories, *The Flood of '64*, was published by The Ecco Press.

JOYCE CAROL OATES is the author of numerous novels and collections of short stories and poems. Her most recent book is *On Boxing*. She lives and teaches in Princeton, N.J.

JAMES PURDY is the author of several novels, plays produced on and off Broadway, and the story collections *Color of Darkness, Children Is All,* and *A Day After the Fair.*

A. L. ROWSE is the author of many books including *Science and History: A New View of History, The Use of History* and *The Early Churchills.*

/ 211

CHARLES SIMIC was born in Yugoslavia and presently teaches at the University of New Hampshire. His twelfth book of poems, *Unending Blues*, was recently published by Harcourt Brace Jovanovich.

JOSEF ŠKVORECKÝ left Czechoslovakia in 1945 and now lives in Toronto where he writes, translates, and teaches. In 1980 he received both a Guggenheim Fellowship and the Neustadt International Prize for Literature.

WILLIAM WILSON is the author of *Why I Don't Write Like Franz Kafka* and a novel, *Birthplace: Moving Into Nearness*, published by North Point Press.

LEE ZACHARIAS grew up in Hammond, Indiana. She is the author of *Helping Muriel Make It Through the Night* (short stories) and *Lessons* (a novel) and was for ten years editor of *The Greensboro Review*. She teaches at the University of North Carolina at Greensboro.

Acknowledgments

Lines from "Notes Toward a Supreme Fiction" are excerpted from the *Collected Poems of Wallace Stevens.* Copyright © 1942 by Wallace Stevens. Reprinted by permission of Alfred A. Knopf, Inc., and Faber and Faber Ltd.

Passages from *To the Lighthouse* by Virginia Woolf are reprinted by permission of Harcourt Brace Jovanovich, Inc., and The Hogarth Press. Copyright © 1927 by Harcourt Brace Jovanovich, Inc.; renewed 1955 by Leonard Woolf.

The less you eat, drink and read books; the less you go to the theatre, the dance hall, the public-house; the less you think, love, theorize, sing, paint, fence, etc. the more you *save* — the *greater* becomes your treasure which neither moths nor dust will devour — your *capital*. The less you *are*, the more you *have*; the less you express your own life, the greater is your alienated life . . .
                KARL MARX

Black Oak Books
1491 SHATTUCK AVE. BERKELEY, CA 94709
415 486-0698

the Jacaranda Review

A Journal
Of Fiction and Poetry

ANNOUNCES ITS FALL ISSUE

Featuring
An Interview with
Carolyn Forché

Submissions Deadline — Spring '88:

March 1, 1988

Subscriptions and Submissions

The Jacaranda Review
Department of English
University of California, Los Angeles
Los Angeles, CA 90024

"Karen Lawrence's success here is in the convincing depiction of a woman's solitude even in the midst of household bustle, sexual love, and physical work."
—*New York Times Book Review*

The acclaimed debut of a superb stylist.

"A gem...in this fine first novel, Karen Lawrence makes your heart race and swell and overflow ...wonderful."
—*San Francisco Chronicle Review*

"A remarkable first novel by any standard."
—*Toronto Star*

**Now in Paperback
Ballantine Books**

$3.95

A NOVEL BY
KAREN LAWRENCE

The Life of
Helen Alone

On a bleak yet beautiful farm, a woman from the city faces life's challenges—love, family, and self....

"SIMPLY STUNNING."
Newsday

Ballantine/Fiction/33042/$3.95

UNDER THE WHEAT

stories

by

RICK

DEMARINIS

paper

$7.50

■

THE ECCO PRESS
26 West 17th Street
New York, NY 10011

Rick DeMarinis' writing carries an almost electrical surge of power. Like shock therapy, his stories jolt us and change our point of view.

—THE CHICAGO TRIBUNE

First Winner of the Barnard New Women Poets Prize

"I am most deeply impressed by the poems in Patricia Storace's collection. There is no one quite like her at the moment. She is clearly one of the most talented and interesting young poets around these days; I look forward to everything she will write."
— **Alfred Kazin**

HEREDITY
PATRICIA STORACE

"At once wryly perceived and lavishly written, these are poems of a distinction not encountered every day."
— **James Merrill**

"Patricia Storace's poetry is a rare combination of the formal and the personal, the rigorously observed and deeply felt. A pleasure equally to senses and to mind."
—**Mary Gordon**

$20.00 cloth $7.95 paper

At your bookstore or direct from

Beacon
PRESS
25 Beacon Street
Boston, MA 02108
(617) 742-2110

MasterCard and VISA accepted.

New *A critical study of expatriation and its origins in the writing of Paul Bowles*

A WORLD OUTSIDE
The Fiction of Paul Bowles
By Richard F. Patteson

"Paul Bowles is one of our finest writers, and Richard Patteson has made a substantial and original contribution to our understanding of his work."   —Tobias Wolff

$18.95 hardcover $7.95 paperback

Now in bookstores or from

University of Texas Press
BOX 7819   AUSTIN, TEXAS 78713-7819
1-800-252-3206 TOLL-FREE FOR ORDERS
$1 shipping on mail orders.   Charge card orders welcome

Antæus 60

will feature an exciting selection of Irish, Scottish, Welsh, and English poetry; contemporary fiction by Richard Elman and Rick Bass; an invaluable reading list of Modern European and Latin American poetry; and an interview with Julio Cortazar.

RARITAN

A Quarterly Review edited by Richard Poirier

Where strong thinking finds its voice

... Leo Bersani, the violence of theory ... Harold Bloom on the epic hero ... Denis Donoghue, reading Bakhtin ... Vicki Hearne on talking with animals ... Christopher Hitchens on Israeli pluralism ... C.L.R. James on cricket in the West Indies ... Frank Kermode on being an enemy of humanity ... George Kateb, the idea of human extinction ... Lincoln Kirstein, an autobiography ... Edward Said on the historical conditions of theory ... Eve Sedgwick, the phenomenology of the closet ... Elaine Showalter on male feminism ...

Cultural conversations reflected upon and extended in every issue.

"RARITAN *is superb*," wrote Ian Hamilton in the TLS.

Subscribe now and receive a complimentary copy of *The Foucault Reader* edited by Paul Rabinow, a comprehensive introduction to the work of Michel Foucault.

Please enter my subscription to RARITAN starting with the current issue.
Individual subscriptions: ☐ $16 (four issues)   ☐ $26 (eight issues)
Institutional subscriptions: ☐ $20 (four issues)   ☐ $30 (eight issues)

☐ Enclosed is my check (payable to RARITAN). Please send me a free FOUCAULT READER. Sorry, we cannot bill.

Name
Institution or Company
Address

RARITAN
165 Colleve Ave.
New Brunswick, NJ 08903

Staying with Relations
A NOVEL BY
Rose Macaulay

*It is a pleasure to have
Staying with Relations
back in print. It reminds us
once more of the
fineness of Rose Macaulay's talent,
her astuteness about character,
and her gift for displaying, just right,
the dramatic elements of the story.
— Elizabeth Hardwick*

PAPER $9.50

THE ECCO PRESS
26 West 17th Street   New York/10011

The Poetry Center
of the 92nd Street Y

CALENDAR OF READINGS, 1987-88

September   Single Tickets*
   21   **Mary McCarthy,** American novelist and critic $8
   28   An Evening of Yiddish Poetry $8

October
   4   **Octavio Paz,** Mexico's foremost poet $8
   5   **Claire Bloom** Reads Virginia Woolf $10
   12   **Amy Clampitt** and **Sherod Santos** $8
   19   **Richard Wordsworth:** The Bliss of Solitude $8
   26   **Joan Didion** and **John Gregory Dunne** $8

November
   2   **W.S. Merwin** and **George Bradley** $8
   9   **Mona Van Duyn** and **Herbert Morris** $8
   16   **Marianne Moore at 100** $8
   23   **Tom Wolfe,** American journalist/novelist $8
   30   **Rolf Hochhuth,** German playwright $8

December
   7   An Evening of Israeli Literature: **Amos Oz, Anton Shammas, Natan Zach** $8
   14   **Galway Kinnell:** An Evening of Romantic Poetry with Music $10

January
   4   **Frank Conroy** and **Mona Simpson** $8
   11   **Maya Angelou,** American autobiographer/poet $8
   18   **Martin Luther King Day Celebration,** featuring **James Earl Jones** $8

February
   1   **Jayne Anne Phillips** and **Paul Rudnick** $8
   8   **William Stafford** and **Liz Rosenberg** $8
   22   **Natalia Ginzburg,** Italian novelist $8

March
   7   **X.J. Kennedy** and **W.D. Snodgrass** $8
   14   **Marsha Norman** and **James Kirkwood,** playwrights $8
   21   **Donald Justice** and **William Logan** $8
   28   **Albert Innaurato** and **Paul Selig,** playwrights $8

April
   4   **Mario Vargas Llosa,** Peruvian novelist $10
   11   **Elizabeth Hardwick** and **Susan Sontag:** An Evening of Literary Essays $8
   18   **Isabelle Allende** and **Eduardo Galeano,** Latin American novelists $8
   25   **Irina Ratushinskaya** and **Adam Zagajewski** $8

May
   2   "Discovery"/*The Nation* 1988 Poetry Contest Winners $6
   9   **Anthony Burgess,** England's revered novelist $10
   16   **Wole Soyinka,** Nigerian playwright $10

*For complete information about the Poetry Center's offerings, please call (212) 427-6000, ext. 176 or 208.
To charge a membership call Y-CHARGE at (212) 996-1100.

The 92nd Street YM-YWHA is an agency of UJA Federation.

Czeslaw Milosz
Unattainable Earth

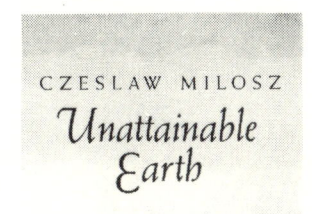

now in paper

$9.50

"A complex, deeply affecting work."
—*Library Journal*

"*Unattainable Earth* is a triumph."
—*Christian Science Monitor*

THE ECCO PRESS • 26 WEST 17th STREET • NEW YORK • 10011

FARRAR STRAUS GIROUX

JOSEPH BRODSKY
Less Than One
Winner, National Book Critics Circle Award for Criticism, 1986
cloth $25.00, paper $12.95
(essays)

CHRISTOPHER LOGUE
War Music
An Account of Books 16-19 of Homer's Iliad
cloth $12.95

ROBERT LOWELL
The Collected Prose
Edited and Introduced by Robert Giroux
cloth $25.00

GJERTRUD SCHNACKENBERG
The Lamplit Answer
cloth $12.95, paper $6.95
Portraits and Elegies
paper $6.95

C.K. WILLIAMS
Flesh and Blood
cloth $12.95

WOLE SOYINKA
Winner, 1986 Nobel Prize for Literature
A Shuttle in the Crypt
cloth $14.95, paper $7.95
Hill and Wang

DEREK WALCOTT
Collected Poems 1948-1984
cloth $25.00, paper $12.95

AILEEN WARD
John Keats
The Making of a Poet
Revised Edition
paper $11.95

ADAM ZAGAJEWSKI
Tremor
Selected Poems
Translated by Renata Gorczynski
Introduction by Czeslaw Milosz
cloth $12.95, paper $7.95

Now at your bookstore, or call 1-800-638-3030

To receive a complete catalogue of poetry books in print, please write
Farrar, Straus & Giroux
19 Union Sq. West, New York, N.Y. 10003
or call (212) 741-6930

*"Our gratitude to The Ecco Press
for its publication of* **THE TALES OF CHEKHOV** *series
can never be too great."* —EUDORA WELTY

"...Chekhov is the greatest short story writer who ever lived.... Anyone who reads literature, anyone who believes, as one must, in the transcendant power of art, sooner or later has to read Chekhov. And just now might be a better time than any.
—RAYMOND CARVER

THE TALES OF CHEKHOV

Volume 1	*The Darling*	*The Bishop*	Volume 7
Volume 2	*The Duel*	*The Chorus Girl*	Volume 8
Volume 3	*The Lady*	*The Schoolmistress*	Volume 9
Volume 4	*The Party*	*The Horse-Stealers*	Volume 10
Volume 5	*The Wife*	*The Schoolmaster*	Volume 11
Volume 6	*The Witch*	*The Cook's Wedding*	Volume 12
	Love	Volume 13	

All thirteen volumes of stories are available for only $95.00—a savings of over $15.00! Individual volumes available for $8.50 paper and $9.50 paper. Don't miss the two companion volumes: *The Unknown Chekhov* $9.50 paper and *The Notebook of Anton Chekhov* $7.50 paper.

THE ECCO PRESS
26 West 17th Street, New York, N.Y. 10011

IOWA Award Winners

Resurrectionists
By Russell Working
Cowinner of the 1986
Iowa Short Fiction Award

"This collection introduces a writer of unusual promise. . . . Raw, abrasive, urgent, these stories jangle the nerves and haunt the memory." — *Tobias Wolff.* "[Working] has an amazing ability to draw the reader immediately into the world about which he is writing. . . . It is the quiet intensity of the writing that is so impressive." — *New York Times Book Review.* "This collection of eight stories . . . proves that [Working] is a writer to watch."
— *Publishers Weekly*
ISBN 0-87745-164-8, $14.95

Eminent Domain
By Dan O'Brien
Cowinner of the 1986
Iowa Short Fiction Award

"Just when a reader is ready to draw a depressing conclusion about the new short story in America, along comes Dan O'Brien." — *New York Times Book Review.* "O'Brien is a capable and lyrical writer. The metaphors that resonate below the surfaces of his tales render them enjoyable, satisfying, and thought-provoking."
— *Publishers Weekly.* "O'Brien takes on some of the larger themes of American fiction — the loss of the wilderness, nostalgia for the west, the end of individualism. . . . O'Brien writes about memory and longing in a voice so strong you cannot help but listen, so gentle you must lean close to hear." — *Mary Morris*
ISBN 0-87745-170-2, $13.95

Available from local bookstores or from the

University of Iowa Press
Iowa City, Iowa 52242

Call 319-335-8777
Visa and MasterCard only